[See page 45

"ON THE DOWN EAST COAST"

# LITERATURE AND LIFE

𝔖𝔱𝔲𝔡𝔦𝔢𝔰

By W. D. HOWELLS

AUTHOR OF

"LITERARY FRIENDS AND ACQUAINTANCE"
"HEROINES OF FICTION"
"MY LITERARY PASSIONS" ETC.

*ILLUSTRATED*

HARPER & BROTHERS PUBLISHERS

NEW YORK AND LONDON

1902

# A WORD OF EXPLANATION

PERHAPS the reader may not feel in these papers that inner solidarity which the writer is conscious of; and it is in this doubt that the writer wishes to offer a word of explanation. He owns, as he must, that they have every appearance of a group of desultory sketches and essays, without palpable relation to one another, or superficial allegiance to any central motive. Yet he ventures to hope that the reader who makes his way through them will be aware, in the retrospect, of something like this relation and this allegiance.

For my own part, if I am to identify myself with the writer who is here on his defence, I have never been able to see much difference between what seemed to me Literature and what seemed to me Life. If I did not find life in what professed to be literature, I disabled its profession, and possibly from this habit, now inveterate with me, I am never quite sure of life unless I find literature in it. Unless the thing seen reveals to me an intrinsic poetry, and puts on phrases that clothe it pleasingly to the imagination, I do not much care for it; but if it will do this, I do not mind how poor or common or squalid it shows at first glance: it challenges my curiosity and keeps my sympathy. Instantly I love it and wish to share my pleasure in it with some one else, or as many ones else as I can get to look or listen. If the thing is something read, rather than seen, I am not anxious about the matter: if it is like life, I know that it is poetry, and take it to my heart.    There can be no offence in it for which its truth will not make me amends.

Out of this way of thinking and feeling about these two great things, about Literature and Life, there may have arisen a confusion as to which is which.    But I do not wish to part them, and in their union I have found, since I learned my letters, a joy in them both which I hope will last till I forget my letters.

> "So was it when my life began;
> So is it, now I am a man;
> So be it when I shall grow old."

It is the rainbow in the sky for me; and I have seldom seen a sky without some bit of rainbow in it. Sometimes I can make others see it, sometimes not; but I always like to try, and if I fail I harbor no worse thought of them than that they have not had their eyes examined and fitted with glasses which would at least have helped their vision.

W. D. H.

# CONTENTS

*in his —*

# CONTENTS

# ILLUSTRATIONS

# ILLUSTRATIONS

# LITERATURE AND LIFE

# LITERATURE AND LIFE

## THE MAN OF LETTERS AS A MAN OF BUSINESS

I THINK that every man ought to work for his living, without exception, and that, when he has once avouched his willingness to work, society should provide him with work and warrant him a living. I do not think any man ought to live by an art. A man's art should be his privilege, when he has proven his fitness to exercise it, and has otherwise earned his daily bread; and its results should be free to all. There is an instinctive sense of this, even in the midst of the grotesque confusion of our economic being; people feel that there is something profane, something impious, in taking money for a picture, or a poem, or a statue. Most of all, the artist himself feels this. He puts on a bold front with the world, to be sure, and brazens it out as Business; but he knows very well that there is something false and vulgar in it; and that the work which cannot be truly priced in money cannot be truly paid in money. He can, of course, say that the priest takes money for reading the marriage service, for christening the new-born babe, and for saying the last office for the dead; that the physician sells healing; that justice itself is paid for; and that he is merely a party to the thing that is and must be. He can say that, as the thing is, unless he sells his

I

art he cannot live, that society will leave him to starve if he does not hit its fancy in a picture, or a poem, or a statue; and all this is bitterly true. He is, and he must be, only too glad if there is a market for his wares. Without a market for his wares he must perish, or turn to making something that will sell better than pictures, or poems, or statues. All the same, the sin and the shame remain, and the averted eye sees them still, with its inward vision. Many will make believe otherwise, but I would rather not make believe otherwise; and in trying to write of Literature as Business I am tempted to begin by saying that Business is the opprobrium of Literature.

## I

Literature is at once the most intimate and the most articulate of the arts. It cannot impart its effect through the senses or the nerves as the other arts can; it is beautiful only through the intelligence; it is the mind speaking to the mind; until it has been put into absolute terms, of an invariable significance, it does not exist at all. It cannot awaken this emotion in one, and that in another; if it fails to express precisely the meaning of the author, if it does not say *him*, it says nothing, and is nothing. So that when a poet has put his heart, much or little, into a poem, and sold it to a magazine, the scandal is greater than when a painter has sold a picture to a patron, or a sculptor has modelled a statue to order. These are artists less articulate and less intimate than the poet; they are more exterior to their work; they are less personally in it; they part with less of themselves in the dicker. It does not change the nature of the case to say that Tennyson and Longfellow and Emerson sold the poems in which they couched the most mystical messages their genius was charged to bear mankind. They submitted to the conditions which none can escape; but that does not justify the conditions, which are none the less the conditions of hucksters because they are imposed upon poets. If it will serve to make my meaning a little clearer, we will suppose that a poet has been crossed in love, or has suffered some real. sorrow, like the loss of a wife or child. He pours out his broken heart in verse that shall bring tears of sacred sympathy from his readers, and an editor pays him a hundred dollars for the right of bringing his verse to their notice. It is perfectly true that the poem was not written for these dollars, but it is perfectly true that it was sold for them. The poet must use his emotions to pay his provision bills; he has no other means; society does not propose to pay his bills for him. Yet, and at the end of the ends, the unsophisticated witness finds the transaction ridiculous, finds it repulsive, finds it shabby. Somehow he knows that if our huckstering civilization did not at every moment violate the eternal fitness of things, the poet's song would have been given to the world, and the poet would have been cared for by the whole human brotherhood, as any man should be who does the duty that every man owes it.

The instinctive sense of the dishonor which money-purchase does to art is so strong that sometimes a man of letters who can pay his way otherwise refuses pay for his work, as Lord Byron did, for a while, from a noble pride, and as Count Tolstoy has tried to do, from a noble conscience. But Byron's publisher profited by a generosity which did not reach his readers; and the Countess Tolstoy collects the copyright which her husband foregoes; so that these two eminent instances of protest against business in literature may be said not to have shaken its money basis. I know of no others; but there may be many that I am culpably ignorant of. Still, I doubt if there are enough to affect the fact that Literature is Business as well as Art, and almost as soon. At present business is the only human solidarity; we are all bound together with that chain, whatever interests and tastes and principles separate us, and I feel quite sure that in writing of the Man of Letters as a Man of Business I shall attract far more readers than I should in writing of him as an Artist. Besides, as an artist he has been done a great deal already; and a commercial state like ours has really more concern in him as a business man. Perhaps it may sometime be different; I do not believe it will till the conditions are different, and that is a long way off.

## II

In the mean time I confidently appeal to the reader's imagination with the fact that there are several men of letters among us who are such good men of business that they can command a hundred dollars a thousand words for all they write. It is easy to write a thousand words a day, and, supposing one of these authors to work steadily, it can be seen that his net earnings during the year would come to some such sum as the President of the United States gets for doing far less work of a much more perishable sort. If the man of letters were wholly a business man, this is what would happen; he would make his forty or fifty thousand dollars a year, and be able to consort with bank presidents, and railroad officials, and rich tradesmen, and other flowers of our plutocracy on equal terms. But, unfortunately, from a business point of view, he is also an artist, and the very qualities that enable him to delight the public disable him from delighting it uninterruptedly. "No rose blooms right along,"

4

as the English boys at Oxford made an American collegian say in a theme which they imagined for him in his national parlance; and the man of letters, as an artist, is apt to have times and seasons when he cannot blossom. Very often it shall happen that his mind will lie fallow between novels or stories for weeks and months at a stretch; when the suggestions of the friendly editor shall fail to fruit in the essays or articles desired; when the muse shall altogether withhold herself, or shall respond only in a feeble dribble of verse which he might sell indeed, but which it would not be good business for him to put on the market. But supposing him to be a very diligent and continuous worker, and so happy as to have fallen on a theme that delights him and bears him along, he may please himself so ill with the result of his labors that he can do nothing less in artistic conscience than destroy a day's work, a week's work, a month's work. I know one man of letters who wrote to-day and tore up to-morrow for nearly a whole summer. But even if part of the mistaken work may be saved, because it is good work out of place, and not intrinsically bad, the task of reconstruction wants almost as much time as the production; and then, when all seems done, comes the anxious and endless process of revision. These drawbacks reduce the earning capacity of what I may call the high-cost man of letters in such measure that an author whose name is known everywhere, and whose reputation is commensurate with the boundaries of his country, if it does not transcend them, shall have the income, say, of a rising young physician, known to a few people in a subordinate city.

In view of this fact, so humiliating to an author in the presence of a nation of business men like ours, I do not know that I can establish the man of letters in the popular esteem as very much of a business man, after all. He must still have a low rank among practical people; and he will be regarded by the great mass of Americans as perhaps a little off, a little funny, a little soft! Perhaps not; and yet I would rather not have a consensus of public opinion on the question; I think I am more comfortable without it.

### III

There is this to be said in defence of men of letters on the business side, that literature is still an infant industry with us, and, so far from having been protected by our laws, it was exposed for ninety years after the foundation of the republic to the vicious competition of stolen goods. It is true that we now have the international copyright law at last, and we can at least begin to forget our shame; but literary property has only forty-two years of life under our unjust statutes, and if it is attacked by robbers the law does not seek out the aggressors and punish them, as it would seek out and punish the trespassers upon any other kind of property; it leaves the aggrieved owner to bring suit against them, and recover damages, if he can. This may be right enough in itself; but I think, then, that all property should be defended by civil suit, and should become public after forty-two years of private tenure. The Constitution guarantees us all equality before the law, but the law-makers seem to have forgotten this in the case of our literary industry. So long as this remains the case, we cannot expect the best business talent to go into literature, and the man of letters must keep his present low grade among business men.

As I have hinted, it is but a little while that he has had any standing at all. I may say that it is only since

6

the Civil War that literature has become a business with us. Before that time we had authors, and very good ones; it is astonishing how good they were; but I do not remember any of them who lived by literature except Edgar A. Poe, perhaps; and we all know how he lived; it was largely upon loans. They were either men of fortune, or they were editors or professors, with salaries or incomes apart from the small gains of their pens; or they were helped out with public offices; one need not go over their names or classify them. Some of them must have made money by their books, but I question whether any one could have lived, even very simply, upon the money his books brought him. No one could do that now, unless he wrote a book that we could not recognize as a work of literature. But many authors live now, and live prettily enough, by the sale of the serial publication of their writings to the magazines. They do not live so nicely as successful tradespeople, of course, or as men in the other professions when they begin to make themselves names; the high state of brokers, bankers, railroad operators, and the like is, in the nature of the case, beyond their fondest dreams of pecuniary affluence and social splendor. Perhaps they do not want the chief seats in the synagogue; it is certain they do not get them. Still, they do very fairly well, as things go; and several have incomes that would seem riches to the great mass of worthy Americans who work with their hands for a living—when they can get the work. Their incomes are mainly from serial publication in the different magazines; and the prosperity of the magazines has given a whole class existence which, as a class, was wholly unknown among us before the Civil War. It is not only the famous or fully recognized authors who live in this way, but the much larger number of clever people who are as yet known chiefly to the editors, and who may never make themselves a public, but who do well a kind of acceptable work. These are the sort who do not get reprinted from the periodicals; but the better recognized authors do get reprinted, and then their serial work in its completed form appeals to the readers who say they do not read serials. The multitude of these is not great, and if an author rested his hopes upon their favor he would be a much more imbittered man than he now generally is. But he understands perfectly well that his reward is in the serial and not in the book; the return from that he may count as so much money found in the road—a few hundreds, a very few thousands, at the most, unless he is the author of an historical romance.

## IV

I doubt, indeed, whether the earnings of literary men are absolutely as great as they were earlier in the century, in any of the English-speaking countries; relatively they are nothing like as great. Scott had forty thousand dollars for *Woodstock*, which was not a very large novel, and was by no means one of his best; and forty thousand dollars then had at least the purchasing power of sixty thousand now. Moore had three thousand guineas for *Lalla Rookh*, but what publisher would be rash enough to pay fifteen thousand dollars for the masterpiece of a minor poet now? The book, except in very rare instances, makes nothing like the return to the author that the magazine makes, and there are few leading authors who find their account in that form of publication. Those who do, those who sell the most widely in book form, are often not at all desired by editors; with difficulty they get a serial accepted by any principal maga-

zine. On the other hand, there are authors whose
books, compared with those of the popular favorites,
do not sell, and yet they are eagerly sought for by
editors; they are paid the highest prices, and nothing
that they offer is refused. These are literary artists;
and it ought to be plain from what I am saying that
in belles-lettres, at least, most of the best literature
now first sees the light in the magazines, and most
of the second-best appears first in book form. The
old-fashioned people who flatter themselves upon their
distinction in not reading magazine fiction or magazine poetry make a great mistake, and simply class
themselves with the public whose taste is so crude that
they cannot enjoy the best. Of course, this is true
mainly, if not merely, of belles-lettres; history, science,
politics, metaphysics, in spite of the many excellent
articles and papers in these sorts upon what used to
be called various emergent occasions, are still to be
found at their best in books. The most monumental
example of literature, at once light and good, which
has first reached the public in book form is in the different publications of Mark Twain; but Mr. Clemens
has of late turned to the magazines too, and now takes
their mint-mark before he passes into general circulation. All this may change again, but at present
the magazines—we have no longer any reviews—
form the most direct approach to that part of our reading public which likes the highest things in literary
art. Their readers, if we may judge from the quality
of the literature they get, are more refined than the
book readers in our community; and their taste has
no doubt been cultivated by that of the disciplined
and experienced editors. So far as I have known
these, they are men of æsthetic conscience and of generous sympathy. They have their preferences in
the different kinds, and they have their theory of what

9

kind will be most acceptable to their readers; but they
exercise their selective function with the wish to give
them the best things they can. I do not know one of
them — and it has been my good fortune to know
them nearly all — who would print a wholly inferior
thing for the sake of an inferior class of readers,
though they may sometimes decline a good thing
because for one reason or another they believe it
would not be liked. Still, even this does not often
happen; they would rather chance the good thing they
doubted of than underrate their readers' judgment.

The young author who wins recognition in a first-
class magazine has achieved a double success, first,
with the editor, and then with the best reading public. Many factitious and fallacious literary reputations have been made through books, but very few
have been made through the magazines, which are
not only the best means of living, but of outliving,
with the author; they are both bread and fame to him.
If I insist a little upon the high office which this modern form of publication fulfils in the literary world, it
is because I am impatient of the antiquated and ignorant prejudice which classes the magazines as ephemeral. They are ephemeral in form, but in substance
they are not ephemeral, and what is best in them
awaits its resurrection in the book, which, as the
first form, is so often a lasting death. An interesting proof of the value of the magazine to literature
is the fact that a good novel will often have wider
acceptance as a book from having been a magazine
serial.

## V

Under the *régime* of the great literary periodicals
the prosperity of literary men would be much greater

than it actually is if the magazines were altogether literary. But they are not, and this is one reason why literature is still the hungriest of the professions. Two-thirds of the magazines are made up of material which, however excellent, is without literary quality. Very probably this is because even the highest class of readers, who are the magazine readers, have small love of pure literature, which seems to have been growing less and less in all classes. I say seems, because there are really no means of ascertaining the fact, and it may be that the editors are mistaken in making their periodicals two-thirds popular science, politics, economics, and the timely topics which I will call contemporanics. But, however that may be, their efforts in this direction have narrowed the field of literary industry, and darkened the hope of literary prosperity kindled by the unexampled prosperity of their periodicals. They pay very well indeed for literature; they pay from five or six dollars a thousand words for the work of the unknown writer to a hundred and fifty dollars a thousand words for that of the most famous, or the most popular, if there is a difference between fame and popularity; but they do not, altogether, want enough literature to justify the best business talent in devoting itself to belles-lettres, to fiction, or poetry, or humorous sketches of travel, or light essays; business talent can do far better in dry goods, groceries, drugs, stocks, real estate, railroads, and the like. I do not think there is any danger of a ruinous competition from it in the field which, though narrow, seems so rich to us poor fellows, whose business talent is small, at the best.

The most of the material contributed to the magazines is the subject of agreement between the editor and the author; it is either suggested by the author or is the fruit of some suggestion from the editor; in any case the price is stipulated beforehand, and it is no longer the custom for a well-known contributor to leave the payment to the justice or the generosity of the publisher; that was never a fair thing to either, nor ever a wise thing. Usually, the price is so much a thousand words, a truly odious method of computing literary value, and one well calculated to make the author feel keenly the hatefulness of selling his art at all. It is as if a painter sold his picture at so much a square inch, or a sculptor bargained away a group of statuary by the pound. But it is a custom that you cannot always successfully quarrel with, and most writers gladly consent to it, if only the price a thousand words is large enough. The sale to the editor means the sale of the serial rights only, but if the publisher of the magazine is also a publisher of books, the re-publication of the material is supposed to be his right, unless there is an understanding to the contrary; the terms for this are another affair. Formerly something more could be got for the author by the simultaneous appearance of his work in an English magazine; but now the great American magazines, which pay far higher prices than any others in the world, have a circulation in England so much exceeding that of any English periodical that the simultaneous publication can no longer be arranged for from this side, though I believe it is still done here from the other side.

## VI

I think this is the case of authorship as it now stands with regard to the magazines. I am not sure that the case is in every way improved for young authors. The magazines all maintain a staff for the careful examination of manuscripts, but as most of the material they print has been engaged, the number of volunteer contributions that they can use is very small; one of the greatest of them, I know, does not use fifty in the course of a year. The new writer, then, must be very good to be accepted, and when accepted he may wait long before he is printed. The pressure is so great in these avenues to the public favor that one, two, three years, are no uncommon periods of delay. If the young writer has not the patience for this, or has a soul above cooling his heels in the courts of fame, or must do his best to earn something at once, the book is his immediate hope. How slight a hope the book is I have tried to hint already, but if a book is vulgar enough in sentiment, and crude enough in taste, and flashy enough in incident, or, better or worse still, if it is a bit hot in the mouth, and promises impropriety if not indecency, there is a very fair chance of its success; I do not mean success with a self-respecting publisher, but with the public, which does not personally put its name to it, and is not openly smirched by it. I will not talk of that kind of book, however, but of the book which the young author has written out of an unspoiled heart and an untainted mind, such as most young men and women write; and I will suppose that it has found a publisher. It is human nature, as competition has deformed human nature, for the publisher to wish the author to take all the risks, and he possibly proposes that the author shall publish it at his own expense, and let him have a percentage of the retail price for managing it. If not that, he proposes that the author shall pay for the stereotype plates, and take fifteen per cent. of the price of the book; or if this will not go, if the author cannot, rather than will not, do it (he is commonly only too glad to do anything he can), then the publisher offers him ten per cent. of the retail price after the first thousand copies

13

have been sold. But if he fully believes in the book,
he will give ten per cent. from the first copy sold, and
pay all the costs of publication himself. The book
is to be retailed for a dollar and a half, and the publisher is not displeased with a new book that sells fifteen hundred copies. Whether the author has as
much reason to be pleased is a question, but if the book
does not sell more he has only himself to blame, and
had better pocket in silence the two hundred and twenty-
five dollars he gets for it, and bless his publisher,
and try to find work somewhere at five dollars a week.
The publisher has not made any more, if quite as much
as the author, and until a book has sold two thousand
copies the division is fair enough. After that, the
heavier expenses of manufacturing have been de-
frayed and the book goes on advertising itself; there
is merely the cost of paper, printing, binding, and
marketing to be met, and the arrangement becomes
fairer and fairer for the publisher. The author has
no right to complain of this, in the case of his first
book, which he is only too grateful to get accepted at
all. If it succeeds, he has himself to blame for making
the same arrangement for his second or third; it is his
fault, or else it is his necessity, which is practically
the same thing. It will be business for the publisher
to take advantage of his necessity quite the same as
if it were his fault; but I do not say that he will always
do so; I believe he will very often not do so.

At one time there seemed a probability of the en-
largement of the author's gains by subscription publication, and one very well-known American author
prospered fabulously in that way. The percentage
offered by the subscription houses was only about
half as much as that paid by the trade, but the sales
were so much greater that the author could very well
afford to take it. Where the book-dealer sold ten, the

book-agent sold a hundred; or at least he did so in the case of Mark Twain's books; and we all thought it reasonable he could do so with ours. Such of us as made experiment of him, however, found the facts illogical. No book of literary quality was made to go by subscription except Mr. Clemens's books, and I think these went because the subscription public never knew what good literature they were. This sort of readers, or buyers, were so used to getting something worthless for their money that they would not spend it for artistic fiction, or, indeed, for any fiction at all except Mr. Clemens's, which they probably supposed bad. Some good books of travel had a measurable success through the book-agents, but not at all the success that had been hoped for; and I believe now the subscription trade again publishes only compilations, or such works as owe more to the skill of the editor than the art of the writer. Mr. Clemens himself no longer offers his books to the public in that way.

It is not common, I think, in this country, to publish on the half-profits system, but it is very common in England, where, owing probably to the moisture in the air, which lends a fairy outline to every prospect, it seems to be peculiarly alluring. One of my own early books was published there on these terms, which I accepted with the insensate joy of the young author in getting any terms from a publisher. The book sold, sold every copy of the small first edition, and in due time the publisher's statement came. I did not think my half of the profits was very great, but it seemed a fair division after every imaginable cost had been charged up against my poor book, and that frail venture had been made to pay the expenses of composition, corrections, paper, printing, binding, advertising, and editorial copies. The wonder ought to have been that there was anything at all coming to me, but I was young and greedy then, and I really thought there ought to have been more. I was disappointed, but I made the best of it, of course, and took the account to the junior partner of the house which employed me, and said that I should like to draw on him for the sum due me from the London publishers. He said, Certainly; but after a glance at the account he smiled and said he supposed I knew how much the sum was? I answered, Yes; it was eleven pounds nine shillings, was not it? But I owned at the same time that I never was good at figures, and that I found English money peculiarly baffling. He laughed now, and said, It was eleven shillings and ninepence. In fact, after all those charges for composition, corrections, paper, printing, binding, advertising, and editorial copies, there was a most ingenious and wholly surprising charge of ten per cent. commission on sales, which reduced my half from pounds to shillings, and handsomely increased the publisher's half in proportion. I do not now dispute the justice of the charge. It was not the fault of the half-profits system; it was the fault of the glad young author who did not distinctly inform himself of its mysterious nature in agreeing to it, and had only to reproach himself if he was finally disappointed.

But there is always something disappointing in the accounts of publishers, which I fancy is because authors are strangely constituted, rather than because publishers are so. I will confess that I have such inordinate expectations of the sale of my books, which I hope I think modestly of, that the sales reported to me never seem great enough. The copyright due me, no matter how handsome it is, appears deplorably mean, and I feel impoverished for several days after I get it. But, then, I ought to add that my balance in the bank is always much less than I have supposed it to be, and my own checks, when they come back to me, have the air of having been in a conspiracy to betray me.

No, we literary men must learn, no matter how we boast ourselves in business, that the distress we feel from our publisher's accounts is simply idiopathic; and I for one wish to bear my witness to the constant good faith and uprightness of publishers. It is supposed that because they have the affair altogether in their hands they are apt to take advantage in it; but this does not follow, and as a matter of fact they have the affair no more in their own hands than any other business man you have an open account with. There is nothing to prevent you from looking at their books, except your own innermost belief and fear that their books are correct, and that your literature has brought you so little because it has sold so little.

The author is not to blame for his superficial delusion to the contrary, especially if he has written a book that has set every one talking, because it is of a vital interest. It may be of a vital interest, without being at all the kind of book people want to buy; it may be the kind of book that they are content to know at second hand; there are such fatal books; but hearing so much, and reading so much about it, the author cannot help hoping that it has sold much more than the publisher says. The publisher is undoubtedly honest, however, and the author had better put away the comforting question of his integrity.

The English writers seem largely to suspect their publishers; but I believe that American authors, when not flown with flattering reviews, as largely trust theirs. Of course there are rogues in every walk of life. I will not say that I ever personally met them

in the flowery paths of literature, but I have heard of
other people meeting them there, just as I have heard
of people seeing ghosts, and I have to believe in both
the rogues and the ghosts, without the witness of my
own senses. I suppose, upon such grounds mainly,
that there are wicked publishers, but, in the case of
our books that do not sell, I am afraid that it is the
graceless and inappreciative public which is far more
to blame than the wickedest of the publishers. It is
true that publishers will drive a hard bargain when
they can, or when they must; but there is nothing to
hinder an author from driving a hard bargain, too,
when he can, or when he must; and it is to be said of
the publisher that he is always more willing to abide
by the bargain when it is made than the author is;
perhaps because he has the best of it. But he has
not always the best of it; I have known publishers
too generous to take advantage of the innocence of
authors; and I fancy that if publishers had to do with
any race less diffident than authors, they would have
won a repute for unselfishness that they do not now
enjoy. It is certain that in the long period when we
flew the black flag of piracy there were many among
our corsairs on the high seas of literature who paid
a fair price for the stranger craft they seized; still
oftener they removed the cargo and released their
capture with several weeks' provision; and although
there was undoubtedly a good deal of actual throat-
cutting and scuttling, still I feel sure that there was
less of it than there would have been in any other line
of business released to the unrestricted plunder of the
neighbor. There was for a long time even a comity
among these amiable buccaneers, who agreed not to
interfere with each other, and so were enabled to pay
over to their victims some portion of the profit from
their stolen goods. Of all business men publishers

are probably the most faithful and honorable, and are only surpassed in virtue when men of letters turn business men.

## VII

Publishers have their little theories, their little superstitions, and their blind faith in the great god Chance which we all worship. These things lead them into temptation and adversity, but they seem to do fairly well as business men, even in their own behalf. They do not make above the usual ninety-five per cent. of failures, and more publishers than authors get rich.

Some theories or superstitions publishers and authors share together. One of these is that it is best to keep your books all in the hands of one publisher if you can, because then he can give them more attention and sell more of them. But my own experience is that when my books were in the hands of three publishers they sold quite as well as when one had them; and a fellow-author whom I approached in question of this venerable belief laughed at it. This bold heretic held that it was best to give each new book to a new publisher, for then the fresh man put all his energies into pushing it; but if you had them all together, the publisher rested in a vain security that one book would sell another, and that the fresh venture would revive the public interest in the stale ones. I never knew this to happen, and I must class it with the superstitions of the trade. It may be so in other and more constant countries, but in our fickle republic each last book has to fight its own way to public favor, much as if it had no sort of literary lineage. Of course this is stating it rather largely, and the truth will be found inside rather than outside of my statement; but there is at least truth enough in it to give the young author pause. While one is preparing to sell his basket of glass, he may as well ask himself whether it is better to part with all to one dealer or not; and if he kicks it over, in spurning the imaginary customer who asks the favor of taking the entire stock, that will be his fault, and not the fault of the customer.

However, the most important question of all with the man of letters as a man of business is what kind of book will sell the best of itself, because, at the end of the ends, a book sells itself or does not sell at all; kissing, after long ages of reasoning and a great deal of culture, still goes by favor, and though innumerable generations of horses have been led to the water, not one horse has yet been made to drink. With the best, or the worst, will in the world, no publisher can force a book into acceptance. Advertising will not avail, and reviewing is notoriously futile. If the book does not strike the popular fancy, or deal with some universal interest, which need by no means be a profound or important one, the drums and the cymbals shall be beaten in vain. The book may be one of the best and wisest books in the world, but if it has not this sort of appeal in it the readers of it, and, worse yet, the purchasers, will remain few, though fit. The secret of this, like most other secrets of a rather ridiculous world, is in the awful keeping of fate, and we can only hope to surprise it by some lucky chance. To plan a surprise of it, to aim a book at the public favor, is the most hopeless of all endeavors, as it is one of the unworthiest; and I can, neither as a man of letters nor as a man of business, counsel the young author to do it. The best that you can do is to write the book that it gives you the most pleasure to write, to put as much heart and soul as you have about you into it, and then hope as hard as you can to reach the heart and soul of the great multitude of your fellow-men.

That, and that alone, is good business for a man of letters.

The man of letters must make up his mind that in the United States the fate of a book is in the hands of the women. It is the women with us who have the most leisure, and they read the most books. They are far better educated, for the most part, than our men, and their tastes, if not their minds, are more cultivated. Our men read the newspapers, but our women read the books; the more refined among them read the magazines. If they do not always know what is good, they do know what pleases them, and it is useless to quarrel with their decisions, for there is no appeal from them. To go from them to the men would be going from a higher to a lower court, which would be honestly surprised and bewildered, if the thing were possible. As I say, the author of light literature, and often the author of solid literature, must resign himself to obscurity unless the ladies choose to recognize him. Yet it would be impossible to forecast their favor for this kind or that. Who could prophesy it for another, who guess it for himself? We must strive blindly for it, and hope somehow that our best will also be our prettiest; but we must remember at the same time that it is not the ladies' man who is the favorite of the ladies.

There are, of course, a few, a very few, of our greatest authors who have striven forward to the first place in our Valhalla without the help of the largest reading-class among us; but I should say that these were chiefly the humorists, for whom women are said nowhere to have any warm liking, and who have generally with us come up through the newspapers, and have never lost the favor of the newspaper readers. They have become literary men, as it were, without the newspaper readers' knowing it; but those who have approached literature from another direction have won fame in it chiefly by grace of the women, who first read them, and then made their husbands and fathers read them. Perhaps, then, and as a matter of business, it would be well for a serious author, when he finds that he is not pleasing the women, and probably never will please them, to turn humorous author, and aim at the countenance of the men. Except as a humorist he certainly never will get it, for your American, when he is not making money, or trying to do it, is making a joke, or trying to do it.

## VIII

I hope that I have not been hinting that the author who approaches literature through journalism is not as fine and high a literary man as the author who comes directly to it, or through some other avenue; I have not the least notion of condemning myself by any such judgment. But I think it is pretty certain that fewer and fewer authors are turning from journalism to literature, though the *entente cordiale* between the two professions seems as great as ever. I fancy, though I may be as mistaken in this as I am in a good many other things, that most journalists would have been literary men if they could, at the beginning, and that the kindness they almost always show to young authors is an effect of the self-pity they feel for their own thwarted wish to be authors. When an author is once warm in the saddle, and is riding his winged horse to glory, the case is different: they have then often no sentiment about him; he is no longer the image of their own young aspiration, and they would willingly see Pegasus buck under him, or have him otherwise brought to grief and shame. They

22

are apt to gird at him for his unhallowed gains, and they would be quite right in this if they proposed any way for him to live without them; as I have allowed at the outset, the gains *are* unhallowed. Apparently it is unseemly for two or three authors to be making half as much by their pens as popular ministers often receive in salary; the public is used to the pecuniary prosperity of some of the clergy, and at least sees nothing droll in it; but the paragrapher can always get a smile out of his readers at the gross disparity between the ten thousand dollars Jones gets for his novel and the five pounds Milton got for his epic. I have always thought Milton was paid too little, but I will own that he ought not to have been paid at all, if it comes to that. Again I say that no man ought to live by any art; it is a shame to the art if not to the artist; but as yet there is no means of the artist's living otherwise and continuing an artist.

The literary man has certainly no complaint to make of the newspaper man, generally speaking. I have often thought with amazement of the kindness shown by the press to our whole unworthy craft, and of the help so lavishly and freely given to rising and even risen authors. To put it coarsely, brutally, I do not suppose that any other business receives so much gratuitous advertising, except the theatre. It is enormous, the space given in the newspapers to literary notes, literary announcements, reviews, interviews, personal paragraphs, biographies, and all the rest, not to mention the vigorous and incisive attacks made from time to time upon different authors for their opinions of romanticism, realism, capitalism, socialism, Catholicism, and Sandemanianism. I have sometimes doubted whether the public cared for so much of it all as the editors gave them, but I have always said this under my breath, and I have thankfully

taken my share of the common bounty. A curious
fact, however, is that this vast newspaper publicity
seems to have very little to do with an author's popularity, though ever so much with his notoriety. Some
of those strange subterranean fellows who never come
to the surface in the newspapers, except for a con-
temptuous paragraph at long intervals, outsell the
famousest of the celebrities, and secretly have their
horses and yachts and country seats, while immodest
merit is left to get about on foot and look up summer
board at the cheaper hotels. That is probably right,
or it would not happen; it seems to be in the general
scheme, like millionairism and pauperism; but it becomes a question, then, whether the newspapers, with
all their friendship for literature, and their actual
generosity to literary men, can really help one much
to fortune, however much they help one to fame. Such
a question is almost too dreadful, and, though I have
asked it, I will not attempt to answer it. I would
much rather consider the question whether, if the
newspapers can make an author, they can also unmake him, and I feel pretty safe in saying that I do not
think they can. The Afreet, once out of the bottle, can
never be coaxed back or cudgelled back; and the author whom the newspapers have made cannot be un-
made by the newspapers. Perhaps he could if they
would let him alone; but the art of letting alone the
creature of your favor, when he has forfeited your
favor, is yet in its infancy with the newspapers. They
consign him to oblivion with a rumor that fills the
land, and they keep visiting him there with an up-
roar which attracts more and more notice to him. An
author who has long enjoyed their favor suddenly
and rather mysteriously loses it, through his opinions on certain matters of literary taste, say. For
the space of five or six years he is denounced with a

unanimity and an incisive vigor that ought to convince him there is something wrong. If he thinks it is his censors, he clings to his opinions with an abiding constancy, while ridicule, obloquy, caricature, burlesque, critical refutation, and personal detraction follow unsparingly upon every expression, for instance, of his belief that romantic fiction is the highest form of fiction, and that the base, sordid, photographic, commonplace school of Tolstoy, Tourguénief, Zola, Hardy, and James is unworthy a moment's comparison with the school of Rider Haggard. All this ought certainly to unmake the author in question, but this is not really the effect. Slowly but surely the clamor dies away, and the author, without relinquishing one of his wicked opinions, or in any wise showing himself repentant, remains apparently whole; and he even returns in a measure to the old kindness— not indeed to the earlier day of perfectly smooth things, but certainly to as much of it as he merits.

I would not have the young author, from this imaginary case, believe that it is well either to court or to defy the good opinion of the press. In fact, it will not only be better taste, but it will be better business, for him to keep it altogether out of his mind. There is only one whom he can safely try to please, and that is himself. If he does this he will very probably please other people; but if he does not please himself he may be sure that he will not please them; the book which he has not enjoyed writing no one will enjoy reading. Still, I would not have him attach too little consequence to the influence of the press. I should say, let him take the celebrity it gives him gratefully but not too seriously; let him reflect that he is often the necessity rather than the ideal of the paragrapher, and that the notoriety the journalists bestow upon him is not the measure of their acquaintance with his

25

work, far less his meaning. They are good fellows, those hard-pushed, poor fellows of the press, but the very conditions of their censure, friendly or unfriendly, forbid it thoroughness, and it must often have more zeal than knowledge in it.

IX

There are some sorts of light literature once greatly in demand, but now apparently no longer desired by magazine editors, who ought to know what their readers desire. Among these is the travel sketch, to me a very agreeable kind, and really to be regretted in its decline. There are some reasons for its decline besides a change of taste in readers, and a possible surfeit. Travel itself has become so universal that everybody, in a manner, has been everywhere, and the foreign scene has no longer the charm of strangeness. We do not think the Old World either so romantic or so ridiculous as we used; and perhaps from an instinctive perception of this altered mood writers no longer appeal to our sentiment or our humor with sketches of outlandish people and places. Of course, this can hold true only in a general way; the thing is still done, but not nearly so much done as formerly. When one thinks of the long line of American writers who have greatly pleased in this sort, and who even got their first fame in it, one must grieve to see it obsolescent. Irving, Curtis, Bayard Taylor, Herman Melville, Ross Browne, Warner, Ik Marvell, Longfellow, Lowell, Story, Mr. James, Mr. Aldrich, Mr. Hay, Mrs. Hunt, Mr. C. W. Stoddard, Mark Twain, and many others whose names will not come to me at the moment, have in their several ways richly contributed to our pleasure in it; but I cannot now fancy

a young author finding favor with an editor in a sketch
of travel or a study of foreign manners and customs;
his work would have to be of the most signal importance and brilliancy to overcome the editor's feeling
that the thing had been done already; and I believe
that a publisher, if offered a book of such things, would
look at it askance and plead the well-known quiet of
the trade. Still, I may be mistaken.

I am rather more confident about the decline of another literary species—namely, the light essay. We
have essays enough and to spare of certain soberer
and severer sorts, such as grapple with problems and
deal with conditions; but the kind that I mean, the
slightly humorous, gentle, refined, and humane kind,
seems no longer to abound as it once did. I do not
know whether the editor discourages them, knowing
his readers' frame, or whether they do not offer themselves, but I seldom find them in the magazines. I
certainly do not believe that if any one were now to
write essays such as Warner's *Backlog Studies*, an
editor would refuse them; and perhaps nobody really
writes them. Nobody seems to write the sort that
Colonel Higginson formerly contributed to the periodicals, or such as Emerson wrote. Without a great
name behind it, I am afraid that a volume of essays
would find few buyers, even after the essays had
made a public in the magazines. There are, of course,
instances to the contrary, but they are not so many or
so striking as to make me think that the essay could
be offered as a good opening for business talent.

I suspect that good poetry by well-known hands
was never better paid in the magazines than it is now.
I must say, too, that I think the quality of the minor
poetry of our day is better than that of twenty-five or
thirty years ago. I could name half a score of young
poets whose work from time to time gives me great

27

pleasure, by the reality of its feeling and the delicate perfection of its art, but I will not name them, for fear of passing over half a score of others equally meritorious. We have certainly no reason to be discouraged, whatever reason the poets themselves have to be so, and I do not think that even in the short story our younger writers are doing better work than they are doing in the slighter forms of verse. Yet the notion of inviting business talent into this field would be as preposterous as that of asking it to devote itself to the essay. What book of verse by a recent poet, if we except some such peculiarly gifted poet as Mr. Whitcomb Riley, has paid its expenses, not to speak of any profit to the author? Of course, it would be rather more offensive and ridiculous that it should do so than that any other form of literary art should do so; and yet there is no more provision in our economic system for the support of the poet apart from his poems than there is for the support of the novelist apart from his novel. One could not make any more money by writing poetry than by writing history, but it is a curious fact that while the historians have usually been rich men, and able to afford the luxury of writing history, the poets have usually been poor men, with no pecuniary justification in their devotion to a calling which is so seldom an election.

To be sure, it can be said for them that it costs far less to set up poet than to set up historian. There is no outlay for copying documents, or visiting libraries, or buying books. In fact, except as historian, the man of letters, in whatever walk, has not only none of the expenses of other men of business, but none of the expenses of other artists. He has no such outlay to make for materials, or models, or studio rent as the painter or the sculptor has, and his income, such as it is, is immediate. If he strikes the fancy

of the editor with the first thing he offers, as he very
well may, it is as well with him as with other men
after long years of apprenticeship. Although he will
always be the better for an apprenticeship, and the
longer apprenticeship the better, he may practically
need none at all. Such are the strange conditions of
his acceptance with the public, that he may please
better without it than with it. An author's first book
is too often not only his luckiest, but really his best;
it has a brightness that dies out under the school he
puts himself to, but a painter or a sculptor is only the
gainer by all the school he can give himself.

## X

In view of this fact it becomes again very hard to
establish the author's status in the business world,
and at moments I have grave question whether he
belongs there at all, except as a novelist. There is,
of course, no outlay for him in this sort, any more than
in any other sort of literature, but it at least supposes
and exacts some measure of preparation. A young
writer may produce a brilliant and very perfect romance, just as he may produce a brilliant and very
perfect poem, but in the field of realistic fiction, or in
what we used to call the novel of manners, a writer
can only produce an inferior book at the outset. For
this work he needs experience and observation, not
so much of others as of himself, for ultimately his characters will all come out of himself, and he will need
to know motive and character with such thoroughness and accuracy as he can acquire only through
his own heart. A man remains in a measure strange
to himself as long as he lives, and the very sources
of novelty in his work will be within himself; he can

continue to give it freshness in no other way than by knowing himself better and better. But a young writer and an untrained writer has not yet begun to be acquainted even with the lives of other men. The world around him remains a secret as well as the world within him, and both unfold themselves simultaneously to that experience of joy and sorrow that can come only with the lapse of time. Until he is well on towards forty, he will hardly have assimilated the materials of a great novel, although he may have amassed them. The novelist, then, is a man of letters who is like a man of business in the necessity of preparation for his calling, though he does not pay store-rent, and may carry all his affairs under his hat, as the phrase is. He alone among men of letters may look forward tc that sort of continuous prosperity which follows from capacity and diligence in other vocations; for story-telling is now a fairly recognized trade, and the story-teller has a money-standing in the economic world. It is not a very high standing, I think, and I have expressed the belief that it does not bring him the respect felt for men in other lines of business. Still our people cannot deny some consideration to a man who gets a hundred dollars a thousand words or whose book sells five hundred thousand copies or less. That is a fact appreciable to business, and the man of letters in the line of fiction may reasonably feel that his place in our civilization, though he may owe it to the women who form the great mass of his readers, has something of the character of a vested interest in the eyes of men. There is, indeed, as yet no conspiracy law which will avenge the attempt to injure him in his business. A critic, or a dark conjuration of critics, may damage him at will and to the extent of their power, and he has no recourse but to write better books, or worse. The law will do noth-

ing for him, and a boycott of his books might be preached with immunity by any class of men not liking his
opinions on the question of industrial slavery or anti-
pædobaptism. Still the market for his wares is stead-
ier than the market for any other kind of literary wares,
and the prices are better. The historian, who is a
kind of inferior realist, has something like the same
steadiness in the market, but the prices he can command are much lower, and the two branches of the
novelist's trade are not to be compared in a business
way. As for the essayist, the poet, the traveller, the
popular scientist, they are nowhere in the competition
for the favor of readers. The reviewer, indeed, has
a pretty steady call for his work, but I fancy the re-
viewers who get a hundred dollars a thousand words
could all stand upon the point of a needle without
crowding one another; I should rather like to see them
doing it. Another gratifying fact of the situation
is that the best writers of fiction, who are most in
demand with the magazines, probably get nearly as
much money for their work as the inferior novelists
who outsell them by tens of thousands, and who make
their appeal to the innumerable multitude of the less
educated and less cultivated buyers of fiction in book
form. I think they earn their money, but if I did not
think all of the higher class of novelists earned so
much money as they get, I should not be so invidious
as to single out for reproach those who did not.

The difficulty about payment, as I have hinted, is
that literature has no objective value really, but only
a subjective value, if I may so express it. A poem,
an essay, a novel, even a paper on political economy,
may be worth gold untold to one reader, and worth
nothing whatever to another. It may be precious to
one mood of the reader, and worthless to another mood
of the same reader. How, then, is it to be priced, and

how is it to be fairly marketed? All people must be
fed, and all people must be clothed, and all people
must be housed; and so meat, raiment, and shelter
are things of positive and obvious necessity, which
may fitly have a market price put upon them. But
there is no such positive and obvious necessity, I am
sorry to say, for fiction, or not for the higher sort of
fiction. The sort of fiction which corresponds in literature to the circus and the variety theatre in the show-
business seems essential to the spiritual health of the
masses, but the most cultivated of the classes can get
on, from time to time, without an artistic novel. This
is a great pity, and I should be very willing that readers might feel something like the pangs of hunger
and cold, when deprived of their finer fiction; but apparently they never do. Their dumb and passive
need is apt only to manifest itself negatively, or in
the form of weariness of this author or that. The
publisher of books can ascertain the fact through the
declining sales of a writer; but the editor of a magazine, who is the best customer of the best writers, must
feel the market with a much more delicate touch. Sometimes it may be years before he can satisfy himself that
his readers are sick of Smith, and are pining for Jones;
even then he cannot know how long their mood will last,
and he is by no means safe in cutting down Smith's
price and putting up Jones's. With the best will in the
world to pay justly, he cannot. Smith, who has been
boring his readers to death for a year, may write to-
morrow a thing that will please them so much that he
will at once be a prime favorite again; and Jones,
whom they have been asking for, may do something
so uncharacteristic and alien that it will be a flat failure in the magazine. The only thing that gives either
writer positive value is his acceptance with the reader;
but the acceptance is from month to month wholly

32

uncertain. Authors are largely matters of fashion, like this style of bonnet, or that shape of gown. Last spring the dresses were all made with lace berthas, and Smith was read; this year the butterfly capes are worn, and Jones is the favorite author. Who shall forecast the fall and winter modes?

## XI

In this inquiry it is always the author rather than the publisher, always the contributor rather than the editor, whom I am concerned for. I study the difficulties of the publisher and editor only because they involve the author and the contributor; if they did not, I will not say with how hard a heart I should turn from them; my only pang now in scrutinizing the business conditions of literature is for the makers of literature, not the purveyors of it.

After all, and in spite of my vaunting title, is the man of letters ever a business man? I suppose that, strictly speaking, he never is, except in those rare instances where, through need or choice, he is the publisher as well as the author of his books. Then he puts something on the market and tries to sell it there, and is a man of business. But otherwise he is an artist merely, and is allied to the great mass of wage-workers who are paid for the labor they have put into the thing done or the thing made; who live by doing or making a thing, and not by marketing a thing after some other man has done it or made it. The quality of the thing has nothing to do with the economic nature of the case; the author is, in the last analysis, merely a working-man, and is under the rule that governs the working-man's life. If he is sick or sad, and cannot work, if he is lazy or tipsy, and will not, then

he earns nothing. He cannot delegate his business
to a clerk or a manager; it will not go on while he is
sleeping. The wage he can command depends strictly
upon his skill and diligence.

I myself am neither sorry nor ashamed for this;
I am glad and proud to be of those who eat their bread
in the sweat of their own brows, and not the sweat of
other men's brows; I think my bread is the sweeter
for it. In the mean time, I have no blame for business
men; they are no more of the condition of things than
we working-men are; they did no more to cause it or
create it; but I would rather be in my place than in
theirs, and I wish that I could make all my fellow-
artists realize that economically they are the same as
mechanics, farmers, day-laborers. It ought to be our
glory that we produce something, that we bring into
the world something that was not choately there before; that at least we fashion or shape something
anew; and we ought to feel the tie that binds us to
all the toilers of the shop and field, not as a galling
chain, but as a mystic bond also uniting us to Him
who works hitherto and evermore.

I know very well that to the vast multitude of our fel-
low-working-men we artists are the shadows of names,
or not even the shadows. I like to look the facts in the
face, for though their lineaments are often terrible,
yet there is light nowhere else; and I will not pretend,
in this light, that the masses care any more for us than
we care for the masses, or so much. Nevertheless,
and most distinctly, we are not of the classes. Except
in our work, they have no use for us; if now and then
they fancy qualifying their material splendor or their
spiritual dulness with some artistic presence, the attempt is always a failure that bruises and abashes.
In so far as the artist is a man of the world, he is the
less an artist, and if he fashions himself upon fashion,

he deforms his art. We all know that ghastly type; it is more absurd even than the figure which is really of the world, which was born and bred in it, and conceives of nothing outside of it, or above it. In the social world, as well as in the business world, the artist is anomalous, in the actual conditions, and he is perhaps a little ridiculous.

Yet he has to be somewhere, poor fellow, and I think that he will do well to regard himself as in a transition state. He is really of the masses, but they do not know it, and what is worse, they do not know him; as yet the common people do not hear him gladly or hear him at all. He is apparently of the classes; they know him, and they listen to him; he often amuses them very much; but he is not quite at ease among them; whether they know it or not, he knows that he is not of their kind. Perhaps he will never be at home anywhere in the world as long as there are masses whom he ought to consort with, and classes whom he cannot consort with. The prospect is not brilliant for any artist now living, but perhaps the artist of the future will see in the flesh the accomplishment of that human equality of which the instinct has been divinely planted in the human soul.

## WORRIES OF A WINTER WALK

THE other winter, as I was taking a morning walk down to the East River, I came upon a bit of our motley life, a fact of our piebald civilization, which has perplexed me from time to time, ever since, and which I wish now to leave with the reader, for his or her more thoughtful consideration.

### I

The morning was extremely cold. It professed to be sunny, and there was really some sort of hard glitter in the air, which, so far from being tempered by this effulgence, seemed all the stonier for it. Blasts of frigid wind swept the streets, and buffeted each other in a fury of resentment when they met around the corners. Although I was passing through a populous tenement-house quarter, my way was not hindered by the sports of the tenement-house children, who commonly crowd one from the sidewalks; no frowzy head looked out over the fire-escapes; there were no peddlers' carts or voices in the road-way; not above three or four shawl-hooded women cowered out of the little shops with small purchases in their hands; not so many tiny girls with jugs opened the doors of the beer saloons. The butchers' windows were painted with patterns of frost, through which I could dimly see the frozen meats hanging like hideous stalactites from

36

the roof. When I came to the river, I ached in sympathy with the shipping painfully atilt on the rocklike surface of the brine, which broke against the piers, and sprayed itself over them like showers of powdered quartz.

But it was before I reached this final point that I received into my consciousness the moments of the human comedy which have been an increasing burden to it. Within a block of the river I met a child so small that at first I almost refused to take any account of her, until she appealed to my sense of humor by her amusing disproportion to the pail which she was lugging in front of her with both of her little mittened hands. I am scrupulous about mittens, though I was tempted to write of her little naked hands, red with the pitiless cold. This would have been more effective, but it would not have been true, and the truth obliges me to own that she had a stout, warm-looking knit jacket on. The pail—which was half her height and twice her bulk—was filled to overflowing with small pieces of coal and coke, and if it had not been for this I might have taken her for a child of the better classes, she was so comfortably clad. But in that case she would have had to be fifteen or sixteen years old, in order to be doing so efficiently and responsibly the work which, as the child of the worse classes, she was actually doing at five or six. We must, indeed, allow that the early self-helpfulness of such children is very remarkable, and all the more so because they grow up into men and women so stupid that, according to the theories of all polite economists, they have to have their discontent with their conditions put into their heads by malevolent agitators.

From time to time this tiny creature put down her heavy burden to rest; it was, of course, only relatively heavy; a man would have made nothing of it. From time to time she was forced to stop and pick up the bits of coke that tumbled from her heaping pail. She could not consent to lose one of them, and at last, when she found she could not make all of them stay on the heap, she thriftily tucked them into the pockets of her jacket, and trudged sturdily on till she met a boy some years older, who planted himself in her path and stood looking at her, with his hands in his pockets. I do not say he was a bad boy, but I could see in his furtive eye that she was a sore temptation to him. The chance to have fun with her by upsetting her bucket, and scattering her coke about till she cried with vexation, was one which might not often present itself, and I do not know what made him forego it, but I know that he did, and that he finally passed her, as I have seen a young dog pass a little cat, after having stopped it, and thoughtfully considered worrying it.

I turned to watch the child out of sight, and when I faced about towards the river again I received the second instalment of my present perplexity. A cart, heavily laden with coke, drove out of the coal-yard which I now perceived I had come to, and after this cart followed two brisk old women, snugly clothed and tightly tucked in against the cold like the child, who vied with each other in catching up the lumps of coke that were jolted from the load, and filling their aprons with them; such old women, so hale, so spry, so tough and tireless, with the withered apples red in their cheeks, I have not often seen. They may have been about sixty years, or sixty-five, the time of life when most women are grandmothers and are relegated on their merits to the cushioned seats of their children's homes, softly silk-gowned and lace-capped, dear visions of lilac and lavender, to be loved and petted by their grandchildren. The fancy can hardly put such sweet ladies in the place of those nimble beldams, who

"IT PROFESSED TO BE SUNNY, AND THERE WAS REALLY SOME SORT OF HARD GLITTER IN THE AIR."

hopped about there in the wind-swept street, plucking
up their day's supply of firing from the involuntary
bounty of the cart. Even the attempt is unseemly,
and whether mine is at best but a feeble fancy, not
bred to strenuous feats of any kind, it fails to bring
them before me in that figure. I cannot imagine ladies
doing that kind of thing; I can only imagine women
who had lived hard and worked hard all their lives
doing it; who had begun to fight with want from their
cradles, like that little one with the pail, and must
fight without ceasing to their graves. But I am not
unreasonable; I understand and I understood what I
saw to be one of the things that must be, for the perfectly good and sufficient reason that they always
have been; and at the moment I got what pleasure I
could out of the stolid indifference of the cart-driver,
who never looked about him at the scene which interested me, but jolted onward, leaving a trail of pungent
odors from his pipe in the freezing eddies of the air behind him.

## II

It is still not at all, or not so much, the fact that
troubles me; it is what to do with the fact. The question began with me almost at once, or at least as soon
as I faced about and began to walk homeward with the
wind at my back. I was then so much more comfortable that the æsthetic instinct thawed out in me, and
I found myself wondering what use I could make of
what I had seen in the way of my trade. Should I
have something very pathetic, like the old grandmother going out day after day to pick up coke for her sick
daughter's freezing orphans till she fell sick herself?
What should I do with the family in that case? They
could not be left at that point, and I promptly imagined

a granddaughter, a girl of about eighteen, very pretty and rather proud, a sort of belle in her humble neighborhood, who should take her grandmother's place. I decided that I should have her Italian, because I knew something of Italians, and could manage that nationality best, and I should call her Maddalena; either Maddalena or Marina; Marina would be more Venetian, and I saw that I must make her Venetian. Here I was on safe ground, and at once the love-interest appeared to help me out. By virtue of the law of contrasts, it appeared to me in the person of a Scandinavian lover, tall, silent, blond, whom I at once felt I could do, from my acquaintance with Scandinavian lovers in Norwegian novels. His name was Janssen, a good, distinctive Scandinavian name; I do not know but it is Swedish; and I thought he might very well be a Swede; I could imagine his manner from that of a Swedish waitress we once had.

Janssen—Jan Janssen, say—drove the coke-cart which Marina's grandmother used to follow out of the coke-yard, to pick up the bits of coke as they were jolted from it, and he had often noticed her with deep indifference. At first he noticed Marina—or Nina, as I soon saw I must call her—with the same unconcern; for in her grandmother's hood and jacket and check apron, with her head held shamefacedly downward, she looked exactly like the old woman. I thought I would have Nina make her self-sacrifice rebelliously, as a girl like her would be apt to do, and follow the coke-cart with tears. This would catch Janssen's notice, and he would wonder, perhaps with a little pang, what the old woman was crying about, and then he would see that it was not the old woman. He would see that it was Nina, and he would be in love with her at once, for she would not only be very pretty, but he would know that she was good, if she were willing to help her family in that way.

He would respect the girl, in his dull, sluggish, Northern way. He would do nothing to betray himself. But little by little he would begin to befriend her. He would carelessly overload his cart before he left the yard, so that the coke would fall from it more lavishly; and not only this, but if he saw a stone or a piece of coal in the street he would drive over it, so that more coke would be jolted from his load.

Nina would get to watching for him. She must not notice him much at first, except as the driver of the overladen, carelessly driven cart. But after several mornings she must see that he is very strong and handsome. Then, after several mornings more, their eyes must meet, her vivid black eyes, with the tears of rage and shame in them, and his cold blue eyes. This must be the climax; and just at this point I gave my fancy a rest, while I went into a drug-store at the corner of Avenue B to get my hands warm.

They were abominably cold, even in my pockets, and I had suffered past several places trying to think of an excuse to go in. I now asked the druggist if he had something which I felt pretty sure he had not, and this put him in the wrong, so that when we fell into talk he was very polite. We agreed admirably about the hard times, and he gave way respectfully when I doubted his opinion that the winters were getting milder. I made him reflect that there was no reason for this, and that it was probably an illusion from that deeper impression which all experiences made on us in the past, when we were younger; I ought to say that he was an elderly man, too. I said I fancied such a morning as this was not very mild for people that had no fires, and this brought me back again to Janssen and Marina, by way of the coke-cart. The

41

thought of them rapt me so far from the druggist that
I listened to his answer with a glazing eye, and did
not know what he said.   My hands had now got warm,
and I bade him good-morning with a parting regret,
which he civilly shared, that he had not the thing I
had not wanted, and I pushed out again into the cold,
which I found not so bad as before.

My hero and heroine were waiting for me there, and
I saw that to be truly modern, to be at once realistic
and mystical, to have both delicacy and strength, I
must not let them get further acquainted with each
other.   The affair must simply go on from day to day,
till one morning Jan must note that it was again the
grandmother and no longer the girl who was following his cart.   She must be very weak from a long
sickness—I was not sure whether to have it the grippe
or not, but I decided upon that provisionally—and she
must totter after Janssen, so that he must get down
after a while to speak to her under pretence of arrang-
ing the tail-board of his cart, or something of that kind ;
I did not care for the detail.   They should get into talk
in the broken English which was the only language
they could have in common, and she should burst into
tears, and tell him that now Nina was sick ; I imagined
making this very simple, but very touching, and I
really made it so touching that it brought the lump
into my own throat, and I knew it would be effective
with the reader.   Then I had Jan get back upon his
cart, and drive stolidly on again, and the old woman
limp feebly after.

There should not be any more, I decided, except
that one very cold morning, like that ; Jan should be
driving through that street, and should be passing
the door of the tenement house where Nina had lived,
just as a little procession should be issuing from it.
The fact must be told in brief sentences, with a total

absence of emotionality. The last touch must be Jan's cart turning the street corner with Jan's figure sharply silhouetted against the clear, cold morning light. Nothing more.

But it was at this point that another notion came into my mind, so antic, so impish, so fiendish, that if there were still any Evil One, in a world which gets on so poorly without him, I should attribute it to his suggestion; and this was that the procession which Jan saw issuing from the tenement-house door was not a funeral procession, as the reader will have rashly fancied, but a wedding procession, with Nina at the head of it, quite well again, and going to be married to the little brown youth with ear-rings who had long had her heart.

With a truly perverse instinct, I saw how strong this might be made, at the fond reader's expense, to be sure, and how much more pathetic, in such a case, the silhouetted figure on the coke-cart would really be. I should, of course, make it perfectly plain that no one was to blame, and that the whole affair had been so tacit on Jan's part that Nina might very well have known nothing of his feeling for her. Perhaps at the very end I might subtly insinuate that it was possible he might have had no such feeling towards her as the reader had been led to imagine.

## III

The question as to which ending I ought to have given my romance is what has ever since remained to perplex me, and it is what has prevented my ever writing it. Here is material of the best sort lying useless on my hands, which, if I could only make up my mind, might be wrought into a short story as affecting as any that wring our hearts in fiction; and I think I could get something fairly unintelligible out of the broken English of Jan and Nina's grandmother, and certainly something novel. All that I can do now, however, is to put the case before the reader, and let him decide for himself how it should end.

The mere humanist, I suppose, might say that I am rightly served for having regarded the fact I had witnessed as material for fiction at all; that I had no business to bewitch it with my miserable art; that I ought to have spoken to that little child and those poor old women, and tried to learn something of their lives from them, that I might offer my knowledge again for the instruction of those whose lives are easy and happy in the indifference which ignorance breeds in us. I own there is something in this, but then, on the other hand, I have heard it urged by nice people that they do not want to know about such squalid lives, that it is offensive and out of taste to be always bringing them in, and that we ought to be writing about good society, and especially creating *grandes dames* for their amusement. This sort of people could say to the humanist that he ought to be glad there are coke-carts for fuel to fall off from for the lower classes, and that here was no case for sentiment; for if one is to be interested in such things at all, it must be æsthetically, though even this is deplorable in the presence of fiction already overloaded with low life, and so poor in *grandes dames* as ours.

## CONFESSIONS OF A SUMMER COLONIST

THE season is ending in the little summer settlement on the Down East coast where I have been passing the last three months, and with each loath day the sense of its peculiar charm grows more poignant. A prescience of the home-sickness I shall feel for it when I go already begins to torment me, and I find myself wishing to imagine some form of words which shall keep a likeness of it at least through the winter; some shadowy semblance which I may turn to hereafter if any chance or change should destroy or transform it, or, what is more likely, if I should never come back to it. Perhaps others in the distant future may turn to it for a glimpse of our actual life in one of its most characteristic phases; I am sure that in the distant present there are many millions of our own inlanders to whom it would be altogether strange.

I

In a certain sort *fragile* is written all over our colony; as far as the visible body of it is concerned it is inexpressibly perishable; a fire and a high wind could sweep it all away; and one of the most American of all American things is the least fitted among them to survive from the present to the future, and impart to it the significance of what may soon be a "portion and parcel" of our extremely forgetful past.

45

It is also in a supremely transitional moment: one might say that last year it was not quite what it is now, and next year it may be altogether different. In fact, our summer colony is in that happy hour when the rudeness of the first summer conditions has been left far behind, and vulgar luxury has not yet cumbrously succeeded to a sort of sylvan distinction.

The type of its simple and sufficing hospitalities is the seven-o'clock supper. Every one, in hotel or in cottage, dines between one and two, and no less scrupulously sups at seven, unless it is a few extremists who sup at half-past seven. At this function, which is our chief social event, it is *de rigueur* for the men *not* to dress, and they come in any sort of sack or jacket or cutaway, letting the ladies make up the pomps which they forego. From this fact may be inferred the informality of the men's day-time attire; and the same note is sounded in the whole range of the cottage life, so that once a visitor from the world outside, who had been exasperated beyond endurance by the absence of form among us (if such an effect could be from a cause so negative), burst out with the reproach, "Oh, you make a fetish of your informality!"

"Fetish" is, perhaps, rather too strong a word, but I should not mind saying that informality was the tutelary genius of the place. American men are everywhere impatient of form. It burdens and bothers them, and they like to throw it off whenever they can. We may not be so very democratic at heart as we seem, but we are impatient of ceremonies that separate us when it is our business or our pleasure to get at one another; and it is part of our splendor to ignore the ceremonies as we do the expenses. We have all the decent grades of riches and poverty in our colony, but our informality is not more the treasure of the humble than of the great. In the nature of things it cannot

46

last, however, and the only question is how long it will last. I think, myself, until some one imagines giving an eight-o'clock dinner; then all the informalities will go, and the whole train of evils which such a dinner connotes will rush in.

## II

The cottages themselves are of several sorts, and some still exist in the earlier stages of mutation from the fishermen's and farmers' houses which formed their germ. But these are now mostly let as lodgings to bachelors and other single or semi-detached folks who go for their meals to the neighboring hotels or boarding-houses. The hotels are each the centre of this sort of centripetal life, as well as the homes of their own scores or hundreds of inmates. A single boarding-house gathers about it half a dozen dependent cottages which it cares for, and feeds at its table; and even where the cottages have kitchens and all the housekeeping facilities, their inmates sometimes prefer to dine at the hotels. By far the greater number of cottagers, however, keep house, bringing their service with them from the cities, and settling in their summer homes for three or four or five months.

The houses conform more or less to one type: a picturesque structure of colonial pattern, shingled to the ground, and stained or left to take a weather-stain of grayish brown, with cavernous verandas, and dormer-windowed roofs covering ten or twelve rooms. Within they are, if not elaborately finished, elaborately fitted up, with a constant regard to health in the plumbing and drainage. The water is brought in a system of pipes from a lake five miles away, and as it is only for summer use the pipes are not buried from the frost, but wander along the surface, through the ferns and brambles of the tough little sea-side knolls on which the cottages are perched, and climb the old tumbling stone walls of the original pastures before diving into the cemented basements.

Most of the cottages are owned by their occupants, and furnished by them; the rest, not less attractive and hardly less tastefully furnished, belong to natives, who have caught on to the architectural and domestic preferences of the summer people, and have built them to let. The rugosities of the stony pasture land end in a wooded point seaward, and curve east and north in a succession of beaches. It is on the point, and mainly short of its wooded extremity, that the cottages of our settlement are dropped, as near the ocean as may be, and with as little order as birds' nests in the grass, among the sweet-fern, laurel, bay, wild rasp-berries, and dog-roses, which it is the ideal to leave as untouched as possible. Wheel-worn lanes that twist about among the hollows find the cottages from the highway, but foot - paths approach one cottage from another, and people walk rather than drive to each other's doors.

From the deep-bosomed, well-sheltered little harbor the tides swim inland, half a score of winding miles, up the channel of a river which without them would be a trickling rivulet. An irregular line of cottages follows the shore a little way, and then leaves the river to the schooners and barges which navigate it as far as the oldest pile-built wooden bridge in New England, and these in their turn abandon it to the fleets of row-boats and canoes in which summer youth of both sexes explore it to its source over depths as clear as glass, past wooded headlands and low, rush-bordered meadows, through reaches and openings of pastoral fields, and under the shadow of dreaming groves.

If there is anything lovelier than the scenery of this gentle river I do not know it; and I doubt if the sky is purer and bluer in paradise. This seems to be the consensus, tacit or explicit, of the youth who visit it, and employ the landscape for their picnics and their water parties from the beginning to the end of summer.

The river is very much used for sunsets by the cottagers who live on it, and who claim a superiority through them to the cottagers on the point. An impartial mind obliges me to say that the sunsets are all good in our colony; there is no place from which they are bad; and yet for a certain tragical sunset, where the dying day bleeds slowly into the channel till it is filled from shore to shore with red as far as the eye can reach, the river is unmatched.

For my own purposes, it is not less acceptable, however, when the fog has come in from the sea like a visible reverie, and blurred the whole valley with its whiteness. I find that particularly good to look at from the trolley-car which visits and revisits the river before finally leaving it, with a sort of desperation, and hiding its passion with a sudden plunge into the woods.


III


The old fishing and seafaring village, which has now almost lost the recollection of its first estate in its absorption with the care of the summer colony, was sparsely dropped along the highway bordering the harbor, and the shores of the river, where the piles of the time-worn wharves are still rotting. A few houses of the past remain, but the type of the summer cottage has impressed itself upon all the later building, and the native is passing architecturally, if not personally, into abeyance. He takes the situation philosophical-

ly, and in the season he caters to the summer colony
not only as the landlord of the rented cottages, and
the keeper of the hotels and boarding-houses, but as
livery-stableman, grocer, butcher, marketman, apoth-
ecary, and doctor; there is not one foreign accent in
any of these callings. If the native is a farmer, he
devotes himself to vegetables, poultry, eggs, and fruit
for the summer folks, and brings these supplies to their
doors; his children appear with flowers; and there are
many proofs that he has accurately sized the cottagers up in their tastes and fancies as well as their
needs. I doubt if we have sized him up so well, or if
our somewhat conventionalized ideal of him is perfectly representative. He is, perhaps, more complex
than he seems; he is certainly much more self-sufficing
than might have been expected. The summer folks
are the material from which his prosperity is wrought,
but he is not dependent, and is very far from sub-
missive. As in all right conditions, it is here the em-
ployer who asks for work, not the employé; and the
work must be respectfully asked for. There are many
fables to this effect, as, for instance, that of the lady
who said to a summer visitor, critical of the week's
wash she had brought home, "I'll wash you and I'll
iron you, but I won't take none of your jaw " A prim-
itive independence is the keynote of the native character, and it suffers no infringement, but rather boasts
itself. "We're independent here, I tell you," said the
friendly person who consented to take off the wire
door. "I was down Bangor way doin' a piece of work,
and a fellow come along, and says he, 'I want you
should hurry up on that job.' 'Hello!' says I, 'I guess
I'll pull out.' Well, we calculate to do our *work*," he
added, with an accent which sufficiently implied that
their consciences needed no bossing in the performance.

"THE COTTAGES . . . ARE DROPPED AS NEAR THE OCEAN AS MAY BE"

# CONFESSIONS OF A SUMMER COLONIST

The native compliance with any summer-visiting request is commonly in some such form as, "Well, I don't know but what I can," or, "I guess there ain't anything to hinder me." This compliance is so rarely, if ever, carried to the point of domestic service that it may fairly be said that all the domestic service, at least of the cottagers, is imported. The natives will wait at the hotel tables; they will come in "to accommodate"; but they will not "live out." I was one day witness of the extreme failure of a friend whose city cook had suddenly abandoned him, and who applied to a friendly farmer's wife in the vain hope that she might help him to some one who would help his family out in their strait. "Why, there ain't a girl in the Hollow that lives out! Why, if you was sick abed, I don't know as I know anybody 't you could git to set up with you." The natives will not live out because they cannot keep their self-respect in the conditions of domestic service. Some people laugh at this self-respect, but most summer folks like it, as I own I do.

In our partly mythical estimate of the native and his relation to us, he is imagined as holding a kind of carnival when we leave him at the end of the season, and it is believed that he likes us to go early. We have had his good offices at a fair price all summer, but as it draws to a close they are rendered more and more fitfully. From some, perhaps flattered, reports of the happiness of the natives at the departure of the sojourners, I have pictured them dancing a sort of *farandole*, and stretching with linked hands from the farthest summer cottage up the river to the last on the wooded point. It is certain that they get tired, and I could not blame them if they were glad to be rid of their guests, and to go back to their own social life. This includes church festivals of divers kinds, lectures

51

and shows, sleigh - rides, theatricals, and reading-clubs, and a plentiful use of books from the excellent-ly chosen free village library. They say frankly that the summer folks have no idea how pleasant it is when they are gone, and I am sure that the gayeties to which we leave them must be more tolerable than those which we go back to in the city. It may be, however, that I am too confident, and that their gayeties are only different. I should really like to know just what the entertainments are which are given in a building de-voted to them in a country neighborhood three or four miles from the village. It was once a church, but is now used solely for social amusements.

IV

The amusements of the summer colony I have al-ready hinted at. Besides suppers, there are also teas, of larger scope, both afternoon and evening. There are hops every week at the two largest hotels, which are practically free to all; and the bathing - beach is, of course, a supreme attraction. The bath-houses, which are very clean and well equipped, are not very cheap, either for the season or for a single bath, and there is a pretty pavilion at the edge of the sands. This is always full of gossiping spectators of the hardy adventurers who brave tides too remote from the Gulf Stream to be ever much warmer than sixty or sixty-five degrees. The bathers are mostly young people, who have the courage of their pretty bathing-costumes or the inextinguishable ardor of their years. If it is not rather serious business with them all, still I admire the fortitude with which some of them remain in fif-teen minutes.

Beyond our colony, which calls itself the Port, there

is a far more populous watering-place, east of the Point, known as the Beach, which is the resort of people several grades of gentility lower than ours: so many, in fact, that we never can speak of the Beach without averting our faces, or, at the best, with a tolerant smile. It is really a succession of beaches, all much longer and, I am bound to say, more beautiful than ours, lined with rows of the humbler sort of summer cottages known as shells, and with many hotels of corresponding degree. The cottages may be hired by the week or month at about two dollars a day, and they are supposed to be taken by inland people of little social importance. Very likely this is true; but they seemed to be very nice, quiet people, and I commonly saw the ladies reading, on their verandas, books and magazines, while the gentlemen sprayed the dusty road before them with the garden hose. The place had also for me an agreeable alien suggestion, and in passing the long row of cottages I was slightly reminded of Scheveningen.

Beyond the cottage settlements is a struggling little park, dedicated to the only Indian saint I ever heard of, though there may be others. His statue, colossal in sheet-lead, and painted the copper color of his race, offers any heathen comer the choice between a Bible in one of his hands and a tomahawk in the other, at the entrance of the park; and there are other sheet-lead groups and figures in the white of allegory at different points. It promises to be a pretty enough little place in future years, but as yet it is not much resorted to by the excursions which largely form the prosperity of the Beach. The concerts and the "high-class vaudeville" promised have not flourished in the pavilion provided for them, and one of two monkeys in the zoological department has perished of the public inattention. This has not fatally affected the

53

captive bear, who rises to his hind legs, and eats pea-
nuts and doughnuts in that position like a fellow-citi-
zen. With the cockatoos and parrots, and the dozen
deer in an inclosure of wire netting, he is no mean
attraction; but he does not charm the excursionists
away from the summer village at the shore, where
they spend long afternoons splashing among the waves,
or in lolling groups of men, women, and children
on the sand. In the more active gayeties, I have
seen nothing so decided during the whole season as
the behavior of three young girls who once came up
out of the sea, and obliged me by dancing a measure
on the smooth, hard beach in their bathing-dresses.

## V

I thought it very pretty, but I do not believe such a
thing could have been seen on *our* beach, which is safe
from all excursionists, and sacred to the cottage and
hotel life of the Port.

Besides our beach and its bathing, we have a read-
ing-club for the men, evolved from one of the old native houses, and verandaed round for summer use;
and we have golf-links and a golf club-house within
easy trolley reach. The links are as energetically,
if not as generally, frequented as the sands, and the
sport finds the favor which attends it everywhere in
the decay of tennis. The tennis-courts which I saw
thronged about by eager girl-crowds, here, seven years
ago, are now almost wholly abandoned to the lovers
of the game, who are nearly always men.

Perhaps the only thing (besides, of course, our common mortality) which we have in common with the
excursionists is our love of the trolley-line. This, by
its admirable equipment, and by the terror it inspires

in horses, has wellnigh abolished driving; and following the old country roads, as it does, with an occasional short-cut through the deep, green-lighted woods or across the prismatic salt meadows, it is of a picturesque variety entirely satisfying. After a year of fervent opposition and protest, the whole community —whether of summer or of winter folks—now gladly accepts the trolley, and the grandest cottager and the lowliest hotel dweller meet in a grateful appreciation of its beauty and comfort.

Some pass a great part of every afternoon on the trolley, and one lady has achieved celebrity by spending four dollars a week in trolley-rides. The exhilaration of these is varied with an occasional apprehension when the car pitches down a sharp incline, and twists almost at right angles on a sudden curve at the bottom without slacking its speed. A lady who ventured an appeal to the conductor at one such crisis was reassured, and at the same time taught her place, by his reply: "That motorman's life, ma'am, is just as precious to him as what yours is to you."

She had, perhaps, really ventured too far, for ordinarily the employés of the trolley do not find occasion to use so much severity with their passengers. They look after their comfort as far as possible, and seek even to anticipate their wants in unexpected cases, if I may believe a story which was told by a witness. She had long expected to see some one thrown out of the open car at one of the sharp curves, and one day she actually saw a woman hurled from the seat into the road. Luckily the woman alighted on her feet, and stood looking round in a daze.

"Oh! oh!" exclaimed another woman in the seat behind, "she's left her umbrella!"

The conductor promptly threw it out to her.

"Why," demanded the witness, "did that lady *wish* to get out here?"

The conductor hesitated before he jerked the bell-pull to go on. Then he said, "Well, she'll want her umbrella, anyway."

The conductors are, in fact, very civil as well as kind. If they see a horse in anxiety at the approach of the car, they considerately stop, and let him get by with his driver in safety. By such means, with their frequent trips and low fares, and with the ease and comfort of their cars, they have conciliated public favor, and the trolley has drawn travel away from the steam railroad in such measure that it ran no trains last winter.

## VI

The trolley, in fact, is a fad of the summer folks this year; but what it will be another no one knows; it may be their hissing and by-word. In the mean time, as I have already suggested, they have other amusements. These are not always of a nature so general as the trolley, or so particular as the tea. But each of the larger hotels has been fully supplied with entertainments for the benefit of their projectors, though nearly everything of the sort had some sort of charitable slant. I assisted at a stereopticon lecture on Alaska for the aid of some youthful Alaskans of both sexes, who were shown first in their savage state, and then as they appeared after a merely rudimental education, in the costumes and profiles of our own civilization. I never would have supposed that education could do so much in so short a time; and I gladly gave my mite for their further development in classic beauty and a final elegance. My mite was taken up in a hat, which, passed round among the audience, is a common means of collecting the spectators' expressions of appreciation. Other entertainments, of a prouder frame, exact an admission fee, but I am not sure that these are better than some of the hat-shows, as they are called.

The tale of our summer amusements would be sadly incomplete without some record of the bull-fights given by the Spanish prisoners of war on the neighboring island, where they were confined the year of the war. Admission to these could be had only by favor of the officers in charge, and even among the élite of the colony those who went were a more elect few. Still, the day I went, there were some fifty or seventy-five spectators, who arrived by trolley near the island, and walked to the stockade which confined the captives. A real bull-fight, I believe, is always given on Sunday, and Puritan prejudice yielded to usage even in the case of a burlesque bull-fight; at any rate, it was on a Sunday that we crouched in an irregular semicircle on a rising ground within the prison pale, and faced the captive audience in another semicircle, across a little alley for the entrances and exits of the performers. The president of the bull-fight was first brought to the place of honor in a hand-cart, and then came the banderilleros, the picadores, and the espada, wonderfully effective and correct in white muslin and colored tissue-paper. Much may be done in personal decoration with advertising placards; and the lofty mural crown of the president urged the public on both sides to Use Plug Cut. The picador's pasteboard horse was attached to his middle, fore and aft, and looked quite the sort of hapless jade which is ordinarily sacrificed to the bulls. The toro himself was composed of two prisoners, whose horizontal backs were covered with a brown blanket; and his feet, sometimes bare and sometimes shod with india-rubber boots, were

of the human pattern. Practicable horns, of a somewhat too yielding substance, branched from a front of
pasteboard, and a cloth tail, apt to come off in the
charge, swung from his rear. I have never seen a
genuine corrida, but a lady present, who had, told me
that this was conducted with all the right circumstance; and it is certain that the performers entered
into their parts with the artistic gust of their race.
The picador sustained some terrific falls, and in his
quality of horse had to be taken out repeatedly and
sewed up; the banderilleros tormented and eluded the
toro with table-covers, one red and two drab, till the
espada took him from them, and with due ceremony,
after a speech to the president, drove his blade home
to the bull's heart. I stayed to see three bulls killed;
the last was uncommonly fierce, and when his hind-
quarters came off or out, his forequarters charged
joyously among the aficionados on the prisoners' side,
and made havoc in their thickly packed ranks. The
espada who killed this bull was showered with cigars
and cigarettes from our side.

I do not know what the Sabbath-keeping shades of
the old Puritans made of our presence at such a fête
on Sunday; but possibly they had got on so far in a
better life as to be less shocked at the decay of piety
among us than pleased at the rise of such Christianity
as had brought us, like friends and comrades, together
with our public enemies in this harmless fun. I wish
to say that the tobacco lavished upon the espada was
collected for the behoof of all the prisoners.

VII

Our fiction has made so much of our summer places
as the *mise en scène* of its love stories that I suppose

58

"IN WHATEVER SORT OUR COLONISTS AMUSE THEMSELVES, IT IS
WITH THE LEAST POSSIBLE CEREMONY"

I ought to say something of this side of our colonial
life. But after sixty I suspect that one's eyes are
poor for that sort of thing, and I can only say that in
its earliest and simplest epoch the Port was particularly famous for the good times that the young people
had. They still have good times, though whether on
just the old terms I do not know. I know that the
river is still here with its canoes and row-boats, its
meadowy reaches apt for dual solitude, and its groves
for picnics. There is not much bicycling—the roads
are rough and hilly—but there is something of it, and
it is mighty pretty to see the youth of both sexes
bicycling with their heads bare. They go about bareheaded on foot and in buggies, too, and the young
girls seek the tan which their mothers used so anxiously to shun.

The sail-boats, manned by weather-worn and weath-
er-wise skippers, are rather for the pleasure of such
older summer folks as have a taste for cod-fishing,
which is here very good. But at every age, and in
whatever sort our colonists amuse themselves, it is
with the least possible ceremony. It is as if, Nature
having taken them so hospitably to her heart, they
felt convention an affront to her. Around their cottages, as I have said, they prefer to leave her primi-
tive beauty untouched, and she rewards their for-
bearance with such a profusion of wild flowers as I
have seen nowhere else. The low, pink laurel flushed
all the stony fields to the edges of their verandas when
we first came; the meadows were milk-white with
daisies; in the swampy places delicate orchids grew,
in the pools the flags and flowering rushes; all the
paths and way-sides were set with dog-roses; the hollows and stony tops were broadly matted with ground
juniper. Since then the golden-rod has passed from
glory to glory, first mixing its yellow-powdered plumes

with the red-purple tufts of the iron-weed, and then with the wild asters everywhere. There has come later a dwarf sort, six or ten inches high, wonderfully rich and fine, which, with a low, white aster, seems to hold the field against everything else, though the taller golden-rod and the masses of the high, blue asters nod less thickly above it. But these smaller blooms deck the ground in incredible profusion, and have an innocent air of being stuck in, as if they had been fancifully used for ornament by children or Indians.

In a little while now, as it is almost the end of September, all the feathery gold will have faded to the soft, pale ghosts of that loveliness. The summer birds have long been silent; the crows, as if they were so many exultant natives, are shouting in the blue sky above the windrows of the rowan, in jubilant prescience of the depopulation of our colony, which fled the hotels a fortnight ago. The days are growing shorter, and the red evenings falling earlier; so that the cottagers' husbands who come up every Saturday from town might well be impatient for a Monday of final return. Those who came from remoter distances have gone back already; and the lady cottagers, lingering hardily on till October, must find the sight of the empty hotels and the windows of the neighboring houses, which no longer brighten after the chilly nightfall, rather depressing. Every one says that this is the loveliest time of year, and that it will be divine here all through October. But there are sudden and unexpected defections; there is a steady pull of the heart cityward, which it is hard to resist. The first great exodus was on the first of the month, when the hotels were deserted by four-fifths of their guests. The rest followed, half of them within the week, and within a fortnight none but an all but inaudible and invisible remnant were left, who made no impression of summer sojourn in the deserted trolleys.

The days now go by in moods of rapid succession. There have been days when the sea has lain smiling in placid derision of the recreants who have fled the lingering summer; there have been nights when the winds have roared round the cottages in wild menace of the faithful few who have remained.

We have had a magnificent storm, which came, as an equinoctial storm should, exactly at the equinox, and for a day and a night heaped the sea upon the shore in thundering surges twenty and thirty feet high. I watched these at their awfulest, from the wide windows of a cottage that crouched in the very edge of the surf, with the effect of clutching the rocks with one hand and holding its roof on with the other. The sea was such a sight as I have not seen on shipboard, and while I luxuriously shuddered at it, I had the advantage of a mellow log-fire at my back, purring and softly crackling in a quiet indifference to the storm.

Twenty-four hours more made all serene again. Blood-curdling tales of lobster-pots carried to sea filled the air; but the air was as blandly unconscious of ever having been a fury as a lady who has found her lost temper. Swift alternations of weather are so characteristic of our colonial climate that the other afternoon I went out with my umbrella against the raw, cold rain of the morning, and had to raise it against the broiling sun. Three days ago I could say that the green of the woods had no touch of hectic in it; but already the low trees of the swamp-land have flamed into crimson. Every morning, when I look out, this crimson is of a fierier intensity, and the trees on the distant uplands are beginning slowly to kindle, with a sort of inner glow which has not yet burst into a blaze. Here and there the golden-rod is rusting; but there seems only to be more and more asters of all sorts; and I have seen ladies coming home with sheaves of blue gentians; I have heard that the orchids are beginning again to light their tender lamps from the burning blackberry vines that stray from the pastures to the edge of the swamps.

After an apparently total evanescence there has been a like resuscitation of the spirit of summer society. In the very last week of September we have gone to a supper, which lingered far out of its season like one of these late flowers, and there has been an afternoon tea which assembled an astonishing number of cottagers, all secretly surprised to find one another still here, and professing openly a pity tinged with contempt for those who are here no longer.

I blamed those who had gone home, but I myself sniff the asphalt afar; the roar of the street calls to me with the magic that the voice of the sea is losing. Just now it shines entreatingly, it shines winningly, in the sun which is mellowing to an October tenderness, and it shines under a moon of perfect orb, which seems to have the whole heavens to itself in "the first watch of the night," except for "the red planet Mars." This begins to burn in the west before the flush of sunset has passed from it; and then, later, a few moonwashed stars pierce the vast vault with their keen points. The stars which so powdered the summer sky seem mostly to have gone back to town, where no doubt people take them for electric lights.

## THE EDITOR'S RELATIONS WITH THE YOUNG
## CONTRIBUTOR

ONE of the trustiest jokes of the humorous paragrapher is that the editor is in great and constant dread of the young contributor; but neither my
experience nor my observation bears out his theory
of the case.

Of course one must not say anything to encourage
a young person to abandon an honest industry in the
vain hope of early honor and profit from literature;
but there have been and there will be literary men and
women always, and these in the beginning have nearly always been young; and I cannot see that there is
risk of any serious harm in saying that it is to the
young contributor the editor looks for rescue from the
old contributor, or from his failing force and charm.

The chances, naturally, are against the young
contributor, and vastly against him; but if any periodical is to live, and to live long, it is by the infusion
of new blood; and nobody knows this better than the
editor, who may seem so unfriendly and uncareful to
the young contributor. The strange voice, the novel
scene, the odor of fresh woods and pastures new, the
breath of morning, the dawn of to-morrow—these are
what the editor is eager for, if he is fit to be an editor
at all; and these are what the young contributor alone
can give him.

A man does not draw near the sixties without wishing people to believe that he is as young as ever, and

he has not written almost as many books as he has lived years without persuading himself that each new work of his has all the surprise of spring; but possibly there are wonted traits and familiar airs and graces in it which forbid him to persuade others. I do not say these characteristics are not charming; I am very far from wishing to say that; but I do say and must say that after the fiftieth time they do not charm for the first time; and this is where the advantage of the new contributor lies, if he happens to charm at all.

## I

The new contributor who does charm can have little notion how much he charms his first reader, who is the editor. That functionary may hide his pleasure in a short, stiff note of acceptance, or he may mask his joy in a check of slender figure; but the contributor may be sure that he has missed no merit in his work, and that he has felt, perhaps far more than the public will feel, such delight as it can give.

The contributor may take the acceptance as a token that his efforts have not been neglected, and that his achievements will always be warmly welcomed; that even his failures will be leniently and reluctantly recognized as failures, and that he must persist long in failure before the friend he has made will finally forsake him.

I do not wish to paint the situation wholly rose color; the editor will have his moods, when he will not see so clearly or judge so justly as at other times; when he will seem exacting and fastidious, and will want this or that mistaken thing done to the story, or poem, or sketch, which the author knows to be simply perfect as it stands; but he is worth bearing with, and he will be constant to the new contributor as long as there is the least hope of him.

The contributor may be the man or the woman of one story, one poem, one sketch, for there are such; but the editor will wait the evidence of indefinite failure to this effect. His hope always is that he or she is the man or the woman of many stories, many poems, many sketches, all as good as the first.

From my own long experience as a magazine editor, I may say that the editor is more doubtful of failure in one who has once done well than of a second success. After all, the writer who can do but one good thing is rarer than people are apt to think in their love of the improbable; but the real danger with a young contributor is that he may become his own rival.

What would have been quite good enough from him in the first instance is not good enough in the second, because he has himself fixed his standard so high. His only hope is to surpass himself, and not begin resting on his laurels too soon; perhaps it is never well, soon or late, to rest upon one's laurels. It is well for one to make one's self scarce, and the best way to do this is to be more and more jealous of perfection in one's work.

The editor's conditions are that having found a good thing he must get as much of it as he can, and the chances are that he will be less exacting than the contributor imagines. It is for the contributor to be exacting, and to let nothing go to the editor as long as there is the possibility of making it better. He need not be afraid of being forgotten because he does not keep sending; the editor's memory is simply relentless; he could not forget the writer who has pleased him if he would, for such writers are few.

I do not believe that in my editorial service on the *Atlantic Monthly*, which lasted fifteen years in all, I forgot the name or the characteristic quality, or even the handwriting, of a contributor who had pleased me, and I forgot thousands who did not. I never lost faith in a contributor who had done a good thing; to the end I expected another good thing from him. I think I was always at least as patient with him as he was with me, though he may not have known it.

At the time I was connected with that periodical it had almost a monopoly of the work of Longfellow, Emerson, Holmes, Lowell, Whittier, Mrs. Stowe, Parkman, Higginson, Aldrich, Stedman, and many others not so well known, but still well known. These distinguished writers were frequent contributors, and they could be counted upon to respond to almost any appeal of the magazine; yet the constant effort of the editors was to discover new talent, and their wish was to welcome it.

I know that, so far as I was concerned, the success of a young contributor was as precious as if I had myself written his paper or poem, and I doubt if it gave him more pleasure. The editor is, in fact, a sort of second self for the contributor, equally eager that he should stand well with the public, and able to promote his triumphs without egotism and share them without vanity.

## II

In fact, my curious experience was that if the public seemed not to feel my delight in a contribution I thought good, my vexation and disappointment were as great as if the work had been my own. It was even greater, for if I had really written it I might have had my misgivings of its merit, but in the case of another I could not console myself with this doubt. The sentiment was at the same time one which I could not cherish for the work of an old contributor; such a one stood more upon his own feet; and the young contributor may be sure that the editor's pride, self-interest, and sense of editorial infallibility will all prompt him to stand by the author whom he has introduced to the public, and whom he has vouched for.

I hope I am not giving the young contributor too high an estimate of his value to the editor. After all, he must remember that he is but one of a great many others, and that the editor's affections, if constant, are necessarily divided. It is good for the literary aspirant to realize very early that he is but one of many; for the vice of our comparatively virtuous craft is that it tends to make each of us imagine himself central, if not sole.

As a matter of fact, however, the universe does not revolve around any one of us; we make our circuit of the sun along with the other inhabitants of the earth, a planet of inferior magnitude. The thing we strive for is recognition, but when this comes it is apt to turn our heads. I should say, then, that it was better it should not come in a great glare and a loud shout, all at once, but should steal slowly upon us, ray by ray, breath by breath.

In the mean time, if this happens, we shall have several chances of reflection, and can ask ourselves whether we are really so great as we seem to other people, or seem to seem.

The prime condition of good work is that we shall get ourselves out of our minds. Sympathy we need, of course, and encouragement; but I am not sure that the lack of these is not a very good thing, too. Praise enervates, flattery poisons; but a smart, brisk snub is always rather wholesome.

I should say that it was not at all a bad thing for a young contributor to get his manuscript back, even after a first acceptance, and even a general newspaper proclamation that he is one to make the immortals tremble for their wreaths of asphodel—or is it amaranth? I am never sure which.

Of course one must have one's hour, or day, or week, of disabling the editor's judgment, of calling him to one's self fool, and rogue, and wretch; but after that, if one is worth while at all, one puts the rejected thing by, or sends it off to some other magazine, and sets about the capture of the erring editor with something better, or at least something else.

III

I think it a great pity that editors ever deal other than frankly with young contributors, or put them off with smooth generalities of excuse, instead of saying they do not like this thing or that offered them. It is impossible to make a criticism of all rejected manuscripts, but in the case of those which show promise I think it is quite possible; and if I were to sin my sins over again, I think I should sin a little more on the side of candid severity. I am sure I should do more good in that way, and I am sure that when I used to dissemble my real mind I did harm to those whose feelings I wished to spare. There ought not, in fact, to be question of feeling in the editor's mind.

I know from much suffering of my own that it is terrible to get back a manuscript, but it is not fatal, or I should have been dead a great many times before I was thirty, when the thing mostly ceased for me. One survives it again and again, and one ought to make the reflection that it is not the first business of a periodical to print contributions of this one or of that, but that its first business is to amuse and instruct its readers.

To do this it is necessary to print contributions, but whose they are, or how the writer will feel if they are not printed, cannot be considered. The editor can consider only what they are, and the young contributor will do well to consider that, although the editor may not be an infallible judge, or quite a good judge, it is his business to judge, and to judge without mercy. Mercy ought no more to qualify judgment in an artistic result than in a mathematical result.

## IV

I suppose, since I used to have it myself, that there is a superstition with most young contributors concerning their geographical position. I used to think that it was a disadvantage to send a thing from a small or unknown place, and that it doubled my insignificance to do so. I believed that if my envelope had borne the postmark of New York, or Boston, or some other city of literary distinction, it would have arrived on the editor's table with a great deal more authority. But I am sure this was a mistake from the first, and when I came to be an editor myself I constantly verified the fact from my own dealings with contributors.

A contribution from a remote and obscure place at once piqued my curiosity, and I soon learned that the fresh things, the original things, were apt to come from such places, and not from the literary centres.

One of the most interesting facts concerning the arts of all kinds is that those who wish to give their lives to them do not appear where the appliances for instruction in them exist. An artistic atmosphere does not create artists a literary atmosphere does not create literators; poets and painters spring up where there was never a verse made or a picture seen.

This suggests that God is no more idle now than He was at the beginning, but that He is still and forever shaping the human chaos into the instruments and means of beauty. It may also suggest to that scholar-pride, that vanity of technique, which is so apt to vaunt itself in the teacher, that the best he can do, after all, is to let the pupil teach himself. If he comes with divine authority to the thing he attempts, he will know how to use the appliances, of which the teacher is only the first.

The editor, if he does not consciously perceive the truth, will instinctively feel it, and will expect the acceptable young contributor from the country, the village, the small town, and he will look eagerly at anything that promises literature from Montana or Texas, for he will know that it also promises novelty.

If he is a wise editor, he will wish to hold his hand as much as possible; he will think twice before he asks the contributor to change this or correct that; he will leave him as much to himself as he can. The young contributor, on his part, will do well to realize this, and to receive all the editorial suggestions, which are veiled commands in most cases, as meekly and as imaginatively as possible.

The editor cannot always give his reasons, however strongly he may feel them, but the contributor, if sufficiently docile, can always divine them. It behooves him to be docile at all times, for this is merely the willingness to learn; and whether he learns that he is wrong, or that the editor is wrong, still he gains knowledge.

A great deal of knowledge comes simply from doing, and a great deal more from doing over, and this is what the editor generally means.

# THE EDITOR AND YOUNG CONTRIBUTOR

I think that every author who is honest with himself must own that his work would be twice as good if it were done twice. I was once so fortunately circumstanced that I was able entirely to rewrite one of my novels, and I have always thought it the best written, or at least indefinitely better than it would have been with a single writing. As a matter of fact, nearly all of them have been rewritten in a certain way. They have not actually been rewritten throughout, as in the case I speak of, but they have been gone over so often in manuscript and in proof that the effect has been much the same.

Unless you are sensible of some strong frame within your work, something vertebral, it is best to renounce it, and attempt something else in which you can feel it. If you are secure of the frame you must observe the quality and character of everything you build about it; you must touch, you must almost taste, you must certainly test, every material you employ; every bit of decoration must undergo the same scrutiny as the structure.

It will be some vague perception of the want of this vigilance in the young contributor's work which causes the editor to return it to him for revision, with those suggestions which he will do well to make the most of; for when the editor once finds a contributor he can trust, he rejoices in him with a fondness which the contributor will never perhaps understand.

It will not do to write for the editor alone; the wise editor understands this, and averts his countenance from the contributor who writes at him; but if he feels that the contributor conceives the situation, and will conform to the conditions which his periodical has invented for itself, and will transgress none of its unwritten laws; if he perceives that he has put artistic conscience in every general and detail, and though he has not done the best, has done the best that he can do, he will begin to liberate him from every trammel except those he must wear himself, and will be only too glad to leave him free. He understands, if he is at all fit for his place, that a writer can do well only what he likes to do, and his wish is to leave him to himself as soon as possible.

## V

In my own case, I noticed that the contributors who could be best left to themselves were those who were most amenable to suggestion and even correction, who took the blue pencil with a smile, and bowed gladly to the rod of the proof-reader. Those who were on the alert for offence, who resented a marginal note as a slight, and bumptiously demanded that their work should be printed just as they had written it, were commonly not much more desired by the reader than by the editor.

Of course the contributor naturally feels that the public is the test of his excellence, but he must not forget that the editor is the beginning of the public; and I believe he is a faithfuller and kinder critic than the writer will ever find again.

Since my time there is a new tradition of editing, which I do not think so favorable to the young contributor as the old. Formerly the magazines were made up of volunteer contributions in much greater measure than they are now. At present most of the material is invited and even engaged; it is arranged for a long while beforehand, and the space that can be given to the aspirant, the unknown good, the potential excellence, grows constantly less and less.

A great deal can be said for either tradition; perhaps some editor will yet imagine a return to the earlier method. In the mean time we must deal with the thing that is, and submit to it until it is changed. The moral to the young contributor is to be better than ever, to leave nothing undone that shall enhance his small chances of acceptance.

If he takes care to be so good that the editor must accept him in spite of all the pressure upon his pages, he will not only be serving himself best, but may be helping the editor to a conception of his duty that shall be more hospitable to all other young contributors. As it is, however, it must be owned that their hope of acceptance is very, very small, and they will do well to make sure that they love literature so much that they can suffer long and often repeated disappointment in its cause.

The love of it is the great and only test of fitness for it. It is really inconceivable how any one should attempt it without this, but apparently a great many do. It is evident to every editor that a vast number of those who write the things he looks at so faithfully, and reads more or less, have no artistic motive.

People write because they wish to be known, or because they have heard that money is easily made in that way, or because they think they will chance that among a number of other things. The ignorance of technique which they often show is not nearly so disheartening as the palpable factitiousness of their product. It is something that they have made; it is not anything that has grown out of their lives.

I should think it would profit the young contributor, before he puts pen to paper, to ask himself why he does so, and, if he finds that he has no motive in the love of the thing, to forbear.

Am I interested in what I am going to write about? Do I feel it strongly? Do I know it thoroughly? Do

I imagine it clearly? The young contributor had better ask himself all these questions, and as many more like them as he can think of. Perhaps he will end by not being a young contributor.

But if he is able to answer them satisfactorily to his own conscience, by all means let him begin. He may at once put aside all anxiety about style; that is a thing that will take care of itself; it will be added unto him if he really has something to say; for style is only a man's way of saying a thing.

If he has not much to say, or if he has nothing to say, perhaps he will try to say it in some other man's way, or to hide his own vacuity with rags of rhetoric and tags and fringes of manner, borrowed from this author and that. He will fancy that in this disguise his work will be more literary, and that there is somehow a quality, a grace, imparted to it which will charm in spite of the inward hollowness. His vain hope would be pitiful if it were not so shameful, but it is destined to suffer defeat at the first glance of the editorial eye.

If he really has something to say, however, about something he knows and loves, he is in the best possible case to say it well. Still, from time to time he may advantageously call a halt, and consider whether he is saying the thing clearly and simply.

If he has a good ear he will say it gracefully and musically; and I would by no means have him aim to say it barely or sparely. It is not so that people talk, who talk well, and literature is only the thought of the writer flowing from the pen instead of the tongue.

To aim at succinctness and brevity merely, as some teach, is to practice a kind of quackery almost as offensive as the charlatanry of rhetoric. In either case the life goes out of the subject.

To please one's self, honestly and thoroughly, is

74

the only way to please others in matters of art. I do not mean to say that if you please yourself you will always please others, but that unless you please yourself you will please no one else. It is the sweet and sacred privilege of work done artistically to delight the doer. Art is the highest joy, but any work done in the love of it is art, in a kind, and it strikes the note of happiness as nothing else can.

We hear much of drudgery, but any sort of work that is slighted becomes drudgery; poetry, fiction, painting, sculpture, acting, architecture, if you do not do your best by them, turn to drudgery sore as digging ditches, hewing wood, or drawing water; and these, by the same blessings of God, become arts if they are done with conscience and the sense of beauty.

The young contributor may test his work before the editor assays it, if he will, and he may know by a rule that is pretty infallible whether it is good or not, from his own experience in doing it. Did it give him pleasure? Did he love it as it grew under his hand? Was he glad and willing with it? Or did he force himself to it, and did it hang heavy upon him?

There is nothing mystical in all this; it is a matter of plain, every-day experience, and I think nearly every artist will say the same thing about it, if he examines himself faithfully.

If the young contributor finds that he has no delight in the thing he has attempted, he may very well give it up, for no one else will delight in it. But he need not give it up at once; perhaps his mood is bad; let him wait for a better, and try it again. He may not have learned how to do it well, and therefore he cannot love it, but perhaps he can learn to do it well.

The wonder and glory of art is that it is without formulas. Or, rather, each new piece of work requires the invention of new formulas, which will not

serve again for another. You must apprentice yourself afresh at every fresh undertaking, and your mastery is always a victory over certain unexpected difficulties, and not a dominion of difficulties overcome before.

I believe, in other words, that mastery is merely
the strength that comes of overcoming, and is never
a sovereign power that smooths the path of all obstacles. The combinations in art are infinite, and almost
never the same; you must make your key and fit it to
each, and the key that unlocks one combination will
not unlock another.

## VI

There is no royal road to excellence in literature,
but the young contributor need not be dismayed at
that. Royal roads are the ways that kings travel,
and kings are mostly dull fellows, and rarely have a
good time. They do not go along singing; the spring
that trickles into the mossy log is not for them, nor

"The wildwood flower that simply blows."

But the traveller on the country road may stop for
each of these; and it is not a bad condition of his progress that he must move so slowly that he can learn
every detail of the landscape, both earth and sky, by
heart.

The trouble with success is that it is apt to leave
life behind, or apart. The successful writer especially is in danger of becoming isolated from the reali-
ties that nurtured in him the strength to win success.
When he becomes famous, he becomes precious to
criticism, to society, to all the things that do not exist
from themselves, or have not the root of the matter in
them.

Therefore, I think that a young writer's upward course should be slow and beset with many obstacles, even hardships. Not that I believe in hardships as having inherent virtues; I think it is stupid to regard them in that way; but they oftener bring out the virtues inherent in the sufferer from them than what I may call the *softships;* and at least they stop him, and give him time to think.

This is the great matter, for if we prosper forward rapidly, we have no time for anything but prospering forward rapidly. We have no time for art, even the art by which we prosper.

I would have the young contributor above all things realize that success is not his concern. Good work, true work, beautiful work is his affair, and nothing else. If he does this, success will take care of itself.

He has no business to think of the thing that will take. It is the editor's business to think of that, and it is the contributor's business to think of the thing that he can do with pleasure, the high pleasure that comes from the sense of worth in the thing done. Let him do the best he can, and trust the editor to decide whether it will take.

It will take far oftener than anything he attempts perfunctorily; and even if the editor thinks it will not take, and feels obliged to return it for that reason, he will return it with a real regret, with the honor and affection which we cannot help feeling for any one who has done a piece of good work, and with the will and the hope to get something from him that will take the next time, or the next, or the next.

# SUMMER ISLES OF EDEN

I T may be all an illusion of the map, where the Summer Islands glimmer a small and solitary little group of dots and wrinkles, remote from continental shores, with a straight line descending southeastwardly upon them, to show how sharp and swift the ship's course is, but they seem so far and alien from my wonted place that it is as if I had slid down a steepy slant from the home-planet to a group of asteroids nebulous somewhere in middle space, and were resting there, still vibrant from the rush of the meteoric fall. There were, of course, facts and incidents contrary to such a theory: a steamer starting from New York in the raw March morning, and lurching and twisting through two days of diagonal seas, with people aboard dining and undining, and talking and smoking and cocktailing and hot-scotching and beef-teaing; but when the ship came in sight of the islands, and they began to lift their cedared slopes from the turquoise waters, and to explain their drifted snows as the white walls and white roofs of houses, then the waking sense became the dreaming sense, and the sweet impossibility of that drop through air became the sole reality.

I

Everything here, indeed, is so strange that you placidly accept whatever offers itself as the simplest

78

and naturalest fact. Those low hills, that climb, with their tough, dark cedars, from the summer sea to the summer sky, might have drifted down across the Gulf Stream from the coast of Maine; but when, upon closer inspection, you find them skirted with palms and bananas, and hedged with oleanders, you merely wonder that you had never noticed these growths in Maine before, where you were so familiar with the cedars. The hotel itself, which has brought the Green Mountains with it, in every detail, from the dormer-windowed mansard-roof, and the white-painted, green-shuttered walls, to the neat, school-mistressly waitresses in the dining-room, has a clump of palmettos beside it, swaying and sighing in the tropic breeze, and you know that when it migrates back to the New England hill-country, at the end of the season, you shall find it with the palmettos still before its veranda, and equally at home, somewhere in the Vermont or New Hampshire July. There will be the same American groups looking out over them, and rocking and smoking, though, alas! not so many smoking as rocking.

But where, in that translation, would be the gold-braided red or blue jackets of the British army and navy which lend their lustre and color here to the veranda groups? Where should one get the house walls of whitewashed stone and the garden walls which everywhere glow in the sun, and belt in little spaces full of roses and lilies? These things must come from some other association, and in the case of him who here confesses, the lustrous uniforms and the glowing walls rise from waters as far away in time as in space, and a long-ago apparition of Venetian Junes haunts the coral shore. (They are beginning to say the shore is not coral; but no matter.) To be sure, the white roofs are not accounted for in this visionary presence; and if one may not relate them to the snowfalls of home winters, then one must frankly own them absolutely tropical, together with the green-pillared and green-latticed galleries. They at least suggest the tropical scenery of *Prue and I* as one remembers seeing it through Titbottom's spectacles; and yet, if one supplies roofs of brown-red tiles, it is all Venetian enough, with the lagoon-like expanses that lend themselves to the fond effect. It is so Venetian, indeed, that it wants but a few silent gondolas and noisy gondoliers, in place of the dark, taciturn oarsmen of the clumsy native boats, to complete the coming and going illusion; and there is no good reason why the rough little isles that fill the bay should not call themselves respectively San Giorgio and San Clemente, and Sant' Elena and San Lazzaro: they probably have no other names!

## II

These summer isles of Eden have this advantage over the scriptural Eden, that apparently it was not woman and her seed who were expelled, when once she set foot here, but the serpent and his seed: women now abound in the Summer Islands, and there is not a snake anywhere to be found. There are some tortoises and a great many frogs in their season, but no other reptiles. The frogs are fabled of a note so deep and hoarse that its vibration almost springs the environing mines of dynamite, though it has never yet done so; the tortoises grow to a great size and a patriarchal age, and are fond of Boston brown bread and baked beans, if their preferences may be judged from those of a colossal specimen in the care of an American family living on the islands. The observer who

"IN THE PRETTY PUBLIC GARDEN"

THE TORTOISE AND HIS FRIENDS

contributes this fact to science is able to report the
case of a parrot-fish, on the same premises, so exactly
like a large brown and purple cockatoo that, seeing
such a cockatoo later on dry land, it was with a sense
of something like cruelty in its exile from its native
waters. The angel-fish he thinks not so much like
angels; they are of a transparent purity of substance,
and a cherubic innocence of expression, but they ter-
minate in two tails, which somehow will not lend themselves to the resemblance.

Certainly the angel-fish is not so well named as
the parrot-fish; it might better be called the ghost-
fish, it is so like a moonbeam in the pools it haunts,
and of such a convertible quality with the iridescent
vegetable growths about it. All things here are of a
weird convertibility to the alien perception, and the
richest and rarest facts of nature lavish themselves
in humble association with the commonest and most
familiar. You drive through long stretches of way-
side willows, and realize only now and then that these
willows are thick clumps of oleanders; and through
them you can catch glimpses of banana-orchards,
which look like dishevelled patches of gigantic corn-
stalks. The fields of Easter lilies do not quite live
up to their photographs; they are presently suffering
from a mysterious blight, and their flowers are not
frequent enough to lend them that sculpturesque effect near to, which they wear as far off as New York.
The potato-fields, on the other hand, are of a tender
delicacy of coloring which compensates for the lilies'
lack, and the palms give no just cause for complaint,
unless because they are not nearly enough to characterize the landscape, which in spite of their presence remains so northern in aspect. They were much
whipped and torn by a late hurricane, which afflicted
all the vegetation of the islands, and some of the royal

palms were blown down. Where these are yet standing, as four or five of them are in a famous avenue now quite one-sided, they are of a majesty befitting that of any king who could pass by them: no sovereign except Philip of Macedon in his least judicial moments could pass between them.

The century-plant, which here does not require pampering under glass, but boldly takes its place outdoors with the other trees of the garden, employs much less than a hundred years to bring itself to bloom. It often flowers twice or thrice in that space of time, and ought to take away the reproach of the inhabitants for a want of industry and enterprise: a century-plant at least could do no more in any air, and it merits praise for its activity in the breath of these languorous seas. One such must be in bloom at this very writing, in the garden of a house which this very writer marked for his own on his first drive ashore from the steamer to the hotel, when he bestowed in its dim, unknown interior one of the many multiples of himself which are now pretty well dispersed among the pleasant places of the earth. It fills the night with a heavy heliotropean sweetness, and on the herb beneath, in the effulgence of the waxing moon, the multiple which has spiritually expropriated the legal owners stretches itself in an interminable reverie, and hears Youth come laughing back to it on the waters kissing the adjacent shore, where other white houses (which also it inhabits) bathe their snowy underpinning. In this dream the multiple drives home from the balls of either hotel with the young girls in the little victorias which must pass its sojourn; and, being but a vision itself, forecasts the shapes of flirtation which shall night-long gild the visions of their sleep with the flash of military and naval uniforms. Of course the multiple has been at the dance too (with a shadowy heartache for the dances of forty years ago), and knows enough not to confuse the uniforms.

### III

In whatever way you walk, at whatever hour, the birds are sweetly calling in the way-side oleanders and the wild sage-bushes and the cedar-tops. They are mostly cat-birds, quite like our own; and bluebirds, but of a deeper blue than ours, and redbirds of as liquid a note, but not so varied, as that of the redbirds of our woods. How came they all here, seven hundred miles from any larger land? Some think, on the stronger wings of tempests, for it is not within the knowledge of men that men brought them. Men did, indeed, bring the pestilent sparrows which swarm about their habitations here, and beat away the gentler and lovelier birds with a ferocity unknown in the human occupation of the islands. Still, the sparrows have by no means conquered, and in the wilder places the cat-bird makes common cause with the bluebird and the redbird, and holds its own against them. The little ground-doves mimic in miniature the form and markings and the gait and mild behavior of our turtle-doves, but perhaps not their melancholy cooing. Nature has nowhere anything prettier than these exquisite creatures, unless it be the long-tailed white gulls which sail over the emerald shallows of the land-locked seas, and take the green upon their translucent bodies as they trail their meteoric splendor against the mid-day sky. Full twenty-four inches they measure from the beak to the tip of the single pen that protracts them a foot beyond their real bulk; but it is said their tempers are shorter than they, and they attack fiercely anything they suspect of too intimate a curiosity concerning their nests.

They are probably the only short-tempered things in the Summer Islands, where time is so long that if you lose your patience you easily find it again. Sweetness, if not light, seems to be the prevailing human quality, and a good share of it belongs to such of the natives as are in no wise light. Our poor brethren of a different pigment are in the large majority, and they have been seventy years out of slavery, with the full enjoyment of all their civil rights, without lifting themselves from their old inferiority. They do the hard work, in their own easy way, and possibly do not find life the burden they make it for the white man, whom here, as in our own country, they load up with the conundrum which their existence involves for him. They are not very gay, and do not rise to a joke with that flashing eagerness which they show for it at home. If you have them against a background of banana-stems, or low palms, or feathery canes, nothing could be more acceptably characteristic of the air and sky; nor are they out of place on the box of the little victorias, where visitors of the more inquisitive sex put them to constant question. Such visitors spare no islander of any color. Once, in the pretty Public Garden which the multiple had claimed for its private property, three unmerciful American women suddenly descended from the heavens and began to question the multiple's gardener, who was peacefully digging at the rate of a spadeful every five minutes. Presently he sat down on his wheelbarrow, and then shifted, without relief, from one handle of it to the other. Then he rose and braced himself desperately against the tool-house, where, when his tormentors drifted away, he seemed to the soft eye of pity pinned to the wall by their cruel interrogations, whose barbed points were buried in the stucco behind him, and whose feathered shafts stuck out half a yard before his breast.

PADRE GIACOMO ISSAVERDENS

Whether he was black or not, pity could not see, but probably he was. At least the garrison of the islands is all black, being a Jamaican regiment of that color; and when one of the warriors comes down the white street, with his swagger-stick in his hand, and flaming in scarlet and gold upon the ground of his own blackness, it is as if a gigantic oriole were coming towards you, or a mighty tulip. These gorgeous creatures seem so much readier than the natives to laugh, that you wish to test them with a joke. But it might fail. The Summer Islands are a British colony, and the joke does not flourish so luxuriantly here as some other things.

To be sure, one of the native fruits seems a sort of joke when you hear it first named, and when you are offered a *loquat,* if you are of a frivolous mind you search your mind for the connection with *loquor* which it seems to intimate. Failing in this, you taste the fruit, and then, if it is not perfectly ripe, you are as far from loquaciousness as if you had bitten a green persimmon. But if it is ripe, it is delicious, and may be consumed indefinitely. It is the only native fruit which one can wish to eat at all, with an unpractised palate, though it is claimed that with experience a relish may come for the pawpaws. These break out in clusters of the size of oranges at the top of a thick pole, which may have some leaves or may not, and ripen as they fancy in the indefinite summer. They are of the color and flavor of a very insipid little muskmelon which has grown too near a patch of squashes.

One may learn to like this pawpaw, yes, but one must study hard. It is best when plucked by a young islander of Italian blood whose father orders him up the bare pole in the sunny Sunday morning air to oblige the signori, and then with a pawpaw in either hand stands talking with them about the two bad

years there have been in Bermuda, and the probability of his doing better in Nuova York. He has not
imagined our winter, however, and he shrinks from
its boldly pictured rigors, and lets the signori go
with a sigh, and a bunch of pink and crimson roses.

The roses are here, budding and blooming in the
quiet bewilderment which attends the flowers and
plants from the temperate zone in this latitude, and
which in the case of the strawberries offered with cream
and cake at another public garden expresses itself in
a confusion of red, ripe fruit and white blossoms on
the same stem. They are a pleasure to the nose and
eye rather than the palate, as happens with so many
growths of the tropics, if indeed the Summer Islands
are tropical, which some plausibly deny; though why
should not strawberries, fresh picked from the plant
in mid-March, enjoy the right to be indifferent sweet?

## IV

What remains? The events of the Summer Islands are few, and none out of the order of athletics
between teams of the army and navy, and what may
be called societetics, have happened in the past en-
chanted fortnight. But far better things than events
have happened: sunshine and rain of such like quality that one could not grumble at either, and gales,
now from the south and now from the north, with the
languor of the one and the vigor of the other in them.
There were drives upon drives that were always to
somewhere, but would have been delightful the same
if they had been mere goings and comings, past the
white houses overlooking little lawns through the
umbrage of their palm-trees. The lawns professed to
be of grass, but were really mats of close little herbs

"... GROTESQUE WITH WIND-WORN AND WAVE-WORN ROCKS"

A BERMUDA HOUSE

which were not grass; but which, where the sparse
cattle were grazing them, seemed to satisfy their in-
exacting stomachs. They are never very green, and
in fact the landscape often has an air of exhaustion
and pause which it wears with us in late August; and
why not, after all its interminable, innumerable summers? Everywhere in the gentle hollows which the
coral hills (if they are coral) sink into are the patches
of potatoes and lilies and onions drawing their geo-
metrical lines across the brown - red, weedless soil;
and in very sheltered spots are banana-orchards which
are never so snugly sheltered there but their broad
leaves are whipped to shreds. The white road winds
between gray walls crumbling in an amiable disin-
tegration, but held together against ruin by a net-
work of maidenhair ferns and creepers of unknown
name, and overhung by trees where the cactus climbs
and hangs in spiky links, or if another sort, pierces
them with speary stems as tall and straight as the
stalks of the neighboring bamboo. The loquat-trees
cluster like quinces in the garden closes, and show
their pale golden, plum-shaped fruit.

For the most part the road runs by still inland waters,
but sometimes it climbs to the high downs beside the
open sea, grotesque with wind-worn and wave-worn
rocks, and beautiful with opalescent beaches, and the
black legs of the negro children paddling in the tints
of the prostrate rainbow.

All this seems probable and natural enough at the
writing; but how will it be when one has turned one's
back upon it? Will it not lapse into the gross fable
of travellers, and be as the things which the liars who
swap them cannot themselves believe? What will
be said to you when you tell that in the Summer Islands one has but to saw a hole in his back yard and
take out a house of soft, creamy sandstone and set it

up and go to living in it? What, when you relate that among the northern and southern evergreens there are deciduous trees which, in a clime where there is no fall or spring, simply drop their leaves when they are tired of keeping them on, and put out others when they feel like it? What, when you pretend that in the absence of serpents there are centipedes a span long, and spiders the bigness of bats, and mosquitoes that sweetly sing in the drowsing ear, but bite not; or that there are swamps but no streams, and in the marshes stand mangrove - trees whose branches grow downward into the ooze, as if they wished to get back into the earth and pull in after them the holes they emerged from?

These every-day facts seem not only incredible to the liar himself, even in their presence, but when you begin the ascent of that steep slant back to New York you foresee that they will become impossible. As impossible as the summit of the slant now appears to the sense which shudderingly figures it a Bermuda pawpaw-tree seven hundred miles high, and fruiting icicles and snowballs in the March air!

# WILD FLOWERS OF THE ASPHALT

LOOKING through Mrs. Caroline A. Creevey's charming book on the *Flowers of Field, Hill, and Swamp*, the other day, I was very forcibly reminded of the number of these pretty, wilding growths which I had been finding all the season long among the streets of asphalt and the sidewalks of artificial stone in this city; and I am quite sure that any one who has been kept in New York, as I have been this year, beyond the natural time of going into the country, can have as real a pleasure in this sylvan invasion as mine, if he will but give himself up to a sense of it.

I

Of course it is altogether too late, now, to look for any of the early spring flowers, but I can recall the exquisite effect of the tender blue hepatica fringing the centre rail of the grip-cars, all up and down Broadway, and apparently springing from the hollow beneath, where the cable ran with such a brooklike gurgle that any damp-living plant must find itself at home there. The water-pimpernel may now be seen, by any sympathetic eye, blowing delicately along the track, in the breeze of the passing cabs, and elastically lifting itself from the rush of the cars. The reader can easily verify it by the picture in Mrs. Creevey's book. He knows it by its other name of brook-weed; and he will have my delight, I am sure, in the cardinal-flower which will be with us in August. It is a shy flower, loving the more sequestered nooks, and may be sought along the shady stretches of Third Avenue, where the Elevated Road overhead forms a shelter as of interlacing boughs. The arrow-head likes such swampy expanses as the converging surface roads form at Dead Man's Curve and the corners of Twenty-third Street. This is in flower now, and will be till September; and St.-John's-wort, which some call the false golden-rod, is already here. You may find it in any moist, low ground, but the gutters of Wall Street, or even the banks of the Stock Exchange, are not too dry for it. The real golden-rod is not much in evidence with us, for it comes only when summer is on the wane. The other night, however, on the promenade of the Madison Square Roof Garden, I was delighted to see it growing all over the oblong dome of the auditorium, in response to the cry of a homesick cricket which found itself in exile there at the base of a potted ever-green. This lonely insect had no sooner sounded its winter-boding note than the fond flower began sym-pathetically to wave and droop along those tarry slopes, as I have seen it on how many hill-side past-ures! But this may have been only a transitory re-sponse to the cricket, and I cannot promise the visitor to the Roof Garden that he will find golden-rod there every night. I believe there is always Golden Seal, but it is the kind that comes in bottles, and not in the gloom of "deep, cool, moist woods," where Mrs. Cree-vey describes it as growing, along with other wildings of such sweet names or quaint as Celandine, and Dwarf Larkspur, and Squirrel-corn, and Dutchman's-breeches, and Pearlwort, and Wood-sorrel, and Bish-op's-cap, and Wintergreen, and Indian-pipe, and

"... SUCH SWAMPY EXPANSES AS THE CONVERGING SURFACE ROADS
FORM AT DEAD MAN'S CURVE"

Snowberry, and Adder's-tongue, and Wakerobin, and
Dragon-root, and Adam-and-Eve, and twenty more,
which must have got their names from some fairy of
genius. I should say it was a female fairy of genius
who called them so, and that she had her own sex
among mortals in mind when she invented their
nomenclature, and was thinking of little girls, and
slim, pretty maids, and happy young wives. The
author tells how they all look, with a fine sense of
their charm in her words, but one would know how
they looked from their names; and when you call them
over they at once transplant themselves to the depths
of the dells between our sky-scrapers, and find a
brief sojourn in the cavernous excavations whence
other sky-scrapers are to rise.

## II

That night on the Roof Garden, when the cricket's
cry flowered the dome with golden-rod, the tall stems
of rye growing among the orchestra sloped all one way
at times, just like the bows of violins, in the half-dollar gale that always blows over the city at that height.
But as one turns the leaves of Mrs. Creevey's magic
book—perhaps one ought to say turns its petals—
the forests and the fields come and make themselves
at home in the city everywhere. By virtue of it I have
been more in the country in a half-hour than if I had
lived all June there. When I lift my eyes from its
pictures or its letter-press my vision prints the eidolons
of wild flowers everywhere, as it prints the image of
the sun against the air after dwelling on his brightness. The rose-mallow flaunts along Fifth Avenue
and the golden threads of the dodder embroider the
house fronts on the principal cross streets; and I might

think at times that it was all mere fancy, it has so much the quality of a pleasing illusion.

Yet Mrs. Creevey's book is not one to lend itself to such a deceit by any of the ordinary arts. It is rather matter of fact in form and manner, and largely owes what magic it has to the inherent charm of its subject. One feels this in merely glancing at the index, and reading such titles of chapters as " Wet Meadows and Low Grounds "; "Dry Fields—Waste Places—Waysides "; " Hills and Rocky Woods, Open Woods "; and "Deep, Cool, Moist Woods "; each a poem in itself, lyric or pastoral, and of a surpassing opulence of suggestion. The spring and summer months pass in stately processional through the book, each with her fillet inscribed with the names of her characteristic flowers or blossoms, and brightened with the blooms themselves.

They are plucked from where nature bade them grow in the wild places, or their own wayward wills led them astray. A singularly fascinating chapter is that called "Escaped from Gardens," in which some of these pretty runagates are catalogued. I supposed in my liberal ignorance that the Bouncing Bet was the only one of these, but I have learned that the Pansy and the Sweet Violet love to gad, and that the Caraway, the Snapdragon, the Prince's Feather, the Summer Savory, the Star of Bethlehem, the Day-Lily, and the Tiger-Lily, and even the sluggish Stone Crop are of the vagrant, fragrant company. One is not surprised to meet the Tiger-Lily in it ; that must always have had the jungle in its heart ; but that the Baby's Breath should be found wandering by the road-sides from Massachusetts and Virginia to Ohio, gives one a tender pang as for a lost child. Perhaps the poor human tramps, who sleep in barns and feed at back doors along those dusty ways, are mind-

ful of the Baby's Breath, and keep a kindly eye
out for the little truant.

### III

As I was writing those homely names I felt again
how fit and lovely they were, how much more fit and
lovely than the scientific names of the flowers.  Mrs.
Creevey will make a botanist of you if you will let her,
and I fancy a very good botanist, though I cannot
speak from experience, but she will make a poet of
you in spite of yourself, as I very well know; and she
will do this simply by giving you first the familiar
name of the flowers she loves to write of.  I am not saying that the Day-Lily would not smell as sweet by her
title of *Hemerocallis Fulva*, or that the homely, hearty
Bouncing Bet would not kiss as deliciously in her
scholar's cap and gown of *Saponaria Officinalis*; but
merely that their college degrees do not lend themselves so willingly to verse, or even melodious prose,
which is what the poet is often after nowadays.  So
I like best to hail the flowers by the names that the
fairies gave them, and the children know them by,
especially when my longing for them makes them
grow here in the city streets.  I have a fancy that
they would all vanish away if I saluted them in botanical terms.  As long as I talk of cat-tail rushes, the
homeless grimalkins of the areas and the back fences
help me to a vision of the swamps thickly studded
with their stiff spears; but if I called them *Typha Lati-
folia*, or even *Typha Angustifolia*, there is not the
hardiest and fiercest prowler of the roof and the fire-
escape but would fly the sound of my voice and leave
me forlorn amid the withered foliage of my dream.
The street sparrows, pestiferous and persistent as they
are, would forsake my sylvan pageant if I spoke of the

Bird-foot Violet as the *Viola Pedata*; and the commonest cur would run howling if he heard the gentle Poison Dogwood maligned as the *Rhus Venenata*. The very milk-cans would turn to their native pumps in disgust from my attempt to invoke our simple American Cowslip as the *Dodecatheon Meadia.*

## IV

Yet I do not deny that such scientific nomenclature has its uses; and I should be far from undervaluing this side of Mrs. Creevey's book. In fact, I secretly respect it the more for its botanical lore, and if ever I get into the woods or fields again I mean to go up to some of the humblest flowers, such as I can feel myself on easy terms with, and tell them what they are in Latin. I think it will surprise them, and I dare say they will some of them like it, and will want their initials inscribed on their leaves, like those signatures which the medicinal plants bear, or are supposed to bear. But as long as I am engaged in their culture amid this stone and iron and asphalt, I find it best to invite their presence by their familiar names, and I hope they will not think them too familiar. I should like to get them all naturalized here, so that the thousands of poor city children, who never saw them growing in their native places, might have some notion of how bountifully the world is equipped with beauty, and how it is governed by many laws which are not enforced by policemen. I think that would interest them very much, and I shall not mind their plucking my Barmecide blossoms, and carrying them home by the armfuls. When good-will costs nothing we ought to practise it even with the tramps, and these are very welcome, in their wanderings over the city pave, to rest their weary limbs in any of my pleached bowers they come to.

"I CANNOT PROMISE THE VISITOR TO THE ROOF GARDEN THAT HE
WILL FIND GOLDEN-ROD THERE EVERY NIGHT"

# LAST DAYS IN A DUTCH HOTEL

(1897)

WHEN we said that we were going to Scheveningen, in the middle of September, the *portier* of
the hotel at The Hague was sure we should be very
cold, perhaps because we had suffered so much in his
house already; and he was right, for the wind blew
with a Dutch tenacity of purpose for a whole week, so
that the guests thinly peopling the vast hostelry seemed
to rustle through its chilly halls and corridors like so
many autumn leaves. We were but a poor hundred
at most where five hundred would not have been a
crowd; and, when we sat down at the long tables d'hôte
in the great dining-room, we had to warm our hands
with our plates before we could hold our spoons. From
time to time the weather varied, as it does in Europe
(American weather is of an exemplary constancy in
comparison), and three or four times a day it rained,
and three or four times it cleared; but through all the
wind blew cold and colder. We were promised, however, that the hotel would not close till October, and
we made shift, with a warm chimney in one room and
three gas-burners in another, if not to keep warm quite,
yet certainly to get used to the cold.

I

In the mean time the sea-bathing went resolutely
on with all its forms. Every morning the bathing-

machines were drawn down to the beach from the esplanade, where they were secured against the gale every night; and every day a half-dozen hardy invalids braved the rigors of wind and wave. At the discreet distance which one ought always to keep one could not always be sure whether these bold bathers were mermen or mermaids; for the sea costume of both sexes is the same here, as regards an absence of skirts and a presence of what are, after the first plunge, effectively tights. The first time I walked down to the beach I was puzzled to make out some object rolling about in the low surf, which looked like a barrel, and which two bathing-machine men were watching with apparently the purpose of fishing it out. Suddenly this object reared itself from the surf and floundered towards the steps of a machine; then I saw that it was evidently not a barrel, but a lady, and after that I never dared carry my researches so far. I suppose that the bathing-tights are more becoming in some cases than in others; but I hold to a modest preference for skirts, however brief, in the sea-gear of ladies. Without them there may sometimes be the effect of beauty, and sometimes the effect of barrel.

For the convenience and safety of the bathers there were, even in the last half of September, some twenty machines, and half as many bath-men and bath-women, who waded into the water and watched that the bathers came to no harm, instead of a solitary life-guard showing his statuesque shape as he paced the shore beside the life-lines, or cynically rocked in his boat beyond the breakers, as the custom is on Long Island. Here there is no need of life-lines, and, unless one held his head resolutely under water, I do not see how he could drown within quarter of a mile of the shore. Perhaps it is to prevent suicide that the bath-men are so plentifully provided.

96

They are a provision of the hotel, I believe, which does not relax itself in any essential towards its guests as they grow fewer. It seems, on the contrary, to use them with a more tender care, and to console them as it may for the inevitable parting near at hand. Now, within three or four days of the end, the kitchen is as scrupulously and vigilantly perfect as it could be in the height of the season; and our dwindling numbers sit down every night to a dinner that we could not get for much more love or vastly more money in the month of August, at any shore hotel in America. It is true that there are certain changes going on, but they are going on delicately, almost silently. A strip of carpeting has come up from along our corridor, but we hardly miss it from the matting which remains. Through the open doors of vacant chambers we can see that beds are coming down, and the dismantling extends into the halls at places. Certain decorative carved chairs which repeated themselves outside the doors have ceased to be there; but the pictures still hang on the walls, and within our own rooms everything is as conscientious as in midsummer. The service is instant, and, if there is some change in it, the change is not for the worse. Yesterday our waiter bade me good-bye, and when I said I was sorry he was going he alleged a boil on his cheek in excuse; he would not allow that his going had anything to do with the closing of the hotel, and he was promptly replaced by another who speaks excellent English. Now that the first is gone, I may own that he seemed not to speak any foreign language long, but, when cornered in English, took refuge in French, and then fled from pursuit in that to German, and brought up in final Dutch, where he was practically inaccessible.

The elevator runs regularly, if not rapidly; the papers arrive unfailingly in the reading-room, including a solitary London *Times*, which even I do not read, perhaps because I have no English-reading rival to contend for it with. Till yesterday, an English artist sometimes got it; but he then instantly offered it to me; and I had to refuse it because I would not be outdone in politeness. Now even he is gone, and on all sides I find myself in an unbroken circle of Dutch and German, where no one would dispute the *Times* with me if he could.

Every night the corridors are fully lighted, and some mornings swept, while the washing that goes on all over Holland, night and morning, does not always spare our unfrequented halls and stairs. I note these little facts, for the contrast with those of an American hotel which we once assisted in closing, and where the elevator stopped two weeks before we left, and we fell from electricity to naphtha-gas, and even this died out before us except at long intervals in the passages; while there were lightning changes in the service, and a final failure of it till we had to go down and get our own ice-water of the lingering room-clerk, after the last bell-boy had winked out.

## II

But in Europe everything is permanent, and in America everything is provisional. This is the great distinction which, if always kept in mind, will save a great deal of idle astonishment. It is in nothing more apparent than in the preparation here at Scheveningen for centuries of summer visitors, while at our Long Island hotel there was a losing bet on a scant generation of them. When it seemed likely that it might be a winning bet the sand was planked there in front of the hotel to the sea with spruce boards. It was very handsomely planked, but it was never afterwards touched,

Europe, attaches to establishment, and which sometimes makes us poor Americans wish for a hereditary
nobility, so that we could all mirror our ancestral value
in the deference of our inferiors. Where we should
get our inferiors is another thing, but I suppose we
could import them for the purpose, if the duties were
not too great under our tariff.

We have not yet imported the idea of a European
hotel in any respect, though we long ago imported
what we call the European plan. No travelled American knows it in the extortionate prices of rooms when
he gets home, or the preposterous charges of our restaurants, where one portion of roast beef swimming in a
lake of lukewarm juice costs as much as a diversi-
fied and delicate dinner in Germany or Holland. But
even if there were any proportion in these things the
European hotel will not be with us till we have the
European *portier*, who is its spring and inspiration.
He must not, dear home-keeping reader, be at all imagined in the moral or material figure of our hotel
porter, who appears always in his shirt-sleeves, and
speaks with the accent of Cork or of Congo. The European *portier* wears a uniform, I do not know why,
and a gold-banded cap, and he inhabits a little office
at the entrance of the hotel. He speaks eight or ten
languages, up to certain limit, rather better than people born to them, and his presence commands an
instant reverence softening to affection under his universal helpfulness. There is nothing he cannot tell
you, cannot do for you; and you may trust yourself
implicitly to him. He has the priceless gift of making
each nationality, each personality, believe that he is
devoted to its service alone. He turns lightly from
one language to another, as if he had each under his
tongue, and he answers simultaneously a fussy French
woman, an angry English tourist, a stiff Prussian

major, and a thin-voiced American girl in behalf of a timorous mother, and he never mixes the replies. He is an inexhaustible bottle of dialects; but this is the least of his merits, of his miracles.

Our *portier* here is a tall, slim Dutchman (most Dutchmen are tall and slim), and in spite of the waning season he treats me as if I were multitude, while at the same time he uses me with the distinction due the last of his guests. Twenty times in as many hours he wishes me good-day, putting his hand to his cap for the purpose; and to oblige me he wears silver braid instead of gilt on his cap and coat. I apologized yesterday for troubling him so often for stamps, and said that I supposed he was much more bothered in the season.

"Between the first of August and the fifteenth," he answered, "you cannot *think*. All that you can do is to say, Yes, No; Yes, No." And he left me to imagine his responsibilities.

I am sure he will hold out to the end, and will smile me a friendly farewell from the door of his office, which is also his dining-room, as I know from often disturbing him at his meals there. I have no fear of the waiters either, or of the little errand-boys who wear suits of sailor blue, and touch their foreheads when they bring you your letters like so many ancient sea-dogs. I do not know why the elevator-boy prefers a suit of snuff-color; but I know that he will salute us as we step out of his elevator for the last time as unfalteringly as if we had just arrived at the beginning of the summer.

### IV

It is our last day in the hotel at Scheveningen, and I will try to recall in their pathetic order the events of the final week.

Nothing has been stranger throughout than the fluctuation of the guests. At times they have dwindled to so small a number that one must reckon chiefly upon their quality for consolation; at other times they swelled to such a tide as to overflow the table, long or short, at dinner, and eddy round a second board beside it. There have been nights when I have walked down the long corridor to my seaward room through a harking solitude of empty chambers; there have been mornings when I have come out to breakfast past door-mats cheerful with boots of both sexes, and door-post hooks where dangling coats and trousers peopled the place with a lively if a somewhat flaccid semblance of human presence. The worst was that, when some one went, we lost a friend, and when some one came we only won a stranger.

Among the first to go were the kindly English folk whose acquaintance we made across the table the first night, and who took with them so large a share of our facile affections that we quite forgot the ancestral enmities, and grieved for them as much as if they had been Americans. There have been, in fact, no Americans here but ourselves, and we have done what we could with the Germans who spoke English. The nicest of these were a charming family from F——, father and mother, and son and daughter, with whom we had a pleasant week of dinners. At the very first we disagreed with the parents so amicably about Ibsen and Sudermann that I was almost sorry to have the son take our modern side of the controversy and declare himself an admirer of those authors with us. Our frank literary difference established a kindness between us that was strengthened by our community of English, and when they went they left us to the sympathy of another German family with whom we had mainly our humanity in common. They spoke

103

no English, and I only a German which they must have understood with their hearts rather than their heads, since it consisted chiefly of good-will. But in the air of their sweet natures it flourished surprisingly, and sufficed each day for praise of the weather after it began to be fine, and at parting for some fond regrets, not unmixed with philosophical reflections, sadly perplexed in the genders and the order of the verbs: with me the verb will seldom wait, as it should in German, to the end. Both of these families, very different in social tradition, I fancied, were one in the amiability which makes the alien forgive so much militarism to the German nation, and hope for its final escape from the drill-sergeant. When they went, we were left for some meals to our own American tongue, with a brief interval of that English painter and his wife with whom we spoke our language as nearly like English as we could. Then followed a desperate lunch and dinner where an unbroken forest of German, and a still more impenetrable morass of Dutch, hemmed us in. But last night it was our joy to be addressed in our own speech by a lady who spoke it as admirably as our dear friends from F——. She was Dutch, and when she found we were Americans she praised our historian Motley, and told us how his portrait is gratefully honored with a place in the Queen's palace, The House in the Woods, near Scheveningen.

## V

She had come up from her place in the country, four hours away, for the last of the concerts here, which have been given throughout the summer by the best orchestra in Europe, and which have been thronged every afternoon and evening by people from The Hague.

One honored day this week even the Queen and the
Queen Mother came down to the concert, and gave
us incomparably the greatest event of our waning
season. I had noticed all the morning a floral per-
turbation about the main entrance of the hotel, which
settled into the form of banks of autumnal bloom on
either side of the specially carpeted stairs, and put
forth on the roof of the arcade in a crown, much bigger
round than a barrel, of orange-colored asters, in honor
of the Queen's ancestral house of Orange. Flags of
blue, white, and red fluttered nervously about in the
breeze from the sea, and imparted to us an agreeable
anxiety not to miss seeing the Queens, as the Dutch
succinctly call their sovereign and her parent; and at
three o'clock we saw them drive up to the hotel. Certain officials in civil dress stood at the door of the concert-room to usher the Queens in, and a bareheaded,
bald-headed dignity of military figure backed up the
stairs before them. I would not rashly commit myself to particulars concerning their dress, but I am
sure that the elder Queen wore black, and the younger
white. The mother has one of the best and wisest
faces I have seen any woman wear (and most of the
good, wise faces in this imperfectly balanced world
are women's) and the daughter one of the sweetest
and prettiest. Pretty is the word for her face, and
it showed pink through her blond veil, as she smiled
and bowed right and left; her features are small and
fine, and she is not above the middle height.

As soon as she had passed into the concert-room,
we who had waited to see her go in ran round to another door and joined the two or three thousand people who were standing to receive the Queens. These
had already mounted to the royal box, and they stood
there while the orchestra played one of the Dutch national airs. (One air is not enough for the Dutch;

they must have two.) Then the mother faded somewhere into the background, and the daughter sat
alone in the front, on a gilt throne, with a gilt crown
at top, and a very uncomfortable carved Gothic back.
She looked so young, so gentle, and so good that the
rudest Republican could not have helped wishing
her well out of a position so essentially and irrepara-
bly false as a hereditary sovereign's. One forgot in
the presence of her innocent seventeen years that most
of the ruling princes of the world had left it the worse
for their having been in it; at moments one forgot her
altogether as a princess, and saw her only as a charming young girl, who had to sit up rather stiffly.

At the end of the programme the Queens rose and
walked slowly out, while the orchestra played the
*other* national air.

## VI

I call them the Queens, because the Dutch do; and
I like Holland so much that I should hate to differ
with the Dutch in anything. But, as a matter of fact,
they are neither of them quite Queens; the mother is
the regent and the daughter will not be crowned till
next year.

But, such as they are, they imparted a supreme
emotion to our dying season, and thrilled the hotel
with a fulness of summer life. Since they went, the
season faintly pulses and respires, so that one can
just say that it is still alive. Last Sunday was fine,
and great crowds came down from The Hague to the
concert, and spread out on the seaward terrace of the
hotel, around the little tables which I fancied that
the waiters had each morning wiped dry of the dew,
from a mere Dutch desire of cleaning something. The
hooded chairs covered the beach; the children played

"PRETTY IS THE WORD FOR HER FACE"

in the edges of the surf and delved in the sand; the lovers wandered up into the hollows of the dunes.

There was only the human life, however. I have looked in vain for the crabs, big and little, that swarm on the Long Island shore, and there are hardly any gulls, even; perhaps because there are no crabs for them to eat, if they eat crabs; I never saw gulls doing it, but they must eat something. Dogs there are, of course, wherever there are people; but they are part of the human life. Dutch dogs are in fact very human; and one I saw yesterday behaved quite as badly as a bad boy, with respect to his muzzle. He did not like his muzzle, and by dint of turning somersaults in the sand he got it off, and went frolicking to his master in triumph to show him what he had done.

## VII

It is now the last day, and the desolation is thickening upon our hotel. This morning the door-posts up and down my corridor showed not a single pair of trousers; not a pair of boots flattered the lonely door-mats. In the lower hall I found the tables of the great dining-room assembled, and the chairs inverted on them with their legs in the air; but decently, decorously, not with the reckless abandon displayed by the chairs in our Long Island hotel for weeks before it closed. In the smaller dining-room the table was set for lunch as if we were to go on dining there forever; in the breakfast-room the service and the provision were as perfect as ever. The coffee was good, the bread delicious, the butter of an unfaltering sweetness; and the glaze of wear on the polished dress-coats of the waiters as respectable as it could have been on the first day of the season. All was correct, and if of a funereal correctness to me, I am sure this effect was purely subjective.

The little bell-boys in sailor suits (perhaps they ought to be spelled bell-buoys) clustered about the elevator-boy like so many Roman sentinels at their posts; the elevator-boy and his elevator were ready to take us up or down at any moment.

The *portier* and I ignored together the hour of parting, which we had definitely ascertained and agreed upon, and we exchanged some compliments to the weather, which is now settled, as if we expected to enjoy it long together. I rather dread going in to lunch, however, for I fear the empty places.

## VIII

All is over; we are off. The lunch was an heroic effort of the hotel to hide the fact of our separation. It was perfect, unless the boiled beef was a confession of human weakness; but even this boiled beef was exquisite, and the horseradish that went with it was so mellowed by art that it checked rather than provoked the parting tear. The table d'hôte had reserved a final surprise for us; and when we sat down with the fear of nothing but German around us, we heard the sound of our own speech from the pleasantest English pair we had yet encountered; and the travelling English *are* pleasant; I will say it, who am said by Sir Walter Besant to be the only American who hates their nation. It was really an added pang to go, on their account, but the carriage was waiting at the door; the *domestique* had already carried our baggage to the steam - tram station; the kindly menial train formed around us for an ultimate *douceur*, and we were off, after the *portier* had shut us into our vehicle and touched his oft-touched cap for the last time, while the hotel façade dissembled its grief by architecturally smiling in the soft Dutch sun.

I liked this manner of leaving better than carrying part of my own baggage to the train, as I had to do on Long Island, though that, too, had its charm; the charm of the whole fresh, pungent American life, which at this distance is so dear.

## SOME ANOMALIES OF THE SHORT STORY

THE interesting experiment of one of our great publishing houses in putting out serially several volumes of short stories, with the hope that a courageous persistence may overcome the popular indifference to such collections when severally administered, suggests some questions as to this eldest form of fiction which I should like to ask the reader's patience with. I do not know that I shall be able to answer them, or that I shall try to do so; the vitality of a question that is answered seems to exhale in the event; it palpitates no longer; curiosity flutters away from the faded flower, which is fit then only to be folded away in the *hortus siccus* of accomplished facts. In view of this I may wish merely to state the problems and leave them for the reader's solution, or, more amusingly, for his mystification.

I

One of the most amusing questions concerning the short story is why a form which is singly so attractive that every one likes to read a short story when he finds it alone is collectively so repellent as it is said to be. Before now I have imagined the case to be somewhat the same as that of a number of pleasant people who are most acceptable as separate householders, but who lose caste and cease to be desirable acquaintances when gathered into a boarding-house.

Yet the case is not the same quite, for we see that the short story where it is ranged with others of its species within the covers of a magazine is so welcome that the editor thinks his number the more brilliant the more short story writers he can call about his board, or under the roof of his *pension*. Here the boarding-house analogy breaks, breaks so signally that I was lately moved to ask a distinguished editor why a book of short stories usually failed and a magazine usually succeeded because of them. He answered, gayly, that the short stories in most books of them were bad; that where they were good, they went; and he alleged several well-known instances in which books of prime short stories had a great vogue. He was so handsomely interested in my inquiry that I could not well say I thought some of the short stories which he had boasted in his last number were indifferent good, and yet, as he allowed, had mainly helped sell it. I had in mind many books of short stories of the first excellence which had failed as decidedly as those others had succeeded, for no reason that I could see; possibly there is really no reason in any literary success or failure that can be predicted, or applied in another case.

I could name these books, if it would serve any purpose, but, in my doubt, I will leave the reader to think of them, for I believe that his indolence or intellectual reluctance is largely to blame for the failure of good books of short stories. He is commonly so averse to any imaginative exertion that he finds it a hardship to respond to that peculiar demand which a book of good short stories makes upon him. He can read one good short story in a magazine with refreshment, and a pleasant sense of excitement, in the sort of spur it gives to his own constructive faculty. But, if this is repeated in ten or twenty stories, he becomes fluttered and exhausted by the draft upon his energies; whereas a continuous fiction of the same quantity acts as an agreeable sedative. A condition that the short story tacitly makes with the reader, through its limitations, is that he shall subjectively fill in the details and carry out the scheme which in its small dimensions the story can only suggest; and the greater number of readers find this too much for their feeble powers, while they cannot resist the incitement to attempt it.

My theory does not wholly account for the fact (no theory wholly accounts for any fact), and I own that the same objections would lie from the reader against a number of short stories in a magazine. But it may be that the effect is not the same in the magazine because of the variety in the authorship, and because it would be impossibly jolting to read all the short stories in a magazine *seriatim*. On the other hand, the identity of authorship gives a continuity of attraction to the short stories in a book which forms that exhausting strain upon the imagination of the involuntary co-partner.

## II

Then, what is the solution as to the form of publication for short stories, since people do not object to them singly but collectively, and not in variety, but in identity of authorship? Are they to be printed only in the magazines, or are they to be collected in volumes combining a variety of authorship? Rather, I could wish, it might be found feasible to purvey them in some pretty shape where each would appeal singly to the reader and would not exhaust him in the subjective after-work required of him. In this event many short stories now cramped into undue limits by the editorial exigencies of the magazines might expand to greater length and breadth, and without ceasing to be each a short story might not make so heavy a demand upon the subliminal forces of the reader.

If any one were to say that all this was a little fantastic, I should not contradict him; but I hope there is some reason in it, if reason can help the short story to greater favor, for it is a form which I have great pleasure in as a reader, and pride in as an American. If we have not excelled all other moderns in it, we have certainly excelled in it; possibly because we are in the period of our literary development which corresponds to that of other peoples when the short story pre-eminently flourished among them. But when one has said a thing like this, it immediately accuses one of loose and inaccurate statement, and requires one to refine upon it, either for one's own peace of conscience or for one's safety from the thoughtful reader. I am not much afraid of that sort of reader, for he is very rare, but I do like to know myself what I mean, if I mean anything in particular.

In this instance I am obliged to ask myself whether our literary development can be recognized separately from that of the whole English-speaking world. I think it can, though, as I am always saying American literature is merely a condition of English literature. In some sense every European literature is a condition of some other European literature, yet the impulse in each eventuates, if it does not originate indigenously. A younger literature will choose, by a sort of natural selection, some things for assimilation from an elder literature, for no more apparent reason than it will reject other things, and it will transform them in the process so that it will give them the effect of indigeneity. The short story among the Italians, who called it the novella, and supplied us with the name devoted solely among us to fiction of epical magnitude, refined indefinitely upon the Greek romance, if it derived from that; it retrenched itself in scope, and enlarged itself in the variety of its types. But still these remained types, and they remained types with the French imitators of the Italian novella. It was not till the Spaniards borrowed the form of the novella and transplanted it to their racier soil that it began to bear character, and to fruit in the richness of their picaresque fiction. When the English borrowed it they adapted it, in the metrical tales of Chaucer, to the genius of their nation, which was then both poetical and humorous. Here it was full of character, too, and more and more personality began to enlarge the bounds of the conventional types and to imbue fresh ones. But in so far as the novella was studied in the Italian sources, the French, Spanish, and English literatures were conditions of Italian literature as distinctly, though, of course, not so thoroughly, as American literature is a condition of English literature. Each borrower gave a national cast to the thing borrowed, and that is what has happened with us, in the full measure that our nationality has differenced itself from the English.

Whatever truth there is in all this, and I will confess that a good deal of it seems to me hardy conjecture, rather favors my position that we are in some such period of our literary development as those other peoples when the short story flourished among them. Or, if I restrict our claim, I may safely claim that they abundantly had the novella when they had not the novel at all, and we now abundantly have the novella, while we have the novel only subordinately and of at least no such quantitative importance as the English, French, Spanish, Norwegians, Russians, and some others of our esteemed contemporaries, not to name the Italians. We surpass the Germans, who, like ourselves, have as distinctly excelled in the modern novella as they have fallen short in the novel. Or, if I may not quite say this, I will make bold to say that I can think of many German novelle that I should like to read again, but scarcely one German novel; and I could honestly say the same of American novelle, though not of American novels.

### III

The abeyance, not to say the desuetude, that the novella fell into for several centuries is very curious, and fully as remarkable as the modern rise of the short story. It began to prevail in the dramatic form, for a play is a short story put on the stage; it may have satisfied in that form the early love of it, and it has continued to please in that form; but in its original shape it quite vanished, unless we consider the little studies and sketches and allegories of the *Spectator* and *Tatler* and *Idler* and *Rambler* and their imitations on the Continent as guises of the novella. The germ of the modern short story may have survived in these, or in the metrical form of the novella which appeared in Chaucer and never wholly disappeared. With Crabbe the novella became as distinctly the short story as it has become in the hands of Miss Wilkins. But it was not till our time that its great merit as a form was felt, for until our time so great work was never done with it. I remind myself of Boccaccio, and of the *Arabian Nights*, without the wish to hedge from my bold stand. They are all elemental; compared with some finer modern work which deepens inward immeasurably, they are all of their superficial limits. They amuse, but they do not hold, the mind and stamp it with large and profound impressions.

An Occidental cannot judge the literary quality

of the Eastern tales; but I will own my suspicion that the perfection of the Italian work is philological rather than artistic, while the web woven by Mr. James or Miss Jewett, by Kielland or Björnson, by Maupassant, by Palacio Valdés, by Giovanni Verga, by Tourguénief, in one of those little frames seems to me of an exquisite color and texture and of an entire literary preciousness, not only as regards the diction, but as regards those more intangible graces of form, those virtues of truth and reality, and those lasting significances which distinguish the masterpiece.

The novella has in fact been carried so far in the short story that it might be asked whether it had not left the novel behind, as to perfection of form; though one might not like to affirm this. Yet there have been but few modern fictions of the novel's dimensions which have the beauty of form many a novella embodies. Is this because it is easier to give form in the small than in the large, or only because it is easier to hide formlessness? It is easier to give form in the novella than in the novel, because the design of less scope can be more definite, and because the persons and facts are fewer, and each can be more carefully treated. But, on the other hand, the slightest error in execution shows more in the small than in the large, and a fault of conception is more evident. The novella must be clearly imagined, above all things, for there is no room in it for those felicities of characterization or comment by which the artist of faltering design saves himself in the novel.

## IV

The question as to where the short story distinguishes itself from the anecdote is of the same nature as that which concerns the bound set between it and the novel. In both cases the difference of the novella is in the motive, or the origination. The anecdote is too palpably simple and single to be regarded as a novella, though there is now and then a novella like *The Father*, by Björnson, which is of the actual brevity of the anecdote, but which, when released in the reader's consciousness, expands to dramatic dimensions impossible to the anecdote. Many anecdotes have come down from antiquity, but not, I believe, one short story, at least in prose; and the Italians, if they did not invent the story, gave us something most sensibly distinguishable from the classic anecdote in the novella. The anecdote offers an illustration of character, or records a moment of action; the novella embodies a drama and develops a type.

It is not quite so clear as to when and where a piece of fiction ceases to be a novella and becomes a novel. The frontiers are so vague that one is obliged to recognize a middle species, or rather a middle magnitude, which paradoxically, but necessarily enough, we call the novelette. First we have the short story, or novella, then we have the long story, or novel, and between these we have the novelette, which is in name a smaller than the short story, though it is in point of fact two or three times longer than a short story. We may realize them physically if we will adopt the magazine parlance and speak of the novella as a one-number story, of the novel as a serial, and of the novelette as a two-number or a three-number story; if it passes the three-number limit it seems to become a novel. As a two-number or three-number story it is the despair of editors and publishers. The interest of so brief a serial will not mount sufficiently to carry strongly over from month to month; when the tale is completed it will not make a book which the Trade (inexorable force!) cares to handle. It is therefore still awaiting its authoritative avatar, which it will be some one's prosperity and glory to imagine; for in the novelette are possibilities for fiction as yet scarcely divined.

The novelette can have almost as perfect form as the novella. In fact, the novel has form in the measure that it approaches the novelette; and some of the most symmetrical modern novels are scarcely more than novelettes, like Tourguénief's *Dmitri Rudine*, or his *Smoke*, or *Spring Floods*. *The Vicar of Wakefield*, the father of the modern novel, is scarcely more than a novelette, and I have sometimes fancied, but no doubt vainly, that the ultimated novel might be of the dimensions of *Hamlet*. If any one should say there was not room in *Hamlet* for the character and incident requisite in a novel, I should be ready to answer that there seemed a good deal of both in *Hamlet*.

But no doubt there are other reasons why the novel should not finally be of the length of *Hamlet*, and I must not let my enthusiasm for the novelette carry me too far, or, rather, bring me up too short. I am disposed to dwell upon it, I suppose, because it has not yet shared the favor which the novella and the novel have enjoyed, and because until somebody invents a way for it to the public it cannot prosper like the one-number story or the serial. I should like to say as my last word for it here that I believe there are many novels which, if stripped of their padding, would turn out to have been all along merely novelettes in disguise.

It does not follow, however, that there are many novelle which, if they were duly padded, would be found novelettes. In that dim, subjective region where the æsthetic origins present themselves almost with the authority of inspirations there is nothing clearer than the difference between the short-story motive and the long-story motive. One, if one is in that line of work, feels instinctively just the size and carrying power of the given motive. Or, if the reader prefers a different figure, the mind which the seed has been dropped into from Somewhere is mystically aware whether the seed is going to grow up a bush or is going to grow up a tree, if left to itself. Of course, the mind to which the seed is intrusted may play it false, and wilfully dwarf the growth, or force it to unnatural dimensions; but the critical observer will easily detect the fact of such treasons. Almost in the first germinal impulse the inventive mind forefeels the ultimate difference and recognizes the essential simplicity or complexity of the motive. There will be a prophetic subdivision into a variety of motives and a multiplication of characters and incidents and situations; or the original motive will be divined indivisible, and there will be a small group of people immediately interested and controlled by a single, or predominant, fact. The uninspired may contend that this is bosh, and I own that something might be said for their contention, but upon the whole I think it is gospel.

The right novel is never a congeries of novelle, as might appear to the uninspired. If it indulges even in episodes, it loses in reality and vitality. It is one stock from which its various branches put out, and form it a living growth identical throughout. The right novella is never a novel cropped back from the size of a tree to a bush, or the branch of a tree stuck into the ground and made to serve for a bush. It is another species, destined by the agencies at work in the realm of unconsciousness to be brought into being of its own kind, and not of another.

## V

This was always its case, but in the process of time the short story, while keeping the natural limits of the primal novella (if ever there was one), has shown almost limitless possibilities within them. It has shown itself capable of imparting the effect of every sort of intention, whether of humor or pathos, of tragedy or comedy or broad farce or delicate irony, of character or action. The thing that first made itself known as a little tale, usually salacious, dealing with conventionalized types and conventionalized incidents, has proved itself possibly the most flexible of all the literary forms in its adaptation to the needs of the mind that wishes to utter itself, inventively or constructively, upon some fresh occasion, or wishes briefly to criticise or represent some phase or fact of life.

The riches in this shape of fiction are effectively inestimable, if we consider what has been done in the short story, and is still doing everywhere. The good novels may be easily counted, but the good novelle, since Boccaccio began (if it was he that first began) to make them, cannot be computed. In quantity they are inexhaustible, and in quality they are wonderfully satisfying. Then, why is it that so very, very few of the most satisfactory of that innumerable multitude stay by you, as the country people say, in characterization or action? How hard it is to recall a person or a fact out of any of them, out of the most signally good! We seem to be delightfully nourished as we read, but is it, after all, a full meal? We become of a perfect intimacy and a devoted friendship with the men and women in the short stories, but not apparently of a lasting acquaintance. It is a single meeting we have with them, and though we instantly love or hate them dearly, recurrence and repetition seem necessary to that familiar knowledge in which we hold the personages in a novel.

It is here that the novella, so much more perfect in

form, shows its irremediable inferiority to the novel, and somehow to the play, to the very farce, which it may quantitatively excel. We can all recall by name many characters out of comedies and farces; but how many characters out of short stories can we recall? Most persons of the drama give themselves away by name for types, mere figments of allegory, and perhaps oblivion is the penalty that the novella pays for the fineness of its characterizations; but perhaps, also, the dramatic form has greater facilities for repetition, and so can stamp its persons more indelibly on the imagination than the narrative form in the same small space. The narrative must give to description what the drama trusts to representation; but this cannot account for the superior permanency of the dramatic types in so great measure as we might at first imagine, for they remain as much in mind from reading as from seeing the plays. It is possible that as the novella becomes more conscious, its persons will become more memorable; but as it is, though we now vividly and with lasting delight remember certain short stories, we scarcely remember by name any of the people in them. I may be risking too much in offering an instance, but who, in even such signal instances as *The Revolt of Mother*, by Miss Wilkins, or *The Dulham Ladies*, by Miss Jewett, can recall by name the characters that made them delightful?

## VI

The defect of the novella which we have been acknowledging seems an essential limitation; but perhaps it is not insuperable; and we may yet have short stories which shall supply the delighted imagination with creations of as much immortality as we can reasonably demand. The structural change would not be greater than the moral or material change which has been wrought in it since it began as a yarn, gross and palpable, which the narrator spun out of the coarsest and often the filthiest stuff, to snare the thick fancy or amuse the lewd leisure of listeners willing as children to have the same persons and the same things over and over again. Now it has not only varied the persons and things, but it has refined and verified them in the direction of the natural and the supernatural, until it is above all other literary forms the vehicle of reality and spirituality. When one thinks of a bit of Mr. James's psychology in this form, or a bit of Verga's or Kielland's sociology, or a bit of Miss Jewett's exquisite veracity, one perceives the immense distance which the short story has come on the way to the height it has reached. It serves equally the ideal and the real; that which it is loath to serve is the unreal, so that among the short stories which have recently made reputations for their authors very few are of that peculiar cast which we have no name for but romanticistic. The only distinguished modern writer of romanticistic novelle whom I can think of is Mr. Bret Harte, and he is of a period when romanticism was so imperative as to be almost a condition of fiction. I am never so enamoured of a cause that I will not admit facts that seem to tell against it, and I will allow that this writer of romanticistic short stories has more than any other supplied us with memorable types and characters. We remember Mr. John Oakhurst by name; we remember Kentuck and Tennessee's Partner, at least by nickname; and we remember their several qualities. These figures, if we cannot quite consent that they are persons, exist in our memories by force of their creator's imagination, and at the moment I cannot think of any others that do, out of the myriad of American short stories, except Rip Van Winkle out of Irving's *Legend of Sleepy Hollow,* and Marjorie Daw out of Mr. Aldrich's famous little caprice of that title, and Mr. James's Daisy Miller.

It appears to be the fact that those writers who have first distinguished themselves in the novella have seldom written novels of prime order. Mr. Kipling is an eminent example, but Mr. Kipling has yet a long life before him in which to upset any theory about him, and one can only instance him provisionally. On the other hand, one can be much more confident that the best novelle have been written by the greatest novelists, conspicuously Maupassant, Verga, Björnson, Mr. Thomas Hardy, Mr. James, Mr. Cable, Tourguénief, Tolstoy, Valdés, not to name others. These have, in fact, all done work so good in this form that one is tempted to call it their best work. It is really not their best, but it is work so good that it ought to have equal acceptance with their novels, if that distinguished editor was right who said that short stories sold well when they were good short stories. That they ought to do so is so evident that a devoted reader of them, to whom I was submitting the anomaly the other day, insisted that they did. I could only allege the testimony of publishers and authors to the contrary, and this did not satisfy him.

It does not satisfy me, and I wish that the general reader, with whom the fault lies, could be made to say why, if he likes one short story by itself and four short stories in a magazine, he does not like, or will not have, a dozen short stories in a book. This was the baffling question which I began with and which I find myself forced to end with, after all the light I have thrown upon the subject. I leave it where I found it, but perhaps that is a good deal for a critic to do. If I had

left it anywhere else the reader might not feel bound
to deal with it practically by reading all the books of
short stories he could lay hands on, and either divin-
ing why he did not enjoy them, or else forever fore-
going his prejudice against them because of his pleasure in them.

# A CIRCUS IN THE SUBURBS

WE dwellers in cities and large towns, if we are well-to-do, have more than our fill of pleasures of all kinds; and for now many years past we have been used to a form of circus where surfeit is nearly as great misery as famine in that kind could be. For our sins, or some of our friends' sins, perhaps, we have now gone so long to circuses of three rings and two raised platforms that we scarcely realize that in the country there are still circuses of one ring and no platform at all. We are accustomed, in the gross and foolish superfluity of these city circuses, to see no feat quite through, but to turn our greedy eyes at the most important instant in the hope of greater wonders in another ring. We have four or five clowns, in as many varieties of grotesque costume, as well as a lady clown in befitting dress; but we hear none of them speak, not even the lady clown, while in the country circus the old clown of our childhood, one and indivisible, makes the same style of jokes, if not the very same jokes, that we used to hear there. It is not easy to believe all this, and I do not know that I should quite believe it myself if I had not lately been witness of it in the suburban village where I was passing the summer.

I

The circus announced itself in the good old way weeks beforehand by the vast posters of former days and by a profusion of small bills which fell upon the

village as from the clouds, and left it littered everywhere with their festive pink.  They prophesied it in
a name borne by the first circus I ever saw, which was
also an animal show, but the animals must all have
died during the fifty years past, for there is now no
menagerie attached to it.  I did not know this when
I heard the band braying through the streets of the
village on the morning of the performance, and for
me the mangy old camels and the pimpled elephants
of yore led the procession through accompanying
ranks of boys who have mostly been in their graves
for half a lifetime; the distracted ostrich thrust an
advertising neck through the top of its cage, and the
lion roared to himself in the darkness of his moving
prison.  I felt the old thrill of excitement, the vain
hope of something preternatural and impossible, and
I do not know what could have kept me from that circus as soon as I had done lunch.  My heart rose at
sight of the large tent (which was yet so very little in
comparison with the tents of the three-ring and two-
platform circuses); the alluring and illusory side-
shows of fat women and lean men; the horses tethered
in the background and stamping under the fly-bites;
the old, weather-beaten grand chariot, which looked
like the ghost of the grand chariot which used to drag
me captive in its triumph; and the canvas shelters
where the cooks were already at work over their ket-
tles on the evening meal of the circus folk.

I expected to be kept a long while from the ticket-
wagon by the crowd, but there was no crowd, and perhaps there never used to be much of a crowd.  I bought
my admittances without a moment's delay, and the
man who sold me my reserve seats had even leisure
to call me back and ask to look at the change he had
given me, mostly nickels.  "I *thought* I didn't give
you enough," he said, and he added one more, and

sent me on to the doorkeeper with my faith in human nature confirmed and refreshed.

It was cool enough outside, but within it was very warm, as it should be, to give the men with palm-leaf fans and ice-cold lemonade a chance. They were already making their rounds, and crying their wares with voices from the tombs of the dead past; and the child of the young mother who took my seat-ticket from me was going to sleep at full length on the lowermost tread of the benches, so that I had to step across its prostrate form. These reserved seats were carpeted; but I had forgotten how little one rank was raised above another, and how very trying they were upon the back and legs. But for the carpeting, I could not see how I was advantaged above the commoner folk in the unreserved seats, and I reflected how often in this world we paid for an inappreciable splendor. I could not see but they were as well off as I; they were much more gayly dressed, and some of them were even smoking cigars, while they were nearly all younger by ten, twenty, forty, or fifty years, and even more. They did not look like the country people whom I rather hoped and expected to see, but were apparently my fellow-villagers, in different stages of excitement. They manifested by the usual signs their impatience to have the performance begin, and I confess that I shared this, though I did not take part in the demonstration.

## II

I have no intention of following the events *seriatim*. From time to time during their progress I renewed my old one-sided acquaintance with the circus-men. They were quite the same people, I believe, but strangely softened and ameliorated, as I hope I am, and looking not a day older, which I cannot say of myself,

exactly. The supernumeraries were patently farmer
boys who had entered newly upon that life in a spirit
of adventure, and who wore their partial liveries, a
braided coat here and a pair of striped trousers there,
with a sort of timorous pride, a deprecating bravado,
as if they expected to be hooted by the spectators and
were very glad when they were not. The man who
went round with a dog to keep boys from hooking in
under the curtain had grown gentler, and his dog did
not look as if he would bite the worst boy in town.
The man came up and asked the young mother about
her sleeping child, and I inferred that the child had
been sick, and was therefore unusually interesting
to all the great, kind-hearted, simple circus family.
He was good to the poor supes, and instructed them,
not at all sneeringly, how best to manage the guy-
ropes for the nets when the trapeze events began.

There was, in fact, an air of pleasing domesticity
diffused over the whole circus. This was, perhaps,
partly an effect from our extreme proximity to its performances; I had never been on quite such intimate
terms with equitation and aërostation of all kinds;
but I think it was also largely from the good hearts
of the whole company. A circus must become, during the season, a great brotherhood and sisterhood,
especially sisterhood, and its members must forget
finally that they are not united by ties of blood. I
dare say they often become so, as husbands and wives
and fathers and mothers, if not as brothers.

The domestic effect was heightened almost poig-
nantly when a young lady in a Turkish-towel bath-
gown came out and stood close by the band, waiting
for her act on a barebacked horse of a conventional ,
pattern. She really looked like a young goddess in
a Turkish-towel bath-gown: goddesses must have
worn bath-gowns, especially Venus, who was often

imagined in the bath, or just out of it.  But when this
goddess threw off her bath-gown, and came bound-
ing into the ring as gracefully as the clogs she wore
on her slippers would let her, she was much more modestly dressed than most goddesses.  What I am trying
to say, however, is that, while she stood there by the
band, she no more interested the musicians than if
she were their collective sister.  They were all in their
shirt-sleeves for the sake of the coolness, and they
banged and trumpeted and fluted away as indifferent
to her as so many born brothers.

Indeed, when the gyrations of her horse brought
her to our side of the ring, she was visibly not so youthful and not so divine as she might have been; but
the girl who did the trapeze acts, and did them wonderfully, left nothing to be desired in that regard;
though really I do not see why we who have neither
youth nor beauty should always expect it of other
people.  I think it would have been quite enough for
her to do the trapeze acts so perfectly; but her being
so pretty certainly added a poignancy to the contem-
plation of her perils.  One could follow every motion
of her anxiety in that close proximity: the tremor of
her chin as she bit her lips before taking her flight
through the air, the straining eagerness of her eye as
she measured the distance, the frown with which she
forbade herself any shrinking or reluctance.

### III

How strange is life, how sad and perplexing its
contradictions!  Why should such an exhibition as
that be supposed to give pleasure?  Perhaps it does
not give pleasure, but is only a necessary fulfilment
of one of the many delusions we are in with regard to
each other in this bewildering world.  They are of

all sorts and degrees, these delusions, and I suppose that in the last analysis it was not pleasure I got from the clown and his clowning, clowned he ever so merrily. I remember that I liked hearing his old jokes, not because they were jokes, but because they were old and endeared by long association. He sang one song which I must have heard him sing at my first circus (I am sure it was he), about "Things that I don't like to see," and I heartily agreed with him that his book of songs, which he sent round to be sold, was fully worth the half-dime asked for it, though I did not buy it.

Perhaps the rival author in me withheld me, but, as a brother man, I will not allow that I did not feel for him and suffer with him because of the thick, white pigment which plentifully coated his face, and, with the sweat drops upon it, made me think of a newly painted wall in the rain. He was infinitely older than his personality, than his oldest joke (though you never can be sure how old a joke is), and, representatively, I dare say he outdated the pyramids. They must have made clowns whiten their faces in the dawn of time, and no doubt there were drolls among the antediluvians who enhanced the effect of their fun by that means. All the same, I pitied this clown for it, and I fancied in his wildest waggery the note of a real irascibility. Shall I say that he seemed the only member of that little circus who was not of an amiable temper? But I do not blame him, and I think it much to have seen a clown once more who jested audibly with the ringmaster and always got the better of him in repartee. It was long since I had known that pleasure.

## IV

Throughout the performance at this circus I was troubled by a curious question, whether it were really of the same moral and material grandeur as the circuses it brought to memory, or whether these were thin and slight, too. We all know how the places of our childhood, the heights, the distances, shrink and dwindle when we go back to them, and was it possible that I had been deceived in the splendor of my early circuses? The doubt was painful, but I was forced to own that there might be more truth in it than in a blind fealty to their remembered magnificence. Very likely circuses have grown not only in size, but in the richness and variety of their entertainments, and I was spoiled for the simple joys of this. But I could see no reflection of my dissatisfaction on the young faces around me, and I must confess that there was at least so much of the circus that I left when it was half over. I meant to go into the side-shows and see the fat woman and the living skeleton, and take the giant by the hand and the armless man by his friendly foot, if I might be so honored. But I did none of these things, and I am willing to believe the fault was in me, if I was disappointed in the circus. It was I who had shrunk and dwindled, and not it. To real boys it was still the size of the firmament, and was a world of wonders and delights. At least I can recognize this fact now, and can rejoice in the peaceful progress all over the country of the simple circuses which the towns never see, but which help to render the summer fairer and brighter to the unspoiled eyes and hearts they appeal to. I hope it will be long before they cease to find profit in the pleasure they give.

## A SHE HAMLET

THE other night as I sat before the curtain of the
Garden Theatre and waited for it to rise upon
the Hamlet of Mme. Bernhardt, a thrill of the rich expectation which cannot fail to precede the rise of any
curtain upon any Hamlet passed through my eager
frame. There is, indeed, no scene of drama which
is of a finer horror (eighteenth-century horror) than
that which opens the great tragedy. The sentry
pacing up and down upon the platform at Elsinore
under the winter night; the greeting between him
and the comrade arriving to relieve him, with its hints
of the bitter cold; the entrance of Horatio and Mar-
cellus to these before they can part; the mention of
the ghost, and, while the soldiers are in the act of pro-
testing it a veridical phantom, the apparition of the
ghost, taking the word from their lips and hushing
all into a pulseless awe: what could be more simply and sublimely real, more naturally supernatural?
What promise of high mystical things to come there
is in the mere syllabling of the noble verse, and how
it enlarges us from ourselves, for that time at least,
to a disembodied unity with the troubled soul whose
martyry seems foreboded in the solemn accents! As
the many Hamlets on which the curtain had risen in
my time passed in long procession through my memory, I seemed to myself so much of their world, and so
little of the world that arrogantly calls itself the actual
one, that I should hardly have been surprised to find

myself one of the less considered persons of the drama
who were seen but not heard in its course.

## I

The trouble in judging anything is that if you have
the materials for an intelligent criticism, the case is
already prejudiced in your hands. You do not bring
a free mind to it, and all your efforts to free your mind
are a species of gymnastics more or less admirable,
but not really effective for the purpose. The best
way is to own yourself unfair at the start, and then
you can have some hope of doing yourself justice,
if not your subject. In other words, if you went to
see the Hamlet of Mme. Bernhardt frankly expecting
to be disappointed, you were less likely in the end to
be disappointed in your expectations, and you could
not blame her if you were. To be ideally fair to that
representation, it would be better not to have known
any other Hamlet, and, above all, the Hamlet of Shakespeare.

From the first it was evident that she had three
things overwhelmingly against her—her sex, her race,
and her speech. You never ceased to feel for a moment that it was a woman who was doing that melancholy Dane, and that the woman was a Jewess, and
the Jewess a French Jewess. These three removes
put a gulf impassable between her utmost skill and
the impassioned irresolution of that inscrutable Northern nature which is in nothing so masculine as its
feminine reluctances and hesitations, or so little French
as in those obscure emotions which the English poetry
expressed with more than Gallic clearness, but which
the French words always failed to convey. The battle
was lost from the first, and all you could feel about

133

it for the rest was that if it was magnificent it was
not war.

While the battle went on I was the more anxious
to be fair, because I had, as it were, pre-espoused the
winning side; and I welcomed, in the interest of critical impartiality, another Hamlet which came to mind,
through readily traceable associations. This was a
Hamlet also of French extraction in the skill and
school of the actor, but as much more deeply derived
than the Hamlet of Mme. Bernhardt as the large imagination of Charles Fechter transcended in its virile
range the effect of her subtlest womanish intuition.
His was the first blond Hamlet known to our stage,
and hers was also blond, if a reddish-yellow wig may
stand for a complexion; and it was of the quality of
his Hamlet in masterly technique.

## II

The Hamlet of Fechter, which rose ghostlike out
of the gulf of the past, and cloudily possessed the stage
where the Hamlet of Mme. Bernhardt was figuring,
was called a romantic Hamlet thirty years ago; and
so it was in being a break from the classic Hamlets of
the Anglo-American theatre. It was romantic as
Shakespeare himself was romantic, in an elder sense
of the word, and not romanticistic as Dumas was romanticistic. It was, therefore, the most realistic Hamlet ever yet seen, because the most naturally poetic.
Mme. Bernhardt recalled it by the perfection of her
school; for Fechter's poetic naturalness differed from
the conventionality of the accepted Hamlets in nothing
so much as the superiority of its self-instruction. In
Mme. Bernhardt's Hamlet, as in his, nothing was
trusted to chance, or "inspiration." Good or bad,

"YOU NEVER CEASED TO FEEL . . . THAT IT WAS A
WOMAN WHO WAS DOING THAT MELANCHOLY DANE"

what one saw was what was meant to be seen. When
Fechter played Edmond Dantes or Claude Melnotte,
he put reality into those preposterous inventions, and
in Hamlet even his alien accent helped him vitalize
the part; it might be held to be nearer the Elizabethan
accent than ours, and after all, you said, Hamlet *was*
a foreigner, and in your high content with what he gave
you did not mind its being in a broken vessel. When
he challenged the ghost with "I call thee keeng, father,
*rawl*-Dane," you would hardly have had the erring
utterance bettered. It sufficed as it was; and when
he said to Rosencrantz, "Will you pleh upon this
pyip?" it was with such a princely authority and com-
radely entreaty that you made no note of the slips in
the vowels except to have pleasure of their quaintness
afterwards. For the most part you were not aware of
these bewrayals of his speech; and in certain high
things it was soul interpreted to soul through the poetry
of Shakespeare so finely, so directly, that there was
scarcely a sense of the histrionic means.

He put such divine despair into the words, "Except my life, except my life, except my life!" following
the mockery with which he had assured Polonius there
was nothing he would more willingly part withal than
his leave, that the heart-break of them had lingered
with me for thirty years, and I had been alert for them
with every Hamlet since. But before I knew, Mme.
Bernhardt had uttered them with no effect whatever.
Her Hamlet, indeed, cut many of the things that we
have learned to think the points of Hamlet, and it so
transformed others by its interpretation of the trans-
lator's interpretation of Shakespeare that they passed
unrecognized. Soliloquies are the weak invention
of the enemy, for the most part, but as such things
go that soliloquy of Hamlet's, "To be or not to be,"
is at least very noble poetry; and yet Mme. Bernhardt

was so unimpressive in it that you scarcely noticed the act of its delivery. Perhaps this happened because the sumptuous and sombre melancholy of Shakespeare's thought was transmitted in phrases that refused it its proper mystery. But there was always a hardness, not always from the translation, upon this feminine Hamlet. It was like a thick shell with no crevice in it through which the tenderness of Shakespeare's Hamlet could show, except for the one moment at Ophelia's grave, where he reproaches Laertes with those pathetic words:

> "What is the reason that you use me thus?
> I loved you ever; but it is no matter."

Here Mme. Bernhardt betrayed a real grief, but as a woman would, and not a man. At the close of the Gonzago play, when Hamlet triumphs in a mad whirl, her Hamlet hopped up and down like a mischievous crow, a mischievous she-crow.

There was no repose in her Hamlet, though there were moments of leaden lapse which suggested physical exhaustion; and there was no range in her elocution expressive of the large vibration of that tormented spirit. Her voice dropped out, or jerked itself out, and in the crises of strong emotion it was the voice of a scolding or a hysterical woman. At times her movements, which she must have studied so hard to master, were drolly womanish, especially those of the whole person. Her quickened pace was a woman's nervous little run, and not a man's swift stride; and to give herself due stature, it was her foible to wear a woman's high heels to her shoes, and she could not help tilting on them.

In the scene with the queen after the play, most English and American Hamlets have required her to look upon the counterfeit presentment of two brothers in miniatures something the size of tea-plates; but Mme. Bernhardt's preferred full-length, life-size family portraits. The dead king's effigy did not appear a flattered likeness in the scene-painter's art, but it was useful in disclosing his ghost by giving place to it in the wall at the right moment. She achieved a novelty by this treatment of the portraits, and she achieved a novelty in the tone she took with the wretched queen. Hamlet appeared to scold her mother, but though it could be said that her mother deserved a scolding, was it the part of a good daughter to give it her?

One should, of course, say a good son, but long before this it had become impossible to think at all of Mme. Bernhardt's Hamlet as a man, if it ever had been possible. She had traversed the bounds which tradition as well as nature has set, and violated the only condition upon which an actress may personate a man. This condition is that there shall be always a hint of comedy in the part, that the spectator shall know all the time that the actress is a woman, and that she shall confess herself such before the play is over; she shall be fascinating in the guise of a man only because she is so much more intensely a woman in in it. Shakespeare had rather a fancy for women in men's rôles, which, as women's rôles in his time were always taken by pretty and clever boys, could be more naturally managed then than now. But when it came to the *éclaircissement*, and the pretty boys, who had been playing the parts of women disguised as men, had to own themselves women, the effect must have been confused if not weakened. If Mme. Bernhardt, in the necessity of doing something Shakespearean, had chosen to do Rosalind, or Viola, or Portia, she could have done it with all the modern advantages of women in men's rôles. These characters are, of course, "lighter motions bounded in a shallower brain" than the creation she aimed at; but she could at least have made much of them, and she does not make much of Hamlet.

### III

The strongest reason against any woman Hamlet is that it does violence to an ideal. Literature is not so rich in great imaginary masculine types that we can afford to have them transformed to women; and after seeing Mme. Bernhardt's Hamlet no one can altogether liberate himself from the fancy that the Prince of Denmark was a girl of uncertain age, with crises of mannishness in which she did not seem quite a lady. Hamlet is in nothing more a man than in the things to which as a man he found himself unequal; for as a woman he would have been easily superior to them. If we could suppose him a woman as Mme. Bernhardt, in spite of herself, invites us to do, we could only suppose him to have solved his perplexities with the delightful precipitation of his putative sex. As the niece of a wicked uncle, who in that case would have had to be a wicked aunt, wedded to Hamlet's father hard upon the murder of her mother, she would have made short work of her vengeance. No fine scruples would have delayed her; she would not have had a moment's question whether she had not better kill herself; she would have out with her bare bodkin and ended the doubt by first passing it through her aunt's breast.

To be sure, there would then have been no play of "Hamlet," as we have it; but a Hamlet like that imagined, a frankly feminine Hamlet, Mme. Bernhardt could have rendered wonderfully. It is in attempting a masculine Hamlet that she transcends the imaginable and violates an ideal. It is not thinkable. After you have seen it done, you say, as Mr. Clemens is said to have said of bicycling: "Yes, I have seen it, but it's impossible. It doesn't stand to reason."

Art, like law, is the perfection of reason, and whatever is unreasonable in the work of an artist is inartistic. By the time I had reached these bold conclusions I was ready to deduce a principle from them, and to declare that in a true civilization such a thing as that Hamlet would be forbidden, as an offence against public morals, a violence to something precious and sacred.

In the absence of any public regulation the precious and sacred ideals in the arts must be trusted to the several artists, who bring themselves to judgment when they violate them. After Mme. Bernhardt was perversely willing to attempt the part of Hamlet, the question whether she did it well or not was of slight consequence. She had already made her failure in wishing to play the part. Her wish impugned her greatness as an artist; of a really great actress it would have been as unimaginable as the assumption of a sublime feminine rôle by a really great actor. There is an obscure law in this matter which it would be interesting to trace, but for the present I must leave the inquiry with the reader. I can note merely that it seems somehow more permissible for women in imaginary actions to figure as men than for men to figure as women. In the theatre we have conjectured how and why this may be, but the privilege, for less obvious reasons, seems yet more liberally granted in fiction. A woman may tell a story in the character of a man and not give offence, but a man cannot write a novel in autobiographical form from the personality of a woman without imparting the sense of something unwholesome. One feels this true even in the work of such a master as Tolstoy, whose *Katia* is a case in point. Perhaps a woman may play Hamlet with a less shocking effect than a man may play Desdemona, but all the same she must not play Hamlet at all. That sublime ideal is the property of the human imagination, and may not be profaned by a talent enamoured of the impossible. No harm could be done by the broadest burlesque, the most irreverent travesty, for these would still leave the ideal untouched. Hamlet, after all the horse-play, would be Hamlet; but Hamlet played by a woman, to satisfy her caprice, or to feed her famine for a fresh effect, is Hamlet disabled, for a long time, at least, in its vital essence. I felt that it would take many returns to the Hamlet of Shakespeare to efface the impression of Mme. Bernhardt's Hamlet; and as I prepared to escape from my row of stalls in the darkening theatre, I experienced a noble shame for having seen the Dane so disnatured, to use Mr. Lowell's word. I had not been obliged to come; I had voluntarily shared in the wrong done; by my presence I had made myself an accomplice in the wrong. It was high ground, but not too high for me, and I recovered a measure of self-respect in assuming it.

## SPANISH PRISONERS OF WAR

CERTAIN summers ago our cruisers, the *St. Louis* and the *Harvard*, arrived at Portsmouth, New Hampshire, with sixteen or seventeen hundred Spanish prisoners from Santiago de Cuba. They were partly soldiers of the land forces picked up by our troops in the fights before the city, but by far the greater part were sailors and marines from Cervera's ill-fated fleet. I have not much stomach for war, but the poetry of the fact I have stated made a very potent appeal to me on my literary side, and I did not hold out against it longer than to let the *St. Louis* get away with Cervera to Annapolis, when only her less dignified captives remained with those of the *Harvard* to feed either the vainglory or the pensive curiosity of the spectator. Then I went over from our summer colony to Kittery Point, and got a boat, and sailed out to have a look at these subordinate enemies in the first hours of their imprisonment.

I

It was an afternoon of the brilliancy known only to an afternoon of the American summer, and the water of the swift Piscataqua River glittered in the sun with a really incomparable brilliancy. But nothing could light up the great monster of a ship, painted the dismal lead-color which our White Squadrons put on with the outbreak of the war, and she lay sullen in the stream

141

with a look of ponderous repose, to which the activities
of the coaling-barges at her side, and of the sailors washing her decks, seemed quite unrelated. A long gun forward and a long gun aft threatened the fleet of launches,
tugs, dories, and cat-boats which fluttered about her,
but the *Harvard* looked tired and bored, and seemed
as if asleep. She had, in fact, finished her mission.
The captives whom death had released had been carried out and sunk in the sea; those who survived to a
further imprisonment had all been taken to the pretty
island a mile farther up in the river, where the tide
rushes back and forth through the Narrows like a torrent. Its defiant rapidity has won it there the graphic
name of Pull-and-be-Damned; and we could only hope
to reach the island by a series of skilful tacks, which
should humor both the wind and the tide, both dead
against us. Our boatman, one of those shore New-
Englanders who are born with a knowledge of sail-
ing, was easily master of the art of this, but it took
time, and gave me more than the leisure I wanted for
trying to see the shore with the strange eyes of the
captives who had just looked upon it. It was beautiful, I had to own, even in my quality of exile and
prisoner. The meadows and the orchards came down
to the water, or, where the wandering line of the land
was broken and lifted in black fronts of rock, they crept
to the edge of the cliff and peered over it. A summer hotel stretched its verandas along a lovely level;
everywhere in clovery hollows and on breezy knolls
were gray old farm-houses and summer cottages—like
weather-beaten birds' nests, and like freshly painted
marten-boxes; but all of a cold New England neatness which made me homesick for my malodorous
Spanish fishing-village, shambling down in stony
lanes to the warm tides of my native seas. Here,
every place looked as if it had been newly scrubbed

with soap and water, and rubbed down with a coarse towel, and was of an antipathetic alertness. The sweet, keen breeze made me shiver, and the northern sky, from which my blinding southern sun was blazing, was as hard as sapphire.

I tried to bewilder myself in the ignorance of a Catalonian or Asturian fisherman, and to wonder with his darkened mind why it should all or any of it have been, and why I should have escaped from the iron hell in which I had fought no quarrel of my own to fall into the hands of strangers, and to be haled over seas to these alien shores for a captivity of unknown term. But I need not have been at so much pains; the intelligence (I do not wish to boast) of an American author would have sufficed; for if there is anything more grotesque than another in war it is its monstrous inconsequence. If we had a grief with the Spanish government, and if it was so mortal we must do murder for it, we might have sent a joint committee of the House and Senate, and, with the improved means of assassination which modern science has put at our command, killed off the Spanish cabinet, and even the queen-mother and the little king. This would have been consequent, logical, and in a sort reasonable; but to butcher and capture a lot of wretched Spanish peasants and fishermen, hapless conscripts to whom personally and nationally we were as so many men in the moon, was that melancholy and humiliating necessity of war which makes it homicide in which there is not even the saving grace of hate, or the excuse of hot blood.

I was able to console myself perhaps a little better for the captivity of the Spaniards than if I had really been one of them, as we drew nearer and nearer their prison isle, and it opened its knotty points and little ravines, overrun with sweet-fern, blueberry-bushes, bay, and low blackberry-vines, and rigidly traversed with a high stockade of yellow pine boards. Six or eight long, low, wooden barracks stretched side by side across the general slope, with the captive officers' quarters, sheathed in weather-proof black paper, at one end of them. About their doors swarmed the common prisoners, spilling out over the steps and on the grass, where some of them lounged smoking. One operatic figure in a long blanket stalked athwart an open space; but there was such poverty of drama in the spectacle at the distance we were keeping that we were glad of so much as a shirt-sleeved contractor driving out of the stockade in his buggy. On the heights overlooking the enclosure Gatling guns were posted at three or four points, and every thirty or forty feet sentries met and parted, so indifferent to us, apparently, that we wondered if we might get nearer. We ventured, but at a certain moment a sentry called to us, "Fifty yards off, please!" Our young skipper answered, "All right," and as the sentry had a gun on his shoulder which we had every reason to believe was loaded, it was easily our pleasure to retreat to the specified limit. In fact, we came away altogether, after that, so little promise was there of our being able to satisfy our curiosity further. We came away carefully nursing such impression as we had got of a spectacle whose historical quality we did our poor best to feel. It related us, after solicitation, to the wars against the Moors, against the Mexicans and Peruvians, against the Dutch; to the Italian campaigns of the Gran Capitan, to the Siege of Florence, to the Sack of Rome, to the wars of the Spanish Succession, and I do not know what others. I do not deny that there was a certain æsthetic joy in having the Spanish prisoners there for this effect; we came away duly grateful for what we had seen of them; and we had long duly re-

SPANISH PRISONERS OF WAR

I wandered vaguely towards a Gatling gun planted on an earthen platform where the laurel and the dog-roses had been cut away for it, the man in charge explained with a smile of apology that I must not pass a certain path I had already crossed.

One always accepts the apologies of a man with a Gatling gun to back them, and I retreated. That seemed the end; and we were going crestfallenly away when the officer of the day came out and allowed us to make his acquaintance. He permitted us, with laughing reluctance, to learn that he had been in the fight at Santiago, and had come with the prisoners, and he was most obligingly sorry that our permit did not let us into the stockade. I said I had some cigarettes for the prisoners, and I supposed I might send them in, but he said he could not allow this, for they had money to buy tobacco; and he answered another of our party, who had not a soul above buttons, and who asked if she could get one from the Spaniards, that so far from promoting her wish, he would have been obliged to take away any buttons she might have got from them.

"The fact is," he explained, "you've come to the wrong end for transactions in buttons and tobacco."

But perhaps innocence so great as ours had wrought upon him. When we said we were going, and thanked him for his unavailing good-will, he looked at his watch and said they were just going to feed the prisoners; and after some parley he suddenly called out, "Music of the guard!" Instead of a regimental band, which I had supposed summoned, a single corporal ran out the barracks, touching his cap.

"Take this party round to the gate," the officer said, and he promised us that he would see us there, and hoped we would not mind a rough walk. We could have answered that to see his prisoners fed we would wade through fathoms of red-tape; but in fact we were arrested at the last point by nothing worse than the barbed wire which fortified the outer gate. Here two marines were willing to tell us how well the prisoners lived, while we stared into the stockade through an inner gate of plank which was run back for us. They said the Spaniards had a breakfast of coffee, and hash or stew and potatoes, and a dinner of soup and roast; and now at five o'clock they were to have bread and coffee, which indeed we saw the white-capped, white-jacketed cooks bringing out in huge tin wash-boilers. Our marines were of opinion, and no doubt rightly, that these poor Spaniards had never known in their lives before what it was to have full stomachs. But the marines said they never acknowledged it, and the one who had a German accent intimated that gratitude was not a virtue of any Roman (I suppose he meant Latin) people. But I do not know that if I were a prisoner, for no fault of my own, I should be very explicitly thankful for being unusually well fed. I thought (or I think now) that a fig or a bunch of grapes would have been more acceptable to me under my own vine and fig-tree than the stew and roast of captors who were indeed showing themselves less my enemies than my own government, but were still not quite my hosts.

### III

How is it the great pieces of good luck fall to us? The clock strikes twelve as it strikes two, and with no more premonition. As we stood there expecting nothing better of it than three at the most, it suddenly struck twelve. Our officer appeared at the inner gate and bade our marines slide away the gate of barbed wire and let us into the enclosure, where he welcomed us to seats on the grass against the stockade, with many polite regrets that the tough little knots of earth beside it were not chairs.

The prisoners were already filing out of their quarters, at a rapid trot towards the benches where those great wash-boilers of coffee were set. Each man had a soup-plate and bowl of enamelled tin, and each in his turn received quarter of a loaf of fresh bread and a big ladleful of steaming coffee, which he made off with to his place at one of the long tables under a shed at the side of the stockade. One young fellow tried to get a place not his own in the shade, and our officer when he came back explained that he was a *guerrillero*, and rather unruly. We heard that eight of the prisoners were in irons, by sentence of their own officers, for misconduct, but all save this *guerrillero* here were docile and obedient enough, and seemed only too glad to get peacefully at their bread and coffee.

First among them came the men of the *Cristóbal Colón*, and these were the best looking of all the captives. From their pretty fair average the others varied to worse and worse, till a very scrub lot, said to be ex-convicts, brought up the rear. They were nearly all little fellows, and very dark, though here and there a six-footer towered up, or a blond showed among them. They were joking and laughing together, harmlessly enough, but I must own that they looked a crew of rather sorry jail-birds; though whether any run of humanity clad in misfits of our navy blue and white, and other chance garments, with close-shaven heads, and sometimes bare feet, would have looked much less like jail-birds I am not sure. Still, they were not prepossessing, and though some of them were pathetically young, they had none of the charm of boyhood. No doubt they did not do themselves justice, and to be herded there like cattle did not improve their chances of

making a favorable impression on the observer. They
were kindly used by our officer and his subordinates,
who mixed among them, and straightened out the confusion they got into at times, and perhaps sometimes
wilfully. Their guards employed a few handy words
of Spanish with them; where these did not avail, they
took them by the arm and directed them; but I did not
hear a harsh tone, and I saw no violence, or even so
much indignity offered them as the ordinary trolley-
car passenger is subjected to in Broadway. At a certain bugle-call they dispersed, when they had finished
their bread and coffee, and scattered about over the
grass, or returned to their barracks. We were told
that these children of the sun dreaded its heat, and
kept out of it whenever they could, even in its decline;
but they seemed not so much to withdraw and hide
themselves from that, as to vanish into the history of
"old, unhappy, far-off" times, where prisoners of war
properly belong. I roused myself with a start as if I
had lost them in the past.

Our officer came towards us and said gayly, "Well,
you have seen the animals fed," and let us take our
grateful leave. I think we were rather a loss, in our
going, to the marines, who seemed glad of a chance to
talk. I am sure we were a loss to the man on guard
at the inner gate, who walked his beat with reluctance when it took him from us, and eagerly when it
brought him back. Then he delayed for a rapid and
comprehensive exchange of opinions and ideas, successfully blending military subordination with American equality in his manner.

The whole thing was very American in the perfect
decorum and the utter absence of ceremony. Those
good fellows were in the clothes they wore through
the fights at Santiago, and they could not have put
on much splendor if they had wished, but apparently

AFTER DINNER

they did not wish. They were simple, straightforward, and adequate. There was some dry joking about the superiority of the prisoners' rations and lodgings, and our officer ironically professed his intention of messing with the Spanish officers. But there was no grudge, and not a shadow of ill will, or of that stupid and atrocious hate towards the public enemy which abominable newspapers and politicians had tried to breed in the popular mind. There was nothing manifest but a sort of cheerful purpose to live up to that military ideal of duty which is so much nobler than the civil ideal of self-interest. Perhaps duty will yet become the civil ideal, when the peoples shall have learned to live for the common good, and are united for the operation of the industries as they now are for the hostilities.

## IV

Shall I say that a sense of something domestic, something homelike, imparted itself from what I had seen? Or was this more properly an effect from our visit, on the way back to the hospital, where a hundred and fifty of the prisoners lay sick of wounds and fevers? I cannot say that a humaner spirit prevailed here than in the camp; it was only a more positive humanity which was at work. Most of the sufferers were stretched on the clean cots of two long, airy, wooden shells, which received them, four days after the orders for their reception had come, with every equipment for their comfort. At five o'clock, when we passed down the aisles between their beds, many of them had a gay, nonchalant effect of having toothpicks or cigarettes in their mouths; but it was really the thermometers with which the nurses were taking their temperature. It suggested a possibility to me, however, and I asked if they were allowed to smoke, and being answered that they *did* smoke, anyway, whenever they could, I got rid at last of those boxes of cigarettes which had been burning my pockets, as it were, all afternoon. I gave them to such as I was told were the most deserving among the sick captives, but Heaven knows I would as willingly have given them to the least. They took my largesse gravely, as became Spaniards; one said, smiling sadly, "*Muchas gracias,*" but the others merely smiled sadly; and I looked in vain for the response which would have twinkled up in the faces of even moribund Italians at our looks of pity. Italians would have met our sympathy halfway; but these poor fellows were of another tradition, and in fact not all the Latin peoples are the same, though we sometimes conveniently group them together for our detestation. Perhaps there are even personal distinctions among their several nationalities, and there are some Spaniards who are as true and kind as some Americans. When we remember Cortez let us not forget Las Casas.

They lay in their beds there, these little Spanish men, whose dark faces their sickness could not blanch to more than a sickly sallow, and as they turned their dull black eyes upon us I must own that I could not "support the government" so fiercely as I might have done elsewhere. But the truth is, I was demoralized by the looks of these poor little men, who, in spite of their character of public enemies, did look so much like somebody's brothers, and even somebody's children. I may have been infected by the air of compassion, of scientific compassion, which prevailed in the place. There it was as wholly business to be kind and to cure as in another branch of the service it was business to be cruel and to kill. How droll these things

152

are! The surgeons had their favorites among the patients, to all of whom they were equally devoted; inarticulate friendships had sprung up between them and certain of their hapless foes, whom they spoke of as "a sort of pets." One of these was very useful in making the mutinous take their medicine; another was liked apparently because he was so likable. At a certain cot the chief surgeon stopped and said, "We did not expect this boy to live through the night." He took the boy's wrist between his thumb and finger, and asked tenderly as he leaned over him, "*Poco mejor?*" The boy could not speak to say that he was a little better; he tried to smile — such things do move the witness; nor does the sight of a man whose bandaged cheek has been half chopped away by a *machete* tend to restore one's composure.

## THE MIDNIGHT PLATOON

HE had often heard of it. Connoisseurs of such
matters, young newspaper men trying to make
literature out of life and smuggle it into print under
the guard of unwary editors, and young authors eager
to get life into their literature, had recommended it to
him as one of the most impressive sights of the city;
and he had willingly agreed with them that he ought
to see it. He imagined it very dramatic, and he was
surprised to find it in his experience so largely subjective. If there was any drama at all it was wholly
in his own consciousness. But the thing was certainly impressive in its way.

### I

He thought it a great piece of luck that he should
come upon it by chance, and so long after he had forgotten about it that he was surprised to recognize it
for the spectacle he had often promised himself the
pleasure of seeing.

Pleasure is the right word; for pleasure of the painful sort that all hedonists will easily imagine was
what he expected to get from it; though upon the face
of it there seems no reason why a man should delight
to see his fellow-men waiting in the winter street for
the midnight dole of bread which must in some cases
be their only meal from the last midnight to the next

midnight.   But the mere thought of it gave him pleasure, and the sight of it, from the very first instant. He was proud of knowing just what it was at once, with the sort of pride which one has in knowing an earthquake, though one has never felt one before. He saw the double file of men stretching up one street, and stretching down the other from the corner of the bakery where the loaves were to be given out on the stroke of twelve, and he hugged himself in a luxurious content with his perspicacity.

It was all the more comfortable to do this because he was in a coupé, warmly shut against the sharp, wholesome Christmas-week weather, and was wrapped to the chin in a long fur overcoat, which he wore that night as a duty to his family, with a conscience against taking cold and alarming them for his health.   He now practised another piece of self-denial: he let the cabman drive rapidly past the interesting spectacle, and carry him to the house where he was going to fetch away the child from the Christmas party.   He wished to be in good time, so as to save the child from anxiety about his coming; but he promised himself to stop, going back, and glut his sensibility in a leisurely study of the scene.   He got the child, with her arms full of things from the Christmas-tree, into the coupé, and then he said to the cabman, respectfully leaning as far over from his box to listen as his thick greatcoat would let him: "When you get up there near that bakery again, drive slowly.   I want to have a look at those men."

"All right, sir," said the driver intelligently, and he found his way skilfully out of the street among the high banks of the seasonable Christmas-week snow, which the street-cleaners had heaped up there till they could get round to it with their carts.

When they were in Broadway again it seemed lonelier and silenter than it was a few minutes be.ore. Except for their own coupé, the cable-cars, with their flaming foreheads, and the mechanical clangor of their gongs at the corners, seemed to have it altogether to themselves. A tall, lumbering United States mail van rolled by, and impressed my friend in the coupé with a cheap and agreeable sense of mystery relative to the letters it was carrying to their varied destination at the Grand Central Station. He listened with half an ear to the child's account of the fun she had at the party, and he watched with both eyes for the sight of the men waiting at the bakery for the charity of the midnight loaves.

He played with a fear that they might all have vanished, and with an apprehension that the cabman might forget and whirl him rapidly by the place where he had left them. But the driver remembered, and checked his horses in good time; and there were the men still, but in even greater number than before, stretching farther up Broadway and farther out along the side street. They stood slouched in dim and solemn phalanx under the night sky, so seasonably clear and frostily atwinkle with Christmas-week stars; two by two they stood, slouched close together, perhaps for their mutual warmth, perhaps in an unconscious effort to get near the door where the loaves were to be given out, in time to share in them before they were all gone.

## II

My friend's heart beat with glad anticipation. He was really to see this important, this representative thing to the greatest possible advantage. He rapidly explained to his companion that the giver of the midnight loaves got rid of what was left of his daily bread

"THEY STOOD SLOUCHED IN DIM AND SOLEMN PHALANX UNDER
THE NIGHT SKY"

in that way: the next day it could not be sold, and he preferred to give it away to those who needed it, rather than try to find his account in it otherwise. She understood, and he tried to think that sometimes coffee was given with the bread, but he could not make sure of this, though he would have liked very much to have it done; it would have been much more dramatic. Afterwards he learned that it was done, and he was proud of having fancied it.

He decided that when he came alongside of the Broadway file he would get out, and go to the side door of the bakery and watch the men receiving the bread. Perhaps he would find courage to speak to them, and ask them about themselves. At the time it did not strike him that it would be indecent.

A great many things about them were open to reasonable conjecture. It was not probable that they were any of them there for their health, as the saying is. They were all there because they were hungry, or else they were there in behalf of some one else who was hungry. But it was always possible that some of them were impostors, and he wondered if any test was applied to them that would prove them deserving or undeserving. If one were poor, one ought to be deserving; if one were rich, it did not so much matter.

It seemed to him very likely that if he asked these men questions they would tell him lies. A fantastic association of their double files and those of the galley-slaves whom Don Quixote released, with the tonguey Gines de Passamonte at their head, came into his mind. He smiled, and then he thought how these men were really a sort of slaves and convicts—slaves to want and self-convicted of poverty. All at once he fancied them actually manacled there together, two by two, a coffle of captives taken in some cruel foray, and driven to a market where no man wanted to buy. He thought how old their slavery was; and he wondered if it would ever be abolished, as other slaveries had been. Would the world ever outlive it? Would some New-Year's day come when some President would proclaim, amid some dire struggle, that their slavery was to be no more? That would be fine.

### III

He noticed how still the most of them were. A few of them stepped a little out of the line, and stamped to shake off the cold; but all the rest remained motionless, shrinking into themselves, and closer together. They might have been their own dismal ghosts, they were so still, with no more need of defence from the cold than the dead have.

He observed now that not one among them had a fur overcoat on; and at a second glance he saw that there was not an overcoat of any kind among them. He made his reflection that if any of them were impostors, and not true men, with real hunger, and if they were alive to feel that stiff, wholesome, Christmas-week cold, they were justly punished for their deceit.

He was interested by the celerity, the simultaneity of his impressions, his reflections. It occurred to him that his abnormal alertness must be something like that of a drowning person, or a person in mortal peril, and being perfectly safe and well, he was obscurely flattered by the fact.

To test his condition further he took note of the fine mass of the great dry-goods store on the hither corner, blocking itself out of the blue-black night, and of the Gothic beauty of the church beyond, so near that the coffle of captives might have issued from its sculptured portal, after vain prayer.

Fragments of conjecture, of speculation, drifted
through his mind. How early did these files begin
to form themselves for the midnight dole of bread?
As early as ten, as nine o'clock? If so, did the fact
argue habitual destitution, or merely habitual leisure?
Did the slaves in the coffle make acquaintance, or remain strangers to one another, though they were closely neighbored night after night by their misery? Perhaps they joked away the weary hours of waiting;
they must have their jokes. Which of them were old-
comers, and which novices? Did they ever quarrel
over questions of precedence? Had they some comity,
some etiquette, which a man forced to leave his place
could appeal to, and so get it back? Could one say to
his next-hand man, "Will you please keep my place?"
and would this man say to an interloper, "Excuse me,
this place is engaged"? How was it with them, when
the coffle worked slowly or swiftly past the door where
the bread and coffee were given out, and word passed
to the rear that the supply was exhausted? This
must sometimes happen, and what did they do then?

## IV

My friend did not quite like to think. Vague, re-
proachful thoughts for all the remote and immediate
luxury of his life passed through his mind. If he reformed that and gave the saving to hunger and cold?
But what was the use? There was so much hunger,
so much cold, that it could not go round.

The cabman was obeying his orders too faithfully.
He was not only walking by the Broadway coffle, he
was creeping by. His action caught the notice of the
slaves, and as the coupé passed them they all turned
and faced it, like soldiers under review making ready

to salute a superior. They were perfectly silent, perfectly respectful, but their eyes seemed to pierce the coupé through and through.

My friend was suddenly aware of a certain quality of representivity; he stood to these men for all the ease and safety that they could never, never hope to know. He was Society: Society that was to be preserved because it embodies Civilization. He wondered if they hated him in his capacity of Better Classes. He no longer thought of getting out and watching their behavior as they took their bread and coffee. He would have liked to excuse that thought, and protest that he was ashamed of it; that he was their friend, and wished them well—as well as might be without the sacrifice of his own advantages or superfluities, which he could have persuaded them would be perfectly useless. He put his hand on that of his companion trembling on his arm with sympathy, or at least with intelligence.

"You mustn't mind. What we are and what we do is all right. It's what they are and what they suffer that's all wrong."

## V

"Does that view of the situation still satisfy you?" I asked, when he had told me of this singular experience; I liked his apparently not coloring it at all.

"I don't know," he answered. "It seems to be the only way out."

"Well, it's an easy way," I admitted, "and it's an idea that ought to gratify the midnight platoon."

# THE BEACH AT ROCKAWAY

I CONFESS that I cannot hear people rejoice in their summer sojourn as beyond the reach of excursionists without a certain rebellion; and yet I have to confess also that after spending a Sunday afternoon of late July, four or five years ago, with the excursionists at one of the beaches near New York, I was rather glad that my own summer sojourn was not within reach of them. I know very well that the excursionists must go somewhere, and as a man and a brother I am willing they should go anywhere, but as a friend of quiet and seclusion I should be sorry to have them come much where I am. It is not because I would deny them a share of any pleasure I enjoy, but because they are so many and I am so few that I think they would get all the pleasure and I none. I hope the reader will see how this attitude distinguishes me from the selfish people who inhumanly exult in their remoteness from excursionists.

I

It was at Rockaway Beach that I saw these fellow-beings whose mere multitude was too much for me. They were otherwise wholly without offence towards me, and so far as I noted, towards each other; they were, in fact, the most entirely peaceable multitude I ever saw in any country, and the very quietest.

There were thousands, mounting well up towards tens of thousands, of them, in every variety of age and sex; yet I heard no voice lifted above the conversational level, except that of some infant ignorant of its privileges in a day at the sea-side, or some showman crying the attractions of the spectacle in his charge. I used to think the American crowds rather boisterous and unruly, and many years ago, when I lived in Italy, I celebrated the greater amiability and self-control of the Italian crowds. But we have certainly changed all that within a generation, and if what I saw the other day was a typical New York crowd, then the popular joy of our poorer classes is no longer the terror it once was to the peaceful observer. The tough was not visibly present, nor the toughness, either of the pure native East Side stock or of the Celtic extraction; yet there were large numbers of Americans with rather fewer recognizable Irish among the masses, who were mainly Germans, Russians, Poles, and the Jews of these several nationalities.

There was eating and drinking without limit, on every hand and in every kind, at the booths abounding in fried sea-food, and at the tables under all the wide-spreading verandas of the hotels and restaurants; yet I saw not one drunken man, and of course not any drunken women. No one that I saw was even affected by drink, and no one was guilty of any rude or unseemly behavior. The crowd was, in short, a monument to the democratic ideal of life in that very important expression of life, personal conduct, I have not any notion who or what the people were, or how virtuous or vicious they privately might be; but I am sure that no society assemblage could be of a goodlier outside; and to be of a goodly outside is all that the mere spectator has a right to ask of any crowd.

162

ROCKAWAY BEACH

# THE BEACH AT ROCKAWAY

I fancied, however, that great numbers of this crowd, or at least all the Americans in it, were Long-Islanders from the inland farms and villages within easy distance of the beach. They had probably the hereditary habit of coming to it, for it was a favorite resort in the time of their fathers and grandfathers, who had—

> —"many an hour whiled away
> Listening to the breakers' roar
> That washed the beach at Rockaway."

But the clothing store and the paper pattern have equalized the cheaper dress of the people so that you can no longer know citizen and countryman apart by their clothes, still less citizeness and countrywoman; and I can only conjecture that the foreign-looking folk I saw were from New York and Brooklyn. They came by boat, and came and went by the continually arriving and departing trains, and last but not least by bicycles, both sexes. A few came in the public carriages and omnibuses of the neighborhood, but by far the vaster number whom neither the boats nor the trains had brought had their own vehicles, the all-pervading bicycles, which no one seemed so poor as not to be able to keep. The bicyclers stormed into the frantic village of the beach the whole afternoon, in the proportion of one woman to five men, and most of these must have ridden down on their wheels from the great cities. Boys ran about in the roadway with bunches of brasses, to check the wheels, and put them for safe-keeping in what had once been the stable-yards of the hotels; the restaurants had racks for them, where you could see them in solid masses, side by side, for a hundred feet, and no shop was without its door-side rack, which the wheelman might slide his wheel into when he stopped for a soda.

a cigar, or a sandwich. All along the road the gay bicycler and bicycless swarmed upon the piazzas of the inns, munching, lunching, while their wheels formed a fantastic decoration for the underpinning of the house and a novel balustering for the steps.

## II

The amusements provided for these throngs of people were not different from those provided for throngs of people everywhere, who must be of much the same mind and taste the world over. I had fine moments when I moved in an illusion of the Midway Plaisance; again I was at the Fête de Neuilly, with all of Paris but the accent about me; yet again the county agricultural fairs of my youth spread their spectral joys before me. At none of these places, however, was there a sounding sea or a mountainous chute, and I made haste to experience the variety these afforded, beginning with the chute, since the sea was always there, and the chute might be closed for the day if I waited to view it last. I meant only to enjoy the pleasure of others in it, and I confined my own participation to the ascent of the height from which the boat plunges down the watery steep into the oblong pool below. When I bought my ticket for the car that carried passengers up, they gave me also a pasteboard medal, certifying for me, "You have shot the chute," and I resolved to keep this and show it to doubting friends as a proof of my daring; but it is a curious evidence of my unfitness for such deceptions that I afterwards could not find the medal. So I will frankly own that for me it was quite enough to see others shoot the chute, and that I came tamely down myself in the car. There is a very charming view from the top, of the sea with its ships, and all the mad gayety of the shore, but of course my main object was to exult in the wild absurdity of those who shot the chute. There was always a lady among the people in the clumsy flat-boat that flew down the long track, and she tried usually to be a pretty girl, who clutched her friends and lovers and shrieked aloud in her flight; but sometimes it was a sober mother of a family, with her brood about her, who was probably meditating, all the way, the inculpation of their father for any harm that came of it. Apparently no harm came of it in any case. The boat struck the water with the impetus gained from a half-perpendicular slide of a hundred feet, bounded high into the air, struck again and again, and so flounced awkwardly across the pond to the farther shore, where the passengers debarked and went away to commune with their viscera, and to get their breath as they could. I did not ask any of them what their emotions or sensations were, but, so far as I could conjecture, the experience of shooting the chute must comprise the rare transport of a fall from a ten-story building and the delight of a tempestuous passage of the Atlantic, powerfully condensed.

The mere sight was so athletic that it took away any appetite I might have had to witness the feats of strength performed by Madame La Noire at the nearest booth on my coming out, though madame herself was at the door to testify, in her own living picture, how much muscular force may be masked in vast masses of adipose. She had a weary, bored look, and was not without her pathos, poor soul, as few of those are who amuse the public; but I could not find her quite justifiable as a Sunday entertainment. One forgot, however, what day it was, and for the time I did not pretend to be so much better than my neighbors that I would not compromise upon a visit to an animal show a little farther on. It was a pretty fair collection of beasts that had once been wild, perhaps, and in the cage of the lions there was a slight, sad-looking, long-haired young man, exciting them to madness by blows of a whip and pistol-shots, whom I was extremely glad to have get away without being torn in pieces, or at least bitten in two. A little later I saw him at the door of the tent, very breathless, di-shevelled, and as to his dress not of the spotlessness one could wish. But perhaps spotlessness is not com-patible with the intimacy of lions and lionesses. He had had his little triumph; one spectator of his feat had declared that you would not see anything like that at Coney Island; and soiled and dusty as he was in his cotton tights, he was preferable to the living pict-ure of a young lady whom he replaced as an attrac-tion of the show. It was professedly a moral show; the manager exhorted us as we came out to say whether it was good or not; and in the box-office sat a kind and motherly faced matron who would have appar-ently abhorred to look upon a living picture at any distance, much less have it at her elbow.

Upon the whole, there seemed a melancholy mis-take in it all; the people to whom the showmen made their appeal were all so much better, evidently, than the showmen supposed; the showmen themselves ap-peared harmless enough, and one could not say that there was personally any harm in the living picture; rather she looked listless and dull, but as to the face respectable enough.

I would not give the impression that most of the amusements were not in every respect decorous. As a means of pleasure, the merry-go-round, both hori-zontal with horses and vertical with swinging cradles, prevailed, and was none the worse for being called by the French name of *carrousel*, for our people an-

glicize the word, and squeeze the last drop of Gallic
wickedness from it by pronouncing it carousal. At
every other step there were machines for weighing
you and ascertaining your height; there were pho-
tographers' booths, and X-ray apparatus for showing you the inside of your watch; and in one open
tent I saw a gentleman (with his back to the public)
having his fortune read in the lines of his hand by
an Egyptian seeress. Of course there was everywhere
soda, and places of the softer drinks abounded.

### III

I think you could only get a hard drink by order-
ing something to eat and sitting down to your wine
or beer at a table. Again I say that I saw no effects
of drink in the crowd, and in one of the great restaurants built out over the sea on piers, where there was
perpetual dancing to the braying of a brass-band, the
cotillon had no fire imparted to its figures by the fumes
of the bar. In fact it was a very rigid sobriety that
reigned here, governing the common behavior by
means of the placards which hung from the roof over
the heads of the dancers, and repeatedly announced
that gentlemen were not allowed to dance together,
or to carry umbrellas or canes while dancing, while
all were entreated not to spit on the floor.

The dancers looked happy and harmless, if not
very wise or splendid; they seemed people of the same
simple neighborhoods, village lovers, young wives
and husbands, and parties of friends who had come
together for the day's pleasure. A slight mother,
much weighed down by a heavy baby, passed, rapt
in an innocent envy of them, and I think she and the
child's father meant to join them as soon as they could

find a place where to lay it. Almost any place would
do; at another great restaurant I saw two chairs faced
together, and a baby sleeping on them as quietly amid
the coming and going of lagers and frankfurters as
if in its cradle at home.

Lagers and frankfurters were much in evidence
everywhere, especially frankfurters, which seemed to
have whole booths devoted to broiling them. They
disputed this dignity with soft-shell crabs, and sections of eels, piled attractively on large platters, or
sizzling to an impassioned brown in deep skillets of
fat. The old acrid smell of frying brought back many
holidays of Italy to me, and I was again at times on
the Riva at Venice, and in the Mercato Vecchio at Florence. But the Continental Sunday cannot be felt to
have quite replaced the old American Sabbath yet;
the Puritan leaven works still, and though so many
of our own people consent willingly to the transforma-
tion, I fancy they always enjoy themselves on Sunday
with a certain consciousness of wrong-doing.

## IV

I have already said that the spectator quite lost
sense of what day it was. Nothing could be more
secular than all the sights and sounds. It was the
Fourth of July, less the fire-crackers and the drunk-
enness, and it was the high day of the week. But
if it was very wicked, and I must recognize that the
scene would be shocking to most of my readers, I feel
bound to say that the people themselves did not look
wicked. They looked harmless; they even looked
good, the most of them. I am sorry to say they were
not very good-looking. The women were pretty enough,
and the men were handsome enough; perhaps the

average was higher in respect of beauty than the average is anywhere else; I was lately from New England, where the people were distinctly more hard-favored; but among all those thousands at Rocka-way I found no striking types. It may be that as we grow older and our satisfaction with our own looks wanes, we become more fastidious as to the looks of others. At any rate, there seems to be much less beauty in the world than there was thirty or forty years ago.

On the other hand, the dresses seem indefinitely prettier, as they should be in compensation. When we were all so handsome we could well afford to wear hoops or peg-top trousers, but now it is different, and the poor things must eke out their personal ungainli-ness with all the devices of the modiste and the tailor. I do not mean that there was any distinction in the dress of the crowd, but I saw nothing positively ugly or grotesquely out of taste. The costumes were as good as the customs, and I have already celebrated the manners of this crowd. I believe I must except the costumes of the bicyclesses, who were unfailingly dumpy in effect when dismounted, and who were all the more lamentable for tottering about, in their short skirts, upon the tips of their narrow little, sharp-point-ed, silly high-heeled shoes. How severe I am! But those high heels seemed to take all honesty from their daring in the wholesome exercise of the wheel, and to keep them in the tradition of cheap coquetry still, and imbecilly dependent.

## V

I have almost forgotten in the interest of the human spectacle that there is a sea somewhere about at Rockaway Beach, and it is this that the people have come for. I might well forget that modest sea, it is so built out of sight by the restaurants and bath-houses and switch-backs and shops that border it, and by the hotels and saloons and shows flaring along the road that divides the village, and the planked streets that intersect this. But if you walk southward on any of the streets, you presently find the planks foundering in sand, which drifts far up over them, and then you find yourself in full sight of the ocean and the ocean bathing. Swarms and heaps of people in all lolling and lying and wallowing shapes strew the beach, and the water is full of slopping and shouting and shrieking human creatures, clinging with bare white arms to the life-lines that run from the shore to the buoys; beyond these the life-guard stays himself in his boat with outspread oars, and rocks on the incoming surf.

All that you can say of it is that it is queer. It is not picturesque, or poetic, or dramatic; it is queer. An enfilading glance gives this impression and no other; if you go to the balcony of the nearest marine restaurant for a flanking eye-shot, it is still queer, with the added effect, in all those arms upstretched to the life-lines, of frogs' legs inverted in a downward plunge.

On the sand before this spectacle I talked with a philosopher of humble condition who backed upon me and knocked my umbrella out of my hand. This made us beg each other's pardon; he said that he did not know I was there, and I said it did not matter. Then we both looked at the bathing, and he said:

"I don't like that."

"Why," I asked, "do you see any harm in it?"

"No. But I don't like the looks of it. It ain't nice. It's—queer."

"IT IS NOT PICTURESQUE, OR POETIC, OR DRAMATIC; IT IS QUEER"

It was indeed like one of those uncomfortable dreams where you are not dressed sufficiently for company, or perhaps at all, and yet are making a very public appearance. This promiscuous bathing was not much in excess of the convention that governs the sea-bathing of the politest people; it could not be; and it was marked by no grave misconduct. Here and there a gentleman was teaching a lady to swim, with his arms round her; here and there a wild nereid was splashing another; a young Jew pursued a flight of naiads with a section of dead eel in his hand. But otherwise all was a damp and dreary decorum. I challenged my philosopher in vain for a specific cause of his dislike of the scene.

Most of the people on the sand were in bathing-dress, but there were a multitude of others who had apparently come for the sea-air and not the sea-bathing. A mother sat with a sick child on her knees; babies were cradled in the sand asleep, and people walked carefully round and over them. There were everywhere a great many poor mothers and children, who seemed getting the most of the good that was going.

## VI

But upon the whole, though I drove away from the beach celebrating the good temper and the good order of the scene to an applausive driver, I have since thought of it as rather melancholy. It was in fact no wiser or livelier than a society function in the means of enjoyment it afforded. The best thing about it was that it left the guests very much to their own devices. The established pleasures were clumsy and tiresome-looking; but one could eschew them. The more of them one eschewed, the merrier perhaps; for I doubt if the race is formed for much pleasure; and even a day's rest is more than most people can bear. They endure it in passing, but they get home weary and cross, even after a twenty-mile run on the wheel. The road, by-the-by, was full of homeward wheels by this time, single and double and tandem, and my driver professed that their multitude greatly increased the difficulties of his profession.

## AMERICAN LITERARY CENTRES

ONE of the facts which we Americans have a difficulty in making clear to a rather inattentive
world outside is that, while we have apparently a literature of our own, we have no literary centre. We
have so much literature that from time to time it seems
even to us we *must* have a literary centre. We say to
ourselves, with a good deal of logic, Where there is so
much smoke there must be some fire, or at least a fireplace. But it is just here that, misled by tradition, and
even by history, we deceive ourselves. Really, we have
no fireplace for such fire as we have kindled; or, if any
one is disposed to deny this, then I say, we have a dozen
fireplaces; which is quite as bad, so far as the notion
of a literary centre is concerned, if it is not worse.

I once proved this fact to my own satisfaction in some
papers which I wrote several years ago; but it appears,
from a question which has lately come to me from England, that I did not carry conviction quite so far as that
island; and I still have my work all before me, if I understand the London friend who wishes "a comparative
view of the centres of literary production" among us;
"how and why they change; how they stand at present;
and what is the relation, for instance, of Boston to other
such centres."

### I

Here, if I cut my coat according to my cloth, I should
have a garment which this whole volume would hard-

173

ly stuff out with its form; and I have a fancy that if I
begin by answering, as I have sometimes rather too
succinctly done, that we have no more a single literary centre than Italy or than Germany has (or had before their unification), I shall not be taken at my word.
I shall be right, all the same, and if I am told that
in those countries there is now a tendency to such a
centre, I can only say that there is none in this, and
that, so far as I can see, we get further every day from
having such a centre. The fault, if it is a fault, grows
upon us, for the whole present tendency of American
life is centrifugal, and just so far as literature is the
language of our life, it shares this tendency. I do not
attempt to say how it will be when, in order to spread
ourselves over the earth, and convincingly to preach
the blessings of our deeply incorporated civilization
by the mouths of our eight-inch guns, the mind of the
nation shall be politically centred at some capital;
that is the function of prophecy, and I am only writing literary history, on a very small scale, with a somewhat crushing sense of limits.

Once, twice, thrice there was apparently an American literary centre: at Philadelphia, from the time
Franklin went to live there until the death of Charles
Brockden Brown, our first romancer; then at New
York, during the period which may be roughly de-
scribed as that of Irving, Poe, Willis, and Bryant;
then at Boston, for the thirty or forty years illumined
by the presence of Longfellow, Lowell, Whittier, Hawthorne, Emerson, Holmes, Prescott, Parkman, and
many lesser lights. These are all still great publishing centres. If it were not that the house with the
largest list of American authors was still at Boston,
I should say New York was now the chief publishing
centre; but in the sense that London and Paris, or
even Madrid and Petersburg, are literary centres, with

a controlling influence throughout England and France, Spain and Russia, neither New York nor Boston is now our literary centre, whatever they may once have been. Not to take Philadelphia too seriously, I may note that when New York seemed our literary centre Irving alone among those who gave it lustre was a New-Yorker, and he mainly lived abroad; Bryant, who was a New-Englander, was alone constant to the city of his adoption; Willis, a Bostonian, and Poe, a Marylander, went and came as their poverty or their prosperity compelled or invited; neither dwelt here unbrokenly, and Poe did not even die here, though he often came near starving. One cannot then strictly speak of any early American literary centre except Boston, and Boston, strictly speaking, was the New England literary centre.

However, we had really no use for an American literary centre before the Civil War, for it was only after the Civil War that we really began to have an American literature. Up to that time we had a Colonial literature, a Knickerbocker literature, and a New England literature. But as soon as the country began to feel its life in every limb with the coming of peace, it began to speak in the varying accents of all the different sections—North, East, South, West, and Farthest West; but not before that time.

## II

Perhaps the first note of this national concord, or discord, was sounded from California, in the voices of Mr. Bret Harte, of Mark Twain, of Mr. Charles Warren Stoddard (I am sorry for those who do not know his beautiful *Idyls of the South Seas*), and others of the remarkable group of poets and humorists whom

these names must stand for. The San Francisco
school briefly flourished from 1867 till 1872 or so, and
while it endured it made San Francisco the first national literary centre we ever had, for its writers were
of every American origin except Californian.

After the Pacific Slope, the great Middle West found
utterance in the dialect verse of Mr. John Hay, and
after that began the exploitation of all the local par-
lances, which has sometimes seemed to stop, and then
has begun again. It went on in the South in the
fables of Mr. Joel Chandler Harris's *Uncle Remus*,
and in the fiction of Miss Murfree, who so long mas-
queraded as Charles Egbert Craddock. Louisiana
found expression in the Creole stories of Mr. G. W.
Cable, Indiana in the Hoosier poems of Mr. James
Whitcomb Riley, and central New York in the novels
of Mr. Harold Frederic; but nowhere was the new impulse so firmly and finely directed as in New England,
where Miss Sarah Orne Jewett's studies of country
life antedated Miss Mary Wilkins's work. To be
sure, the portrayal of Yankee character began before
either of these artists was known; Lowell's *Bigelow
Papers* first reflected it; Mrs. Stowe's *Old Town Stories*
caught it again and again; Mrs. Harriet Prescott
Spofford, in her unromantic moods, was of an excellent fidelity to it; and Mrs. Rose Terry Cooke was
even truer to the New England of Connecticut. With
the later group Mrs. Lily Chase Wyman has pictured
Rhode Island work-life with truth pitiless to the beholder, and full of that tender humanity for the material which characterizes Russian fiction.

Mr. James Lane Allen has let in the light upon
Kentucky; the *Red Men and White* of the great plains
have found their interpreter in Mr. Owen Wister, a
young Philadelphian witness of their dramatic conditions and characteristics; Mr. Hamlin Garland had

already expressed the sad circumstances of the rural
Northwest in his pathetic idyls, colored from the experience of one who had been part of what he saw.
Later came Mr. Henry B. Fuller, and gave us what
was hardest and most sordid, as well as something
of what was most touching and most amusing, in the
hurly-burly of Chicago.

### III

A survey of this sort imparts no just sense of the
facts, and I own that I am impatient of merely nam-
ing authors and books that each tempt me to an expansion far beyond the limits of this essay; for, if I
may be so personal, I have watched the growth of our
literature in Americanism with intense sympathy.
In my poor way I have always liked the truth, and in
times past I am afraid that I have helped to make it
odious to those who believed beauty was something
different; but I hope that I shall not now be doing our
decentralized literature a disservice by saying that its
chief value is its honesty, its fidelity to our decentralized life. Sometimes I wish this were a little more
constant; but upon the whole I have no reason to complain; and I think that as a very interested spectator of
New York I have reason to be content with the veracity with which some phases of it have been rendered.
The lightning—or the flash-light, to speak more accurately—has been rather late in striking this un-
gainly metropolis, but it has already got in its work
with notable effect at some points. This began, I
believe, with the local dramas of Mr. Edward Harrigan, a species of farces, or sketches of character,
loosely hung together, with little sequence or relevancy,
upon the thread of a plot which would keep the stage
for two or three hours. It was very rough magic, as

a whole, but in parts it was exquisite, and it held the mirror up towards politics on their social and political side, and gave us East-Side types—Irish, German, negro, and Italian—which were instantly recognizable and deliciously satisfying. I never could understand why Mr. Harrigan did not go further, but perhaps he had gone far enough; and, at any rate, he left the field open for others. The next to appear noticeably in it was Mr. Stephen Crane, whose *Red Badge of Courage* wronged the finer art which he showed in such New York studies as *Maggie: A Girl of the Streets,* and *George's Mother.* He has been followed by Abraham Cahan, a Russian Hebrew, who has done portraits of his race and nation with uncommon power. They are the very Russian Hebrews of Hester Street translated from their native Yiddish into English, which the author mastered after coming here in his early manhood. He brought to his work the artistic qualities of both the Slav and the Jew, and in his *Jekl: A Story of the Ghetto,* he gave proof of talent which his more recent book of sketches—*The Imported Bridegroom* — confirms. He sees his people humorously, and he is as unsparing of their sordidness as he is compassionate of their hard circumstance and the somewhat frowsy pathos of their lives. He is a Socialist, but his fiction is wholly without "tendentiousness."

A good many years ago—ten or twelve, at least— Mr. Harry Harland had shown us some politer New York Jews, with a romantic coloring, though with genuine feeling for the novelty and picturesqueness of his material; but I do not think of any one who has adequately dealt with our Gentile society. Mr. James has treated it historically in *Washington Square,* and more modernly in some passages of *The Bostonians,* as well as in some of his shorter stories; Mr. Edgar Fawcett has dealt with it intelligently and authoritatively in a novel or two; and Mr. Brander Matthews has sketched it, in this aspect, and that with his Gallic cleverness, neatness, and point. In the novel, *His Father's Son*, he in fact faces it squarely and renders certain forms of it with masterly skill. He has done something more distinctive still in *The Action and the Word*, one of the best American stories I know. But except for these writers, our literature has hardly taken to New York society.

## IV

It is an even thing: New York society has not taken to our literature. New York publishes it, criticises it, and circulates it, but I doubt if New York society much reads it or cares for it, and New York is therefore by no means the literary centre that Boston once was, though a large number of our literary men live in or about New York. Boston, in my time at least, had distinctly a literary atmosphere, which more or less pervaded society; but New York has distinctly nothing of the kind, in any pervasive sense. It is a vast mart, and literature is one of the things marketed here; but our good society cares no more for it than for some other products bought and sold here; it does not care nearly so much for books as for horses or for stocks, and I suppose it is not unlike the good society of any other metropolis in this. To the general, here, journalism is a far more appreciable thing than literature, and has greater recognition, for some very good reasons; but in Boston literature had vastly more honor, and even more popular recognition, than journalism. There journalism desired to be literary, and here literature has to try hard not to be journalistic. If New York is a literary centre on the business side, as London is, Boston was a literary centre, as Weimar was, and as Edinburgh was. It felt literature, as those capitals felt it, and if it did not love it quite so much as might seem, it always respected it.

To be quite clear in what I wish to say of the present relation of Boston to our other literary centres, I must repeat that we have now no such literary centre as Boston was. Boston itself has perhaps outgrown the literary consciousness which formerly distinguished it from all our other large towns. In a place of near-ly a million people (I count in the outlying places) newspapers must be more than books; and that alone says everything.

Mr. Aldrich once noticed that whenever an author died in Boston, the New-Yorkers thought they had a literary centre; and it is by some such means that the primacy has passed from Boston, even if it has not passed to New York. But still there is enough literature left in the body at Boston to keep her first among equals in some things, if not easily first in all.

Mr. Aldrich himself lives in Boston, and he is, with Mr. Stedman, the foremost of our poets. At Cam-bridge live Colonel T. W. Higginson, an essayist in a certain sort without rival among us; and Mr. William James, the most interesting and the most literary of psychologists, whose repute is European as well as American. Mr. Charles Eliot Norton alone survives of the earlier Cambridge group — Longfellow, Lowell, Richard Henry Dana, Louis Agassiz, Francis J. Child, and Henry James, the father of the novelist and the psychologist.

To Boston Mr. James Ford Rhodes, the latest of our abler historians, has gone from Ohio; and there Mr. Henry Cabot Lodge, the Massachusetts Senator, whose work in literature is making itself more and more known, was born and belongs, politically, socially, and intellectually. Mrs. Julia Ward Howe, a poet of wide fame in an elder generation, lives there; Mr. T. B. Aldrich lives there; and thereabouts live Mrs. Elizabeth Stuart Phelps Ward and Mrs. Harriet Prescott Spofford, the first of a fame beyond the last, who was known to us so long before her. Then at Boston, or near Boston, live those artists supreme in the kind of short story which we have carried so far: Miss Jewett, Miss Wilkins, Miss Alice Brown, Mrs. Chase-Wyman, and Miss Gertrude Smith, who comes from Kansas, and writes of the prairie farm-life, though she leaves Mr. E. W. Howe (of *The Story of a Country Town* and presently of the *Atchison Daily Globe*) to constitute, with the humorous poet Ironquill, a frontier literary centre at Topeka. Of Boston, too, though she is of western Pennsylvania origin, is Mrs. Margaret Deland, one of our most successful novelists. Miss Wilkins has married out of Massachusetts into New Jersey, and is the neighbor of Mr. H. M. Alden at Metuchen.

All these are more or less embodied and represented in the *Atlantic Monthly*, still the most literary, and in many things still the first of our magazines. Finally, after the chief publishing house in New York, the greatest American publishing house is in Boston, with by far the largest list of the best American books. Recently several firms of younger vigor and valor have recruited the wasted ranks of the Boston publishers, and are especially to be noted for the number of rather nice new poets they give to the light.

## V

Dealing with the question geographically, in the right American way, we descend to Hartford obliquely by way of Springfield, Massachusetts, where, in a little city of fifty thousand, a newspaper of metropolitan influence and of distinctly literary tone is published. At Hartford while Charles Dudley Warner lived, there was an indisputable literary centre; Mark Twain lives there no longer, and now we can scarcely count Hartford among our literary centres, though it is a publishing centre of much activity in subscription books.

At New Haven, Yale University has latterly attracted Mr. William H. Bishop, whose novels I always liked for the best reasons, and has long held Professor J. T. Lounsbury, who is, since Professor Child's death at Cambridge, our best Chaucer scholar. Mr. Donald G. Mitchell, once endeared to the whole fickle American public by his *Reveries of a Bachelor* and his *Dream Life*, dwells on the borders of the pleasant town, which is also the home of Mr. J. W. De Forest, the earliest real American novelist, and for certain gifts in seeing and telling our life also one of the greatest.

As to New York (where the imagination may arrive daily from New Haven, either by a Sound boat or by eight or ten of the swiftest express trains in the world), I confess I am more and more puzzled. Here abide the poets, Mr. R. H. Stoddard, Mr. E. C. Stedman, Mr. R. W. Gilder, and many whom an envious etcetera must hide from view; the fictionists, Mr. R. H. Davis, Mrs. Kate Douglas Wiggin, Mr. Brander Matthews, Mr. Frank Hopkinson Smith, Mr. Abraham Cahan, Mr. Frank Norris, and Mr. James Lane Allen, who has left Kentucky to join the large Southern contingent, which includes Mrs. Burton Harrison and Mrs. McEnery Stuart; the historians, Professor William M. Sloane and Dr. Eggleston (reformed from a novelist); the literary and religious and economic essayists, Mr. Hamilton W. Mabie, Mr. H. M. Alden,

Mr. J. J. Chapman, and Mr. E. L. Godkin, with critics, dramatists, satirists, magazinists, and journalists of literary stamp in number to convince the wavering reason against itself that here beyond all question is the great literary centre of these States. There is an Authors' Club, which alone includes a hundred and fifty authors, and, if you come to editors, there is simply no end. Magazines are published here and circulated hence throughout the land by millions; and books by the ton are the daily output of our publishers, who are the largest in the country.

If these things do not mean a great literary centre, it would be hard to say what does; and I am not going to try for a reason against such facts. It is not quality that is wanting, but perhaps it is the quantity of the quality; there is leaven, but not for so large a lump. It may be that New York is going to be our literary centre, as London is the literary centre of England, by gathering into itself all our writing talent, but it has by no means done this yet. What we can say is that more authors come here from the West and South than go elsewhere; but they often stay at home, and I fancy very wisely. Mr. Joel Chandler Harris stays at Atlanta, in Georgia; Mr. James Whitcomb Riley stays at Indianapolis; Mr. Maurice Thompson spent his whole literary life, and General Lew. Wallace still lives at Crawfordsville, Indiana; Mr. Madison Cawein stays at Louisville, Kentucky; Miss Murfree stays at St. Louis, Missouri; Francis R. Stockton spent the greater part of the year at his place in West Virginia, and came only for the winter months to New York; Mr. Edward Bellamy, until his failing health exiled him to the Far West, remained at Chicopee, Massachusetts; and I cannot think of one of these writers whom it would have advantaged in any literary wise to dwell in New York. He would not have found greater incentive than at home; and in society he would not have found that literary tone which all society had, or wished to have, in Boston when Boston was a great town and not yet a big town.

In fact, I doubt if anywhere in the world there was ever so much taste and feeling for literature as there was in that Boston. At Edinburgh (as I imagine it) there was a large and distinguished literary class, and at Weimar there was a cultivated court circle; but in Boston there was not only such a group of authors as we shall hardly see here again for hundreds of years, but there was such regard for them and their calling, not only in good society, but among the extremely well-read people of the whole intelligent city, as hardly another community has shown. New York, I am quite sure, never was such a centre, and I see no signs that it ever will be. It does not influence the literature of the whole country as Boston once did through writers whom all the young writers wished to resemble; it does not give the law, and it does not inspire the love that literary Boston inspired. There is no ideal that it represents.

A glance at the map of the Union will show how very widely our smaller literary centres are scattered; and perhaps it will be useful in following me to other more populous literary centres. Dropping southward from New York, now, we find ourselves in a literary centre of importance at Philadelphia, since that is the home of Mr. J. B. McMasters, the historian of the American people; of Mr. Owen Wister, whose fresh and vigorous work I have mentioned; and of Dr. Weir Mitchell, a novelist of power long known to the better public, and now recognized by the larger in the immense success of his historical romance, *Hugh Wynne*.

If I skip Baltimore, I may ignore a literary centre of great promise, but while I do not forget the excellent work of Johns Hopkins University in training men for the solider literature of the future, no Baltimore names to conjure with occur to me at the moment; and we must really get on to Washington. This, till he became ambassador at the Court of St. James, was the home of Mr. John Hay, a poet whose biography of Lincoln must rank him with the historians, and whose public service as Secretary of State classes him high among statesmen. He blotted out one literary centre at Cleveland, Ohio, when he removed to Washington, and Mr. Thomas Nelson Page another at Richmond, Virginia, when he came to the national capital. Mr. Paul Dunbar, the first negro poet to divine and utter his race, carried with him the literary centre of Dayton, Ohio, when he came to be an employé in the Congressional Library; and Mr. Charles Warren Stoddard, in settling at Washington as Professor of Literature in the Catholic University, brought somewhat indirectly away with him the last traces of the old literary centre at San Francisco.

A more recent literary centre in the Californian metropolis went to pieces when Mr. Gelett Burgess came to New York and silenced the *Lark*, a bird of as new and rare a note as ever made itself heard in this air; but since he has returned to California, there is hope that the literary centre may form itself there again. I do not know whether Mrs. Charlotte Perkins Stetson wrecked a literary centre in leaving Los Angeles or not. I am sure only that she has enriched the literary centre of New York by the addition of a talent in sociological satire which would be extraordinary even if it were not altogether unrivalled among us.

Could one say too much of the literary centre at Chicago? I fancy, yes; or too much, at least, for the taste of the notable people who constitute it. In Mr. Henry B. Fuller we have reason to hope, from what he has already done, an American novelist of such greatness that he may well leave being the great American novelist to any one who likes taking that rôle. Mr. Hamlin Garland is another writer of genuine and original gift who centres at Chicago; and Mrs. Mary Catherwood has made her name well known in romantic fiction. Miss Edith Wyatt is a talent, newly known, of the finest quality in minor fiction; Mr. Robert Herrick, Mr. Will Payne in their novels, and Mr. George Ade and Mr. Peter Dunn in their satires form with those named a group not to be matched elsewhere in the country. It would be hard to match among our critical journals the *Dial* of Chicago; and with a fair amount of publishing in a sort of books often as good within as they are uncommonly pretty without, Chicago has a claim to rank with our first literary centres.

It is certainly to be reckoned not so very far below London, which, with Mr. Henry James, Mr. Harry Harland, and Mr. Bret Harte, seems to me an American literary centre worthy to be named with contemporary Boston. Which is our chief literary centre, however, I am not, after all, ready to say. When I remember Mr. G. W. Cable, at Northampton, Massachusetts, I am shaken in all my preoccupations; when I think of Mark Twain, it seems to me that our greatest literary centre is just now at Riverdale-on-the-Hudson.

## SAWDUST IN THE ARENA

IT was in the old Roman arena of beautiful Verona
that the circus events I wish to speak of took place;
in fact, I had the honor and profit of seeing two circuses there. Or, strictly speaking, it was one entire
circus that I saw, and the unique speciality of another,
the dying glory of a circus on its last legs, the trium-
phal fall of a circus superb in adversity.

### I

The entire circus wás altogether Italian, with the
exception of the clowns, who, to the credit of our nation, are always Americans, or advertised as such,
in Italy. Its chief and almost absorbing event was
a reproduction of the tournament which had then
lately been held at Rome in celebration of Prince Tom-
maso's coming of age, and for a copy of a copy it was
really fine. It had fitness in the arena, which must
have witnessed many such mediæval shows in their
time, and I am sensible still of the pleasure its effects
of color gave me. There was one beautiful woman,
a red blonde in a green velvet gown, who might have
ridden, as she was, out of a canvas of Titian's, if he
had ever painted equestrian pictures, and who at any
rate was an excellent Carpaccio. Then, the *Clowns
Americani* were very amusing, from a platform devoted solely to them, and it was a source of pride if

not of joy with me to think that we were almost the
only people present who understood their jokes. In
the vast oval of the arena, however, the circus ring
looked very little, not half so large, say, as the rim
of a lady's hat in front of you at the play; and on
the gradines of the ancient amphitheatre we were all
such a great way off that a good field-glass would
have been needed to distinguish the features of the
actors. I could not make out, therefore, whether the
*Clowns Americani* had the national expression or
not, but one of them, I am sorry to say, spoke the
United States language with a cockney accent. I
suspect that he was an Englishman who had passed
himself off upon the Italian management as a true
Yankee, and who had formed himself upon our school
of clowning, just as some of the recent English humorists have patterned after certain famous wits of ours.
I do not know that I would have exposed this impos-
tor, even if occasion had offered, for, after all, his fraud
was a tribute to our own primacy in clowning, and the
Veronese were none the worse for his erring aspirates.

The audience was for me the best part of the spectacle, as the audience always is in Italy, and I indulged
my fancy in some cheap excursions concerning the
place and people. I reflected that it was the same
race essentially as that which used to watch the glad-
iatorial shows in that arena when it was new, and that
very possibly there were among these spectators persons of the same blood as those Veronese patricians
who had left their names carved on the front of the
gradines in places, to claim this or that seat for their
own. In fact, there was so little difference, probably,
in their qualities, from that time to this, that I felt the
process of the generations to be a sort of impertinence;
and if Nature had been present, I might very well
have asked her why, when she had once arrived at a

given expression of humanity, she must go on repeating it indefinitely? How were all those similar souls to know themselves apart in their common eternity? Merely to have been differently circumstanced in time did not seem enough; and I think Nature would have been puzzled to answer me. But perhaps not; she may have had her reasons, as that you cannot have too much of a good thing, and that when the type was so fine in most respects as the Italian you could not do better than go on repeating impressions from it.

Certainly I myself could have wished no variation from it in the young officer of *bersaglieri*, who had come down from antiquity to the topmost gradine of the arena over against me, and stood there defined against the clear evening sky, one hand on his hip, and the other at his side, while his thin cockerel plumes streamed in the light wind. I have since wondered if he knew how beautiful he was, and I am sure that, if he did not, all the women there did, and that was doubtless enough for the young officer of *bersaglieri*.

## II

I think that he was preliminary to the sole event of that partial circus I have mentioned. This event was one that I have often witnessed elsewhere, but never in such noble and worthy keeping. The top of the outer arena wall must itself be fifty feet high, and the pole in the centre of its oval seemed to rise fifty feet higher yet. At its base an immense net was stretched, and a man in a Prince Albert coat and a derby hat was figuring about, anxiously directing the workmen who were fixing the guy-ropes, and testing every particular of the preparation with his own hands. While this went on, a young girl ran out into the arena, and, after a bow to the spectators, quickly mounted to the top of the pole, where she presently stood in statuesque beauty that took all eyes even from the loveliness of the officer of *bersaglieri*. Then the man in the Prince Albert coat and the derby hat stepped back from the net and looked up at her.

She called down, in English that sounded like some delocalized, denaturalized speech, it was so strange then and there, "Is it all right?"

He shouted back in the same alienated tongue, "Yes; keep to the left," and she dived straight downward in the long plunge, till, just before she reached the net, she turned a quick somersault into its elastic mesh.

It was all so exquisitely graceful that one forgot how wickedly dangerous it was; but I think that the brief English colloquy was the great wonder of the event for me, and I doubt if I could ever have been perfectly happy again, if chance had not amiably suffered me to satisfy my curiosity concerning the speakers. A few evenings after that, I was at that copy of a copy of a tournament, and, a few gradines below me, I saw the man of the Prince Albert coat and the derby hat. I had already made up my mind that he was an American, for I supposed that an Englishman would rather perish than wear such a coat with such a hat, and as I had wished all my life to speak to a circus-man, I went down and boldly accosted him. "Are you a brother Yankee?" I asked, and he laughed, and confessed that he was an Englishman, but he said he was glad to meet any one who spoke English, and he made a place for me by his side. He was very willing to tell how he happened to be there, and he explained that he was the manager of a circus, which had been playing to very good business all winter in Spain. In an evil hour he decided to come to Italy, but he found the prices so ruinously low that he was forced to disband his company. This diving-girl was all that remained to him of its many attractions, and he was trying to make a living for both in a country where the admission to a circus was six of our cents, with fifty for a reserved seat. But he was about to give it up and come to America, where he said Barnum had offered him an engagement. I hope he found it profitable, and is long since an American citizen, with as good right as any of us to wear a Prince Albert coat with a derby hat.

### III

There used to be very good circuses in Venice, where many Venetians had the only opportunity of their lives to see a horse. The horses were the great attraction for them, and, perhaps in concession to their habitual destitution in this respect, the riding was providentially very good. It was so good that it did not bore me, as circus-riding mostly does, especially that of the silk-clad jockey who stands in his high boots, on his backbared horse, and ends by waving an American flag in triumph at having been so tiresome.

I am at a loss to know why they make such an ado about the lady who jumps through paper hoops, which have first had holes poked in them to render her transit easy, or why it should be thought such a merit in her to hop over a succession of banners which are swept under her feet in a manner to minify her exertion almost to nothing, but I observe it is so at all circuses. At my first Venetian circus, which was on a broad expanse of the Riva degli Schiavoni, there was a girl who flung herself to the ground and back to her horse again, holding by his mane with one hand, quite like the goddess out of the bath-gown at my village circus the other day; and apparently there are more circuses in the world than circus events. It must be as hard to think up anything new in that kind as in romanticistic fiction, which circus-acting otherwise largely resembles.

At a circus which played all one winter in Florence I saw for the first time—outside of polite society—the clown in evening dress, who now seems essential to all circuses of metropolitan pretensions, and whom I missed so gladly at my village circus. He is nearly as futile as the lady clown, who is one of the saddest and strangest developments of New Womanhood.

Of the clowns who do not speak, I believe I like most the clown who catches a succession of peak-crowned soft hats on his head, when thrown across the ring by an accomplice. This is a very pretty sight always, and at the Hippodrome in Paris I once saw a gifted creature take his stand high up on the benches among the audience and catch these hats on his head from a flight of a hundred feet through the air. This made me proud of human nature, which is often so humiliating; and altogether I do not think that after a real country circus there are many better things in life than the Hippodrome. It had a state, a dignity, a smoothness, a polish, which I should not know where to match, and when the superb coach drove into the ring to convey the lady performers to the scene of their events, there was a majesty in the effect which I doubt if courts have the power to rival. Still, it should be remembered that I have never been at court, and speak from a knowledge of the Hippodrome only.

## AT A DIME MUSEUM

"I SEE," said my friend, "that you have been writing a good deal about the theatre during the past winter. You have been attacking its high hats and its high prices, and its low morals; and I suppose that you think you have done good, as people call it."

### I

This seemed like a challenge of some sort, and I prepared myself to take it up warily. I said I should be very sorry to do good, as people called it; because such a line of action nearly always ended in spiritual pride for the doer and general demoralization for the doee. Still, I said, a law had lately been passed in Ohio giving a man who found himself behind a high hat at the theatre a claim for damages against the manager; and if the passage of this law could be traced ever so faintly and indirectly to my teachings, I should not altogether grieve for the good I had done. I added that if all the States should pass such a law, and other laws fixing a low price for a certain number of seats at the theatres, or obliging the managers to give one free performance every month, as the law does in Paris, and should then forbid indecent and immoral plays—

"I see what you mean," said my friend, a little impatiently. "You mean sumptuary legislation. But I have not come to talk to you upon that subject, for then you would probably want to do all the talking yourself. I want to ask you if you have visited any of the cheaper amusements of this metropolis, or know anything of the really clever and charming things one may see there for a very little money."

"Ten cents, for instance?"

"Yes."

I answered that I would never own to having come as low down as that; and I expressed a hardy and somewhat inconsistent doubt of the quality of the amusement that could be had for that money. I questioned if anything intellectual could be had for it.

"What do you say to the ten-cent magazines?" my friend retorted. "And do you pretend that the two-dollar drama is intellectual?"

I had to confess that it generally was not, and that this was part of my grief with it.

Then he said: "I don't contend that it is intellectual, but I say that it is often clever and charming at the ten-cent shows, just as it is less often clever and charming in the ten-cent magazines. I think the average of propriety is rather higher than it is at the two-dollar theatres; and it is much more instructive at the ten-cent shows, if you come to that. The other day," said my friend, and in squaring himself comfortably in his chair and finding room for his elbow on the corner of my table he knocked off some books for review, "I went to a dime museum for an hour that I had between two appointments, and I must say that I never passed an hour's time more agreeably. In the curio hall, as one of the lecturers on the curios called it— they had several lecturers in white wigs and scholars' caps and gowns—there was not a great deal to see, I confess; but everything was very high-class. There was the inventor of a perpetual motion, who lectured upon it and explained it from a diagram. There was a fortune-teller in a three-foot tent whom I did not interview; there were five macaws in one cage, and two gloomy apes in another. On a platform at the end of the hall was an Australian family a good deal gloomier than the apes, who sat in the costume of our latitude, staring down the room with varying expressions all verging upon melancholy madness, and who gave me such a pang of compassion as I have seldom got from the tragedy of the two-dollar theatres. They allowed me to come quite close up to them, and to feed my pity upon their wild dejection in exile without stint. I couldn't enter into conversation with them, and express my regret at finding them so far from their native boomerangs and kangaroos and pine-tree grubs, but I know they felt my sympathy, it was so evident. I didn't see their performance, and I don't know that they had any. They may simply have been there ethnologically, but this was a good object, and the sight of their spiritual misery was alone worth the price of admission.

"After the inventor of the perpetual motion had brought his harangue to a close, we all went round to the dais where a lady in blue spectacles lectured us upon a fire-escape which she had invented, and operated a small model of it. None of the events were so exciting that we could regret it when the chief lecturer announced that this was the end of the entertainment in the curio hall, and that now the performance in the theatre was about to begin. He invited us to buy tickets at an additional charge of five, ten, or fifteen cents for the gallery, orchestra circle, or orchestra.

"I thought I could afford an orchestra stall, for once. We were three in the orchestra, another man and a young mother, not counting the little boy she had with her; there were two people in the gallery, and a dozen at least in the orchestra circle. An attendant shouted, 'Hats off!' and the other man and I uncovered, and a lady came up from under the stage and began to play the piano in front of it. The curtain rose, and the entertainment began at once. It was a passage apparently from real life, and it involved a dissatisfied boarder and the daughter of the landlady. There was not much coherence in it, but there was a good deal of conscience on the part of the actors, who toiled through it with unflagging energy. The young woman was equipped for the dance she brought into it at one point rather than for the part she had to sustain in the drama. It was a very blameless dance, and she gave it as if she was tired of it, but was not going to falter. She delivered her lines with a hard, Southwestern accent, and I liked fancying her having come up in a simpler-hearted section of the country than ours, encouraged by a strong local belief that she was destined to do Juliet and Lady Macbeth, or Peg Woffington at the least; but very likely she had not.

"Her performance was followed by an event involving a single character. The actor, naturally, was blackened as to his skin, but as to his dress he was all in white, and at the first glance I could see that he had temperament. I suspect that he thought I had, too, for he began to address his entire drama to me. This was not surprising, for it would not have been the thing for him to single out the young mother; and the other man in the orchestra stalls seemed a vague and inexperienced youth, whom he would hardly have given the preference over me. I felt the compliment, but upon the whole it embarrassed me; it was too intimate, and it gave me a publicity I would willingly have foregone. I did what I could to reject it, by feigning an indifference to his jokes; I even frowned

a measure of disapproval; but this merely stimulated
his ambition.  He was really a merry creature, and
when he had got off a number of very good things
which were received in perfect silence, and looked over
his audience with a woe-begone eye, and said, with
an effect of delicate apology, 'I hope I'm not disturbing you any,' I broke down and laughed, and that
delivered me into his hand.  He immediately said
to me that now he would tell me about a friend of his,
who had a pretty large family, eight of them living,
and one in Philadelphia; and then for no reason he
seemed to change his mind, and said he would sing
me a song written expressly for him—by an express-
man; and he went on from one wild gayety to another, until he had worked his audience up to quite a
frenzy of enthusiasm, and almost had a recall when
he went off.

"I was rather glad to be rid of him, and I was glad
that the next performers, who were a lady and a gentleman contortionist of Spanish-American extraction,
behaved more impartially.  They were really remarkable artists in their way, and though it's a painful way, I couldn't help admiring their gift in bow-
knots and other difficult poses.  The gentleman got
abundant applause, but the lady at first got none.  I
think perhaps it was because, with the correct feeling
that prevailed among us, we could not see a lady contort herself with so much approval as a gentleman,
and that there was a wound to our sense of propriety
in witnessing her skill.  But I could see that the poor
girl was hurt in her artist pride by our severity, and
at the next thing she did I led off the applause with
my umbrella.  She instantly lighted up with a joyful smile, and the young mother in the orchestra leaned
forward to nod her sympathy to me while she clapped.
We were fast becoming a domestic circle, and it was

very pleasant, but I thought that upon the whole I had better go."

"And do you think you had a profitable hour at that show?" I asked, with a smile that was meant to be sceptical.

"Profitable?" said my friend. "I said agreeable. I don't know about the profit. But it was very good variety, and it was very cheap. I understand that this is the kind of thing you want the two-dollar theatre to come down to, or up to."

"Not exactly, or not quite," I returned, thoughtfully, "though I must say I think your time was as well spent as it would have been at most of the plays I have seen this winter."

My friend left the point, and said, with a dreamy air: "It was all very pathetic, in a way. Three out of those five people were really clever, and certainly artists. That colored brother was almost a genius, a very common variety of genius, but still a genius, with a gift for his calling that couldn't be disputed. He was a genuine humorist, and I sorrowed over him —after I got safely away from his intimacy—as I should over some author who was struggling along without winning his public. Why not? One is as much in the show business as the other. There is a difference of quality rather than of kind. Perhaps by-and-by my colored humorist will make a strike with his branch of the public, as you are always hoping to do with yours."

"You don't think you're making yourself rather offensive?" I suggested.

"Not intentionally. Aren't the arts one? How can you say that any art is higher than the others? Why is it nobler to contort the mind than to contort the body?"

"I am always saying that it is not at all noble to

"'I HOPE I'M NOT DISTURBING YOU ANY'"

contort the mind," I returned, "and I feel that to aim at nothing higher than the amusement of your readers is to bring yourself most distinctly to the level of the show business."

"Yes, I know that is your pose," said my friend. "And I dare say you really think that you make a distinction in facts when you make a distinction in terms. If you don't amuse your readers, you don't keep them; practically, you cease to exist. You may call it interesting them, if you like; but, really, what is the difference? You do your little act, and because the stage is large and the house is fine, you fancy you are not of that sad brotherhood which aims to please in humbler places, with perhaps cruder means—"

"I don't know whether I like your saws less than your instances, or your instances less than your saws," I broke in. "Have you been at the circus yet?"

## II

"Yet?" demanded my friend. "I went the first night, and I have been a good deal interested in the examination of my emotions ever since. I can't find out just why I have so much pleasure in the trapeze. Half the time I want to shut my eyes, and a good part of the time I do look away; but I wouldn't spare any actor the most dangerous feat. One of the poor girls, that night, dropped awkwardly into the net after her performance, and limped off to the dressing-room with a sprained ankle. It made me rather sad to think that now she must perhaps give up her perilous work for a while, and pay a doctor, and lose her salary, but it didn't take away my interest in the other trapezists flying through the air above another net.

"If I had honestly complained of anything it would

have been of the superfluity which glutted rather than
fed me.  How can you watch three sets of trapezists
at once?  You really see neither well.  It's the same
with the three rings.  There should be one ring, and
each act should have a fair chance with the spectator,
if it took six hours; I would willingly give the time.
Fancy three stages at the theatre, with three plays
going on at once!"

"No, *don't* fancy that!" I entreated.  "One play is
bad enough."

"Or fancy reading three novels simultaneously,
and listening at the same time to a lecture and a sermon, which could represent the two platforms between
the rings," my friend calmly persisted.  "The three
rings are an abuse and an outrage, but I don't know
but I object still more to the silencing of the clowns.
They have a great many clowns now, but they are
all dumb, and you only get half the good you used to
get out of the single clown of the old one-ring circus.
Why, it's as if the literary humorist were to lead up
to a charming conceit or a subtle jest, and then put
asterisks where the humor ought to come in."

"Don't you think you are going from bad to worse?"
I asked.

My friend went on: "I'm afraid the circus is spoiled
for me.  It has become too much of a good thing; for
it *is* a good thing; almost the best thing in the way of
an entertainment that there is.  I'm still very fond
of it, but I come away defeated and defrauded because
I have been embarrassed with riches, and have been
given more than I was able to grasp.  My greed has
been overfed.  I think I must keep to those entertainments where you can come at ten in the morning and
stay till ten at night, with a perpetual change of bill,
only one stage, and no fall of the curtain.  I suppose
*you* would object to them because they're getting rather

dear; at the best of them now they ask you a dollar for the first seats."

I said that I did not think this too much for twelve hours, if the intellectual character of the entertainment was correspondingly high.

"It's as high as that of some magazines," said my friend, "though I could sometimes wish it were higher. It's like the matter in the Sunday papers—about that average. Some of it's good, and most of it isn't. Some of it could hardly be worse. But there is a great deal of it, and you get it consecutively and not simultaneously. That constitutes its advantage over the circus."

My friend stopped, with a vague smile, and I asked: "Then, do I understand that you would advise me to recommend the dime museums, the circus, and the perpetual-motion varieties in the place of the theatres?"

"You have recommended books instead, and that notion doesn't seem to have met with much favor, though you urged their comparative cheapness. Now, why not suggest something that is really level with the popular taste?"

# AMERICAN LITERATURE IN EXILE

A RECENTLY lecturing Englishman is reported
to have noted the unenviable primacy of the
United States among countries where the struggle
for material prosperity has been disastrous to the pursuit of literature.  He said, or is said to have said
(one cannot be too careful in attributing to a public
man the thoughts that may be really due to an imaginative frame in the reporter), that among us, "the
old race of writers of distinction, such as Longfellow,
Bryant, Holmes, and Washington Irving, have (*sic*)
died out, and the Americans who are most prominent
in cultivated European opinion in art or literature,
like Sargent, Henry James, or Marion Crawford, live
habitually out of America, and draw their inspiration
from England, France, and Italy."

I

If this were true, I confess that I am so indifferent
to what many Americans glory in that it would not
distress me, or wound me in the sort of self-love which
calls itself patriotism.  If it would at all help to put
an end to that struggle for material prosperity which
has eventuated with us in so many millionaires and
so many tramps, I should be glad to believe that it was
driving our literary men out of the country.  This
would be a tremendous object-lesson, and might be a

warning to the millionaires and the tramps. But I am afraid it would not have this effect, for neither our very rich nor our very poor care at all for the state of polite learning among us; though for the matter of that, I believe that economic conditions have little to do with it; and that if a general mediocrity of fortune prevailed and there were no haste to be rich and to get poor, the state of polite learning would not be considerably affected. As matters stand, I think we may reasonably ask whether the Americans "most prominent in cultivated European opinion," the Americans who "live habitually out of America," are not less exiles than advance agents of the expansion now advertising itself to the world. They may be the vanguard of the great army of adventurers destined to overrun the earth from these shores, and exploit all foreign countries to our advantage. They probably themselves do not know it, but in the act of "drawing their inspiration" from alien scenes, or taking their own where they find it, are not they simply transporting to Europe "the struggle for material prosperity" which Sir Lepel supposes to be fatal to them here?

There is a question, however, which comes before this, and that is the question whether they have quitted us in such numbers as justly to alarm our patriotism. Qualitatively, in the authors named and in the late Mr. Bret Harte, Mr. Harry Harland, and the late Mr. Harold Frederic, as well as in Mark Twain, once temporarily resident abroad, the defection is very great; but quantitatively it is not such as to leave us without a fair measure of home-keeping authorship. Our destitution is not nearly so great now in the absence of Mr. James and Mr. Crawford as it was in the times before the "struggle for material prosperity" when Washington Irving went and lived in England and on the European continent wellnigh half his life.

Sir Lepel Griffin—or Sir Lepel Griffin's reporter—seems to forget the fact of Irving's long absenteeism when he classes him with "the old race" of eminent American authors who stayed at home. But really none of those he names were so constant to our air as he seems—or his reporter seems—to think. Longfellow sojourned three or four years in Germany, Spain, and Italy; Holmes spent as great time in Paris; Bryant was a frequent traveller, and each of them "drew his inspiration" now and then from alien sources. Lowell was many years in Italy, Spain, and England; Motley spent more than half his life abroad; Hawthorne was away from us nearly a decade.

## II

If I seem to be proving too much in one way, I do not feel that I am proving too much in another. My facts go to show that the literary spirit is the true world-citizen, and is at home everywhere. If any good American were distressed by the absenteeism of our authors, I should first advise him that American literature was not derived from the folk-lore of the red Indians, but was, as I have said once before, a condition of English literature, and was independent even of our independence. Then I should entreat him to consider the case of foreign authors who had found it more comfortable or more profitable to live out of their respective countries than in them. I should allege for his consolation the case of Byron, Shelley, and Leigh Hunt, and more latterly that of the Brownings and Walter Savage Landor, who preferred an Italian to an English sojourn; and yet more recently that of Mr. Rudyard Kipling, who voluntarily lived several years in Vermont, and has "drawn his inspiration" in notable

instances from the life of these States. It will serve
him also to consider that the two greatest Norwegian
authors, Björnsen and Ibsen, have both lived long in
France and Italy. Heinrich Heine loved to live in
Paris much better than in Düsseldorf, or even in Ham-
burg; and Tourguénief himself, who said that any
man's country could get on without him, but no man
could get on without his country, managed to dis-
pense with his own in the French capital, and died
there after he was quite free to go back to St. Petersburg. In the last century Rousseau lived in France
rather than Switzerland; Voltaire at least tried to live
in Prussia, and was obliged to a long exile elsewhere;
Goldoni left fame and friends in Venice for the favor
of princes in Paris.

Literary absenteeism, it seems to me, is not peculiarly an American vice or an American virtue. It is
an expression and a proof of the modern sense which
enlarges one's country to the bounds of civilization.
I cannot think it justly a reproach in the eyes of the
world, and if any American feels it a grievance, I suggest that he do what he can to have embodied in the
platform of his party a plank affirming the right of
American authors to a public provision that will enable them to live as agreeably at home as they can
abroad on the same money. In the mean time, their
absenteeism is not a consequence of "the struggle
for material prosperity," not a high disdain of the strife
which goes on not less in Europe than in America,
and must, of course, go on everywhere as long as
competitive conditions endure, but is the result of
chances and preferences which mean nothing nationally calamitous or discreditable.

## THE HORSE SHOW

"AS good as the circus—not so good as the circus—better than the circus." These were my varying impressions, as I sat looking down upon the tanbark, the other day, at the Horse Show in Madison Square Garden; and I came away with their blend for my final opinion.

I might think that the Horse Show (which is so largely a Man Show and a Woman Show) was better or worse than the circus, or about as good; but I could not get away from the circus, in my impression of it. Perhaps the circus is the norm of all splendors where the horse and his master are joined for an effect upon the imagination of the spectator. I am sure that I have never been able quite to dissociate from it the picturesqueness of chivalry, and that it will hereafter always suggest to me the last correctness of fashion. It is through the horse that these far extremes meet; in all times the horse has been the supreme expression of aristocracy; and it may very well be that a dream of the elder world prophesied the ultimate type of the future, when the Swell shall have evolved into the Centaur.

Some such teasing notion of their mystical affinity is what haunts you as you make your round of the vast ellipse, with the well-groomed men about you and the well-groomed horses beyond the barrier.

In this first affair of the new-comer, the horses are not so much on show as the swells; you get only glimpses of shining coats and tossing manes, with a glint here and there of a flying hoof through the lines of people coming and going, and the ranks of people, three or four feet deep, against the rails of the ellipse; but the swells are there in perfect relief, and it is they who finally embody the Horse Show to you. The fact is that they are there to see, of course, but the effect is that they are there to be seen.

The whole spectacle had an historical quality, which I tasted with pleasure. It was the thing that had eventuated in every civilization, and the American might feel a characteristic pride that what came to Rome in five hundred years had come to America in a single century. There was something fine in the absolutely fatal nature of the result, and I perceived that nowhere else in our life, which is apt to be seclusive in its exclusiveness, is the prime motive at work in it so dramatically apparent. "Yes," I found myself thinking, "this is what it all comes to: the *subiti guadagni* of the new rich, made in large masses and seeking a swift and eager exploitation, and the slowly accumulated fortunes, put together from sparing and scrimping, from slaving and enslaving, in former times, and now in the stainless white hands of the second or third generation, they both meet here to the purpose of a common ostentation, and create a Horse Show."

I cannot say that its creators looked much as if they liked it, now they had got it; and, so far as I have been able to observe them, people of wealth and fashion always dissemble their joy, and have the air of being bored in the midst of their amusements. This reserve of rapture may be their delicacy, their unwillingness to awaken envy in the less prospered; and I

should not have objected to the swells at the Horse
Show looking dreary if they had looked more like
swells; except for a certain hardness of the countenance (which I found my own sympathetically taking
on) I should not have thought them very patrician,
and this hardness may have been merely the consequence of being so much stared at. Perhaps, indeed,
they were not swells whom I saw in the boxes, but
only companies of ordinary people who had clubbed
together and hired their boxes; I understand that this
can be done, and the student of civilization so far misled. But certainly if they were swells they did not look
quite up to themselves; though, for that matter, neither
do the nobilities of foreign countries, and on one or
two occasions when I have seen them, kings and em-
perors have failed me in like manner. They have all
wanted that indescribable something which I have
found so satisfying in aristocracies and royalties on
the stage; and here at the Horse Show, while I made
my tour, I constantly met handsome, actor-like folk
on foot who could much better have taken the rôle of
the people in the boxes. The promenaders may not
have been actors at all; they may have been the real
thing for which I was in vain scanning the boxes,
but they looked like actors, who indeed set an example to us all in personal beauty and in correctness of
dress.

I mean nothing offensive either to swells or to actors.
We have not distinction, as a people; Matthew Arnold
noted that; and it is not our business to have it. When
it is our business our swells will have it, just as our
actors now have it, especially our actors of English
birth. I had not this reflection about me at the time
to console me for my disappointment, and it only now
occurs to me that what I took for an absence of distinction may have been such a universal prevalence of it

"THE EFFECT IS THAT THEY ARE THERE TO BE SEEN"

that the result was necessarily a species of indistinc-
tion. But in the complexion of any social assembly
we Americans are at a disadvantage with Europeans
from the want of uniforms. A few military scattered
about in those boxes, or even a few sporting bishops in
shovel-hats and aprons, would have done much to relieve them from the reproach I have been heaping
upon them. Our women, indeed, poor things, always
do their duty in personal splendor, and it is not of a
poverty in their modes at the Horse Show that I am
complaining. If the men had borne their part as
well, there would not have been these tears; and yet,
what am I saying? There was here and there a clean-
shaven face (which I will not believe was always an
actor's), and here and there a figure superbly set up,
and so faultlessly appointed as to shoes, trousers,
coat, tie, hat, and gloves as to have a salience from
the mass of good looks and good clothes which I will
not at last call less than distinction.

## II

At any rate, I missed these marked presences when
I left the lines of the promenaders around the ellipse,
and climbed to a seat some tiers above the boxes. I
am rather anxious to have it known that my seat was
not one of those cheap ones in the upper gallery, but
was with the virtuous poor who could afford to pay a
dollar and a half for their tickets. I bought it of a
speculator on the sidewalk, who said it was his last,
so that I conceived it the last in the house; but I found
the chairs by no means all filled, though it was as
good an audience as I have sometimes seen in the
same place at other circuses. The people about me
were such as I had noted at the other circuses, hotel-

sojourners, kindly - looking comers from provincial towns and cities, whom I instantly felt myself at home with, and free to put off that gloomy severity of aspect which had grown upon me during my association with the swells below. My neighbors were sufficiently well dressed, and if they had no more distinction than their betters, or their richers, they had not the burden of the occasion upon them, and seemed really glad of what was going on in the ring.

There again I was sensible of the vast advantage of costume. The bugler who stood up at one end of the central platform and blew a fine fanfare (I hope it was a fanfare) towards the gates where the horses were to enter from their stalls in the basement was a hussar-like shape that filled my romantic soul with joy; and the other figures of the management I thought very fortunate compromises between grooms and ring-masters. At any rate, their 'nondescript costumes were gay, and a relief from the fashions in the boxes and the promenade; they were costumes, and costumes are always more sincere, if not more effective, than fashions. As I have hinted, I do not know just what costumes they were, but they took the light well from the girandole far aloof and from the thousands of little electric bulbs that beaded the roof in long lines, and dispersed the sullenness of the dull, rainy afternoon. When the knights entered the lists on the seats of their dog-carts, with their squires beside them, and their shining tandems before them, they took the light well, too, and the spectacle was so brilliant that I trust my imagery may be forgiven a novelist pining for the pageantries of the past. I do not know to this moment whether these knights were bona fide gentlemen, or only their deputies, driving their tandems for them, and I am equally at a loss to account for the variety of their hats. Some wore tall, shining silk hats; some flat-topped, brown derbys; some simple black pot-hats;—and is there, then, no rigor as to the head-gear of people driving tandems? I felt that there ought to be, and that there ought to be some rule as to where the number of each tandem should be displayed. As it was, this was sometimes carelessly stuck into the seat of the cart; sometimes it was worn at the back of the groom's waist, and sometimes full upon his stomach. In the last position it gave a touch of burlesque which wounded me; for these are vital matters, and I found myself very exacting in them.

With the horses themselves I could find no fault upon the grounds of my censure of the show in some other ways. *They* had distinction; *they* were patrician; *they* were swell. They felt it, they showed it, they rejoiced in it; and the most reluctant observer could not deny them the glory of blood, of birth, which the thoroughbred horse has expressed in all lands and ages. Their lordly port was a thing that no one could dispute, and for an aristocracy I suppose that they had a high average of intelligence, though there might be two minds about this. They made me think of mettled youths and haughty dames; they abashed the humble spirit of the beholder with the pride of their high-stepping, their curvetting and caracoling, as they jingled in their shining harness around the long ring. Their noble uselessness took the fancy, for I suppose that there is nothing so superbly superfluous as a tandem, outside or inside of the best society. It is something which only the ambition of wealth and unbroken leisure can mount to; and I was glad that the display of tandems was the first event of the Horse Show which I witnessed, for it seemed to me that it must beyond all others typify the power which created the Horse Show. I wished that the human side of it could have been more unquestionably adequate, but the equine side of the event was perfect. Still, I felt a certain relief, as in something innocent and simple and childlike, in the next event.

### III

This was the inundation of the tan-bark with troops of pretty Shetland ponies of all ages, sizes, and colors. A cry of delight went up from a group of little people near me, and the spell of the Horse Show was broken. It was no longer a solemnity of fashion, it was a sweet and kindly pleasure which every one could share, or every one who had ever had, or ever wished to have, a Shetland pony; the touch of nature made the whole show kin. I could not see that the freakish, kittenish creatures did anything to claim our admiration, but they won our affection by every trait of ponyish caprice and obstinacy. The small colts broke away from the small mares, and gambolled over the tan-bark in wanton groups, with gay or plaintive whinnyings, which might well have touched a responsive chord in the bosom of fashion itself; I dare say it is not so hard as it looks. The scene remanded us to a moment of childhood; and I found myself so fond of all the ponies that I felt it invidious of the judges to choose among them for the prizes; they ought every one to have had the prize.

I suppose a Shetland pony is not a very useful animal in our conditions; no doubt a good, tough, stubbed donkey would be worth all their tribe when it came down to hard work; but we cannot all be hard-working donkeys, and some of us may be toys and playthings without too great reproach. I gazed after the broken, refluent wave of these amiable creatures, with the vague toleration here formulated, but I was not quite

"WITH THE HORSES THEMSELVES I COULD FIND NO FAULT"

at peace in it, or fully consoled in my habitual ethicism till the next event brought the hunters with their high-jumping into the ring. These noble animals unite use and beauty in such measure that the censor must be of Catonian severity who can refuse them his praise. When I reflected that by them and their devoted riders our civilization had been assimilated to that of the mother-country in its finest expression, and another tie added to those that bind us to her through the language of Shakespeare and Milton; that they had tamed the haughty spirit of the American farmer in several parts of the country so that he submitted for a consideration to have his crops ridden over, and that they had all but exterminated the ferocious anise-seed bag, once so common and destructive among us, I was in a fit mood to welcome the bars and hurdles which were now set up at four or five places for the purposes of the high-jumping.

As to the beauty of the hunting-horse, though, I think I must hedge a little, while I stand firmly to my admiration of his use. To be honest, the tandem horse is more to my taste. He is better shaped, and he bears himself more proudly. The hunter is apt to behave, whatever his reserve of intelligence, like an excited hen; he is apt to be ewe-necked and bred away to nothing where the ideal horse abounds; he has the behavior of a turkey-hen when not behaving like the common or garden hen. But there can be no question of his jumping, which seems to be his chief business in a world where we are all appointed our several duties, and I at once began to take a vivid pleasure in his proficiency. I have always felt a blind and insensate joy in running races, which has no relation to any particular horse, and I now experienced an impartial rapture in the performances of these hunters. They looked very much alike, and if it had not been for the changing numbers on the sign-board in the centre of the ring announcing that 650, 675, or 602 was now jumping, I might have thought it was 650 all the time.

A high jump is not so fine a sight as a running race when the horses have got half a mile away and look like a covey of swift birds, but it is still a fine sight. I became very fastidious as to which moment of it was the finest, whether when the horse rose in profile, or when his aërial hoof touched the ground (with the effect of half jerking his rider's head half off), or when he showed a flying heel in perspective; and I do not know to this hour which I prefer. But I suppose I was becoming gradually spoiled by my pleasure, for as time went on I noticed that I was not satisfied with the monotonous excellence of the horses' execution. Will it be credited that I became willing something should happen, anything, to vary it? I asked myself why, if some of the more exciting incidents of the hunting-field which I had read of *must* befall, I should not see them. Several of the horses had balked at the barriers, and almost thrown their riders across them over their necks, but not quite done it; several had carried away the green-tufted top rail with their heels; when suddenly there came a loud clatter from the farther side of the ellipse, where a whole panel of fence had gone down. I looked eagerly for the prostrate horse and rider under the bars, but they were cantering safely away

## IV

It was enough, however. I perceived that I was becoming demoralized, and that if I were to write of the Horse Show with at all the superiority one likes to feel towards the rich and great, I had better come

away. But I came away critical, even in my down-
fall, and feeling that, circus for circus, the Greatest
Show on Earth which I had often seen in that place
had certain distinct advantages of the Horse Show.
It had three rings and two platforms; and, for another
thing, the drivers and riders in the races, when they
won, bore the banner of victory aloft in their hands,
instead of poorly letting a blue or red ribbon flicker at
their horses' ears. The events were more frequent
and rapid; the costumes infinitely more varied and
picturesque. As for the people in the boxes, I do not
know that they were less distinguished than these at
the Horse Show, but if they were not of the same high
level in which distinction was impossible, they did
not show it in their looks.

The Horse Show, in fine, struck me as a circus of
not all the first qualities; and I had moments of sus-
pecting that it was no more than the evolution of the
county cattle show. But in any case I had to own
that its great success was quite legitimate; for the
horse, upon the whole, appeals to a wider range of
humanity, vertically as well as horizontally, than
any other interest, not excepting politics or religion.
I cannot, indeed, regard him as a civilizing influence;
but then we cannot be always civilizing.

## THE PROBLEM OF THE SUMMER

IT has sometimes seemed to me that the solution of the problem how and where to spend the summer was simplest with those who were obliged to spend it as they spent the winter, and increasingly difficult in the proportion of one's ability to spend it wherever and however one chose. Few are absolutely released to this choice, however, and those few are greatly to be pitied. I know that they are often envied and hated for it by those who have no such choice, but that is a pathetic mistake. If we could look into their hearts, indeed, we should witness there so much misery that we should wish rather to weep over them than to reproach them with their better fortune, or what appeared so.

### I

For most people choice is a curse, and it is this curse that the summer brings upon great numbers who would not perhaps otherwise be afflicted. They are not in the happy case of those who must stay at home; their hard necessity is that they can go away, and try to be more agreeably placed somewhere else; but although I say they are in great numbers, they are an infinitesimal minority of the whole bulk of our population. Their bane is not, in its highest form, that of the average American who has no choice of the kind; and when one begins to speak of the summer problem, one must begin at once to distinguish. It is the problem of the East rather than of the West (where people are much more in the habit of staying at home the year round), and it is the problem of the city and not of the country. I am not sure that there is one practical farmer in the whole United States who is obliged to witness in his household those sad dissensions which almost separate the families of professional men as to where and how they shall pass the summer. People of this class, which is a class with some measure of money, ease, and taste, are commonly of varying and decided minds, and I once knew a family of the sort whose combined ideal for their summer outing was summed up in the simple desire for society and solitude, mountain-air and sea-bathing. They spent the whole months of April, May, and June in a futile inquiry for a resort uniting these attractions, and on the first of July they drove to the station with no definite point in view. But they found that they could get return tickets for a certain place on an inland lake at a low figure, and they took the first train for it. There they decided next morning to push on to the mountains, and sent their baggage to the station, but before it was checked they changed their minds, and remained two weeks where they were. Then they took train for a place on the coast, but in the cars a friend told them they ought to go to another place; they decided to go there, but before arriving at the junction they decided again to keep on. They arrived at their original destination, and the following day telegraphed for rooms at a hotel farther down the coast. The answer came that there were no rooms, and being by this time ready to start, they started, and in due time reported themselves at the hotel. The landlord saw that something must be done, and he got them rooms, at a smaller house, and *mealed* them (as it used to be called at Mt. Desert) in his own. But upon experiment of the fare at the smaller house they liked it so well that they resolved to live there altogether, and they spent a summer of the greatest comfort there, so that they would hardly come away when the house closed in the fall.

This was an extreme case, and perhaps such a venture might not always turn out so happily; but I think that people might oftener trust themselves to Providence in these matters than they do. There is really an infinite variety of pleasant resorts of all kinds now, and one could quite safely leave it to the man in the ticket-office where one should go, and check one's baggage accordingly. I think the chances of an agreeable summer would be as good in that way as in making a hard-and-fast choice of a certain place and sticking to it. My own experience is that in these things chance makes a very good choice for one, as it does in most non-moral things.

II

A joke dies hard, and I am not sure that the life is yet quite out of the kindly ridicule that was cast for a whole generation upon the people who left their comfortable houses in town to starve upon farm-board or stifle in the narrow rooms of mountain and seaside hotels. Yet such people were in the right, and their mockers were in the wrong, and their patient persistence in going out of town for the summer in the face of severe discouragements has multiplied indefinitely the kinds of summer resorts, and reformed them altogether. I believe the city boarding-house remains very much what it used to be; but I am bound to say that the country boarding-house has vastly improved since I began to know it. As for the summer hotel, by steep or by strand, it leaves little to be complained of except the prices. I take it for granted, therefore, that the out-of-town summer has come to stay, for all who can afford it, and that the chief sorrow attending it is that curse of choice, which I have already spoken of.

I have rather favored chance than choice, because, whatever choice you make, you are pretty sure to regret it, with a bitter sense of responsibility added, which you cannot feel if chance has chosen for you. I observe that people who own summer cottages are often apt to wish they did not, and were foot-loose to roam where they listed, and I have been told that even a yacht is not a source of unmixed content, though so eminently detachable. To great numbers Europe looks from this shore like a safe refuge from the American summer problem; and yet I am not sure that it is altogether so; for it is not enough merely to go to Europe; one has to choose where to go when one has got there. A European city is certainly always more tolerable than an American city, but one cannot very well pass the summer in Paris, or even in London. The heart there, as here, will yearn for some blessed seat

" Where falls not hail, or rain, or any snow,
　　Nor ever wind blows loudly; but it lies
　　Deep-meadow'd, happy, fair with orchard lawns
　　And bowery hollows crown'd with summer sea,"

and still, after your keel touches the strand of that alluring old world, you must buy your ticket and register your trunk for somewhere in particular.

### III

It is truly a terrible stress, this summer problem, and, as I say, my heart aches much more for those who

have to solve it and suffer the consequences of their
choice than for those who have no choice, but must
stay the summer through where their work is, and be
humbly glad that they have any work to keep them
there. I am not meaning now, of course, business
men obliged to remain in the city to earn the bread—or,
more correctly, the cake—of their families in the country, or even their clerks and bookkeepers, and porters
and messengers, but such people as I sometimes catch
sight of from the elevated trains (in my reluctant
midsummer flights through the city), sweltering in
upper rooms over sewing-machines or lap-boards, or
stewing in the breathless tenement streets, or driving
clangorous trucks, or monotonous cars, or bending
over wash-tubs at open windows for breaths of the
no-air without.

These all get on somehow, and at the end of the
summer they have not to accuse themselves of folly
in going to one place rather than another. Their
fate is decided for them, and they submit to it; whereas
those who decide their fate are always rebelling against
it. They it is whom I am truly sorry for, and whom I
write of with tears in my ink. Their case is hard, and
it will seem all the harder if we consider how foolish
they will look and how flat they will feel at the judg-
ment-day, when they are asked about their summer
outings. I do not really suppose we shall be held to
a very strict account for our pleasures because everybody else has not enjoyed them, too; that would be a
pity of our lives; and yet there is an old-fashioned
compunction which will sometimes visit the heart if
we take our pleasures ungraciously, when so many
have no pleasures to take. I would suggest, then,
to those on whom the curse of choice between pleasures
rests, that they should keep in mind those who have
chiefly pains to their portion in life.

I am not, I hope, urging my readers to any active
benevolence, or counselling them to share their pleasures with others; it has been accurately ascertained
that there are not pleasures enough to go round, as
things now are; but I would seriously entreat them
to consider whether they could not somewhat alleviate
the hardships of their own lot at the sea-side or among
the mountains, by contrasting it with the lot of others
in the sweat-shops and the boiler-factories of life. I
know very well that it is no longer considered very
good sense or very good morality to take comfort in
one's advantages from the disadvantages of others,
and this is not quite what I mean to teach. Perhaps
I mean nothing more than an overhauling of the whole
subject of advantages and disadvantages, which would
be a light and agreeable occupation for the leisure of
the summer outer. It might be very interesting, and
possibly it might be amusing, for one stretched upon
the beach or swaying in the hammock to inquire into
the reasons for his or her being so favored, and it is
not beyond the bounds of expectation that a consensus
of summer opinion on this subject would go far to en-
lighten the world upon a question that has vexed the
world ever since mankind was divided into those who
work too much and those who rest too much.

# ÆSTHETIC NEW YORK FIFTY-ODD YEARS AGO

A STUDY of New York civilization in 1849 has lately come into my hands, with a mortifying effect, which I should like to share with the reader, to my pride of modernity. I had somehow believed that after half a century of material prosperity, such as the world has never seen before, New York in 1902 must be very different from New York in 1849, but if I am to trust either the impressions of the earlier student or my own, New York is essentially the same now that it was then. The spirit of the place has not changed; it is as it was, splendidly and sordidly commercial. Even the body of it has undergone little or no alteration; it was as shapeless, as incongruous, as ugly when the author of *New York in Slices* wrote as it is at this writing; it has simply grown, or overgrown, on the moral and material lines which seem to have been structural in it from the beginning. He felt in his time the same vulgarity, the same violence, in its architectural anarchy that I have felt in my time, and he noted how all dignity and beauty perished, amid the warring forms, with a prescience of my own affliction, which deprives me of the satisfaction of a discoverer and leaves me merely the sense of being rather old-fashioned in my painful emotions.

I

I wish I could pretend that my author philosophized the facts of his New York with something less than

222

the raw haste of the young journalist; but I am afraid I must own that *New York in Slices* affects one as having first been printed in an evening paper, and that the writer brings to the study of the metropolis something like the eager horror of a country visitor. This probably enabled him to heighten the effect he wished to make with readers of a kindred tradition, and for me it adds a certain innocent charm to his work. I may make myself better understood if I say that his attitude towards the depravities of a smaller New York is much the same as that of Mr. Stead towards the wickedness of a much larger Chicago. He seizes with some such avidity upon the darker facts of the prisons, the slums, the gambling-houses, the mock auctions, the toughs (who then called themselves b'hoys and g'hals), the quacks, the theatres, and even the intelligence offices, and exploits their iniquities with a ready virtue which the wickedest reader can enjoy with him.

But if he treated of these things alone, I should not perhaps have brought his curious little book to the polite notice of my readers. He treats also of the press, the drama, the art, and, above all, "the literary soirées" of that remote New York of his in a manner to make us latest New-Yorkers feel our close proximity to it. Fifty-odd years ago journalism had already become "the absorbing, remorseless, clamorous thing" we now know, and very different from the thing it was when "expresses were unheard of, and telegraphs were uncrystallized from the lightning's blue and fiery film." Reporterism was beginning to assume its present importance, but it had not yet become the paramount intellectual interest, and did not yet "stand shoulder to shoulder" with the counting-room in authority. Great editors, then as now, ranked great authors in the public esteem, or achieved a double primacy by uniting journalism and literature in the same personality. They were often the owners as well as the writers of their respective papers, and they indulged for the advantage of the community the rancorous rivalries, recriminations, and scurrilities which often form the charm, if not the chief use, of our contemporaneous journals. Apparently, however, notarially authenticated boasts of circulation had not yet been made the delight of their readers, and the press had not become the detective agency that it now is, nor the organizer and distributer of charities.

But as dark a cloud of doubt rested upon its relations to the theatre as still eclipses the popular faith in dramatic criticism. "How can you expect," our author asks, "a frank and unbiassed criticism upon the performance of George Frederick Cooke Snooks . . . when the editor or reporter who is to write it has just been supping on beefsteak and stewed potatoes at Windust's, and regaling himself on brandy-and-water cold, without, at the expense of the aforesaid George Frederick Cooke Snooks?" The severest censor of the press, however, would hardly declare now that "as to such a thing as impartial and independent criticism upon theatres in the present state of the relations between editors, reporters, managers, actors—and actresses—the thing is palpably out of the question," and if matters were really at the pass hinted, the press has certainly improved in fifty years, if one may judge from its present frank condemnations of plays and players. The theatre apparently has not, for we read that at that period "a very great majority of the standard plays and farces on the stage depend mostly for their piquancy and their power of interesting an audience upon intrigues with married women, elopements, seductions, bribery, cheating, and fraud of every description. . . . Stage costume, too,

224

wherever there is half a chance, is usually made as lascivious and immodest as possible; and a freedom and impropriety prevails among the characters of the piece which would be kicked out of private society the instant it would have the audacity to make its appearance there."

## II

I hope private society in New York would still be found as correct if not quite so violent; and I wish I could believe that the fine arts were presently in as flourishing a condition among us as they were in 1849. That was the prosperous day of the Art Unions, in which the artists clubbed their output, and the subscribers parted the works among themselves by something so very like raffling that the Art Unions were finally suppressed under the law against lotteries. While they lasted, however, they had exhibitions thronged by our wealth, fashion, and intellect (to name them in the order they hold the New York mind), as our private views now are, or ought to be; and the author "devotes an entire number" of his series "to a single institution—fearless of being accused of partiality by any who rightly appreciate the influences of the fine arts upon the morals and refinement of mankind."

He devotes even more than an entire number to literature; for, besides treating of various literary celebrities at the "literary soirées," he imagines encountering several of them at the high-class restaurants. At Delmonico's, where if you had "French and money" you could get in that day "a dinner which, as a work of art, ranks with a picture by Huntington, a poem by Willis, or a statue by Powers," he meets such a musical critic as Richard Grant White, such an in-

tellectual epicurean as N. P. Willis, such a lyric poet
as Charles Fenno Hoffman. But it would be a warm
day for Delmonico's when the observer in this epoch
could chance upon so much genius at its tables, perhaps because genius among us has no longer the
French or the money. Indeed, the author of *New
York in Slices* seems finally to think that he has gone
too far, even for his own period, and brings himself
up with the qualifying reservation that if Willis and
Hoffman never did dine together at Delmonico's, they
ought to have done so. He has apparently no misgivings as to the famous musical critic, and he has no
scruple in assembling for us at his "literary soirée"
a dozen distinguished - looking men and "twice as
many women . . . listening to a tall, deaconly man,
who stands between two candles held by a couple of
sticks summoned from the recesses of the back parlor, reading a basketful of gilt-edged notes. It is . . .
the annual Valentine Party, to which all the male
and female authors have contributed for the purpose
of saying on paper charming things of each other,
and at which, for a few hours, all are gratified with
the full meed of that praise which a cold world is chary
of bestowing upon its literary cobweb-spinners."

It must be owned that we have no longer anything
so like a *salon* as this. It is, indeed, rather terrible,
and it is of a quality in its celebrities which may well
carry dismay to any among us presently intending
immortality. Shall we, one day, we who are now in
the rich and full enjoyment of our far-reaching fame,
affect the imagination of posterity as these phantoms
of the past affect ours? Shall we, too, appear in some
pale limbo of unimportance as thin and faded as " John
Inman, the getter-up of innumerable things for the
annuals and magazines," or as Dr. Rufus Griswold,
supposed for picturesque purposes to be " stalking

about with an immense quarto volume under his arm
. . . an early copy of his forthcoming *Female Poets
of America*"; or as Lewis Gaylord Clark, the "sunny-
faced, smiling" editor of the *Knickerbocker Magazine,* "who don't look as if the Ink-Fiend had ever
heard of him," as he stands up to dance a polka with
"a demure lady who has evidently spilled the ink-
stand over her dress"; or as "the stately Mrs. Seba
Smith, bending aristocratically over the centre-table,
and talking in a bright, cold, steady stream, like an
antique fountain by moonlight"; or as "the spiritual
and dainty Fanny Osgood, clapping her hands and
crowing like a baby," where she sits "nestled under
a shawl of heraldic devices, like a bird escaped from
its cage"; or as Margaret Fuller, "her large, gray
eyes lamping inspiration, and her thin, quivering
lip prophesying like a Pythoness"?

I hope not; I earnestly hope not. Whatever I said
at the outset, affirming the persistent equality of New
York characteristics and circumstances, I wish to take
back at this point; and I wish to warn malign foreign
observers, of the sort who have so often refused to see
us as we see ourselves, that they must not expect to
find us now grouped in the taste of 1849. Possibly
it was not so much the taste of 1849 as the author of
*New York in Slices* would have us believe; and perhaps any one who trusted his pictures of life among
us otherwise would be deceived by a parity of the spirit
in which they are portrayed with that of our modern
"society journalism."

## FROM NEW YORK INTO NEW ENGLAND

THERE is, of course, almost a world's difference between England and the Continent anywhere; but I do not recall just now any transition between Continental countries which involves a more distinct change in the superficial aspect of things than the passage from the Middle States into New England. It is all American, but American of diverse ideals; and you are hardly over the border before you are sensible of diverse effects, which are the more apparent to you the more American you are. If you want the contrast at its sharpest you had better leave New York on a Sound boat; for then you sleep out of the Middle State civilization and wake into the civilization of New England, which seems to give its stamp to nature herself. As to man, he takes it whether native or alien; and if he is foreign-born it marks him another Irishman, Italian, Canadian, Jew, or negro from his brother in any other part of the United States.

### I

When you have a theory of any kind, proofs of it are apt to seek you out, and I, who am rather fond of my faith in New England's influence of this sort, had as pretty an instance of it the day after my arrival as I could wish. A colored brother of Massachusetts birth, as black as a man can well be, and of a merely an-

thropoidal profile, was driving me along shore in search
of a sea-side hotel when we came upon a weak-minded
young chicken in the road.   The natural expectation is that any chicken in these circumstances will
wait for your vehicle, and then fly up before it with a
loud screech; but this chicken may have been overcome by the heat (it was a land breeze and it drew like
the breath of a furnace over the hay-cocks and the
clover), or it may have mistimed the wheel, which
passed over its head and left it to flop a moment in the
dust and then fall still.   The poor little tragedy was
sufficiently distressful to me, but I bore it well, compared with my driver.   He could hardly stop lamenting
it; and when presently we met a young farmer, he
pulled up.   "You goin' past Jim Marden's?"  "Yes."
"Well, I wish you'd tell him I just run over a chicken
of his, and I killed it, I guess.   I guess it was a pretty
big one."  "Oh no," I put in, "it was only a broiler.
What do you think it was worth?"   I took out some
money, and the farmer noted the largest coin in my
hand; "About half a dollar, I guess."   On this I put
it all back in my pocket, and then he said, "Well, if
a chicken don't know enough to get out of the road,
I guess *you* ain't to blame."   I expressed that this was
my own view of the case, and we drove on.   When we
parted I gave the half-dollar to my driver, and begged
him not to let the owner of the chicken come on me for
damages; and though he chuckled his pleasure in the
joke, I could see that he was still unhappy, and I have
no doubt that he has that pullet on his conscience yet,
unless he has paid for it.   He was of a race which elsewhere has so immemorially plundered hen-roosts that
chickens are as free to it as the air it breathes, without
any conceivable taint of private ownership.   But the
spirit of New England had so deeply entered into him
that the imbecile broiler of another, slain by pure ac-

cident and by its own contributory negligence, was
saddening him, while I was off in my train without a
pang for the owner and with only an agreeable pathos
for the pullet.

## II

The instance is perhaps extreme; and, at any rate,
it has carried me in a psychological direction away
from the simpler differences which I meant to note in
New England. They were evident as soon as our
train began to run from the steamboat landing into
the country, and they have intensified, if they have not
multiplied, themselves as I have penetrated deeper
and deeper into the beautiful region. The land is
poorer than the land to the southward—one sees that
at once; the soil is thin, and often so thickly burdened
with granite bowlders that it could never have borne
any other crop since the first Puritans, or Pilgrims,
cut away the primeval woods and betrayed its hopeless sterility to the light. But wherever you come to
a farm-house, whether standing alone or in one of the
village groups that New England farm-houses have
always liked to gather themselves into, it is of a neatness that brings despair, and of a repair that ought to
bring shame to the beholder from more easy-going
conditions. Everything is kept up with a strenuous
virtue that imparts an air of self-respect to the landscape, which the bleaching and blackening stone
walls, wandering over the hill-slopes, divide into wood
lots of white birch and pine, stony pastures, and
little patches of potatoes and corn. The mowing-
lands alone are rich; and if the New England year
is in the glory of the latest June, the breath of the
clover blows honey-sweet into the car windows,
and the fragrance of the new-cut hay rises hot

" THE MOWING-LANDS ALONE ARE RICH "

from the heavy swaths that seem to smoke in the sun.

We have struck a hot spell, one of those torrid moods of continental weather which we have telegraphed us ahead to heighten our suffering by anticipation. But the farmsteads and village houses are safe in the shade of their sheltering trees amid the fluctuation of the grass that grows so tall about them that the June roses have to strain upward to get themselves free of it. Behind each dwelling is a billowy mass of orchard, and before it the Gothic archway of the elms stretches above the quiet street. There is no tree in the world so full of sentiment as the American elm, and it is nowhere so graceful as in these New England villages, which are themselves, I think, the prettiest and wholesomest of mortal sojourns. By a happy instinct, their wooden houses are all painted white, to a marble effect that suits our meridional sky, and the contrast of their dark-green shutters is deliciously refreshing. There was an evil hour, the terrible moment of the æsthetic revival now happily past, when white walls and green blinds were thought in bad taste, and the village houses were often tinged a dreary ground color, or a doleful olive, or a gloomy red, but now they have returned to their earlier love. Not the first love; that was a pale buff with white trim; but I doubt if it were good for all kinds of village houses; the eye rather demands the white. The pale buff does very well for large colonial mansions, like Lowell's or Longfellow's in Cambridge; but when you come, say, to see the great square houses built in Portsmouth, New Hampshire, early in this century, and painted white, you find that white, after all, is the thing for our climate, even in the towns.

In such a village as my colored brother drove me through on the way to the beach it was of an absolute fitness; and I wish I could convey a due sense of the exquisite keeping of the place. Each white house was more or less closely belted in with a white fence, of panels or pickets; the grassy door-yards glowed with flowers, and often a climbing rose embowered the door-way with its bloom. Away backward or sidewise stretched the woodshed from the dwelling to the barn, and shut the whole under one cover; the turf grew to the wheel-tracks of the road-way, over which the elms rose and drooped; and from one end of the village to the other you could not, as the saying is, find a stone to throw at a dog. I know Holland; I have seen the wives of Scheveningen scrubbing up for Sunday to the very middle of their brick streets, but I doubt if Dutch cleanliness goes so far without, or comes from so deep a scruple within, as the cleanliness of New England. I felt so keenly the feminine quality of its motive as I passed through that village, that I think if I had dropped so much as a piece of paper in the street I must have knocked at the first door and begged the lady of the house (who would have opened it in person after wiping her hands from her work, taking off her apron, and giving a glance at herself in the mirror and at me through the window-blind) to report me to the selectmen in the interest of good morals.

### III

I did not know at once quite how to reconcile the present foulness of the New England capital with the fairness of the New England country; and I am still somewhat embarrassed to own that after New York (even under the relaxing rule of Tammany) Boston seemed very dirty when we arrived there. At best I was never more than a naturalized Bostonian; but it

used to give me great pleasure—so penetratingly does
the place qualify even the sojourning Westerner—to
think of the defect of New York in the virtue that is
next to godliness; and now I had to hang my head
for shame at the mortifying contrast of the Boston
streets to the well-swept asphalt which I had left frying
in the New York sun the afternoon before. Later,
however, when I began to meet the sort of Boston faces
I remembered so well — good, just, pure, but set and
severe, with their look of challenge, of interrogation,
almost of reproof—they not only ignored the disgrace-
ful untidiness of the streets, but they convinced me of
a state of transition which would leave the place swept
and garnished behind it; and comforted me against
the litter of the winding thoroughfares and narrow
lanes, where the dust had blown up against the brick
walls, and seemed permanently to have smutched and
discolored them.

In New York you see the American face as Europe
characterizes it; in Boston you see it as it characterizes
Europe; and it is in Boston that you can best imagine
the strenuous grapple of the native forces which all
alien things must yield to till they take the American
cast. It is almost dismaying, that physiognomy, before it familiarizes itself anew; and in the brief first
moment while it is yet objective, you ransack your
conscience for any sins you may have committed in
your absence from it and make ready to do penance
for them. I felt almost as if I had brought the dirty
streets with me, and were guilty of having left them
lying about, so impossible were they with reference
to the Boston face.

It is a face that expresses care, even to the point of
anxiety, and it looked into the window of our carriage
with the serious eyes of our elderly hackman to make
perfectly sure of our destination before we drove away

from the station. It was a little rigorous with us, as requiring us to have a clear mind; but it was not unfriendly, not unkind, and it was patient from long experience. In New York there are no elderly hackmen; but in Boston they abound, and I cannot believe they would be capable of bad faith with travellers. In fact, I doubt if this class is anywhere as predatory as it is painted; but in Boston it appears to have the public honor in its keeping. I do not mean that it was less mature, less self-respectful in Portsmouth, where we were next to arrive; more so it could not be; an equal sense of safety, of ease, began with it in both places, and all through New England it is of native birth, while in New York it is composed of men of many nations, with a weight in numbers towards the Celtic strain. The prevalence of the native in New England helps you sensibly to realize from the first moment that here you are in America as the first Americans imagined and meant it; and nowhere in New England is the original tradition more purely kept than in the beautiful old seaport of New Hampshire. In fact, without being quite prepared to defend a thesis to this effect, I believe that Portsmouth is pre-eminently American, and in this it differs from Newburyport and from Salem, which have suffered from different causes an equal commercial decline, and, though among the earliest of the great Puritan towns after Boston, are now largely made up of aliens in race and religion; these are actually the majority, I believe, in Newburyport.

## IV

The adversity of Portsmouth began early in the century, but before that time she had prospered so greatly that her merchant princes were able to build

"THE GREAT SQUARE HOUSES . . . PAINTED WHITE"

themselves wooden palaces with white walls and green shutters, of a grandeur and beauty unmatched elsewhere in the country. I do not know what architect had his way with them, though his name is richly worth remembrance, but they let him make them habitations of such graceful proportion and of such delicate ornament that they have become shrines of pious pilgrimage with the young architects of our day who hope to house our well-to-do people fitly in country or suburbs. The decoration is oftenest spent on a porch or portal, or a frieze of peculiar refinement; or perhaps it feels its way to the carven casements or to the delicate iron-work of the transoms; the rest is a simplicity and a faultless propriety of form in the stately mansions which stand under the arching elms, with their gardens sloping, or dropping by easy terraces behind them to the river, or to the borders of other pleasances. They are all of wood, except for the granite foundations and doorsteps, but the stout edifices rarely sway out of the true line given them, and they look as if they might keep it yet another century.

Between them, in the sun-shotten shade, lie the quiet streets, whose gravelled stretch is probably never cleaned because it never needs cleaning. Even the business streets, and the quaint square which gives the most American of towns an air so foreign and Old Worldly, look as if the wind and rain alone cared for them; but they are not foul, and the narrower avenues, where the smaller houses of gray, unpainted wood crowd each other, flush upon the pavements, towards the water-side, are doubtless unvisited by the hoe or broom, and must be kept clean by a New England conscience against getting them untidy.

When you get to the river-side there is one stretch of narrow, high-shouldered warehouses which recall

Holland, especially in a few with their gables broken in steps, after the Dutch fashion. These, with their mouldering piers and grass-grown wharves, have their pathos, and the whole place embodies in its architecture an interesting record of the past, from the time when the homesick exiles huddled close to the water's edge till the period of post-colonial prosperity, when proud merchants and opulent captains set their vast square houses each in its handsome space of gardened ground.

My adjectives might mislead as to size, but they could not as to beauty, and I seek in vain for those that can duly impart the peculiar charm of the town. Portsmouth still awaits her novelist; he will find a rich field when he comes; and I hope he will come of the right sex, for it needs some minute and subtle feminine skill, like that of Jane Austen, to express a fit sense of its life in the past. Of its life in the present I know nothing. I could only go by those delightful, silent houses, and sigh my longing soul into their dim interiors. When now and then a young shape in summer silk, or a group of young shapes in diaphanous muslin, fluttered out of them, I was no wiser; and doubtless my elderly fancy would have been unable to deal with what went on in them. Some girl of those flitting through the warm, odorous twilight must become the creative historian of the place; I can at least imagine a Jane Austen now growing up in Portsmouth.

## V

If Miss Jewett were of a little longer breath than she has yet shown herself in fiction, I might say the Jane Austen of Portsmouth was already with us, and had merely not yet begun to deal with its precious material. One day when we crossed the Piscataqua from

New Hampshire into Maine, and took the trolley-line for a run along through the lovely coast country, we suddenly found ourselves in the midst of her own people, who are a little different sort of New-Englanders from those of Miss Wilkins. They began to flock into the car, young maidens and old, mothers and grandmothers, and nice boys and girls, with a very, very few farmer youth of marriageable age, and more rustic and seafaring elders long past it, all in the Sunday best which they had worn to the graduation exercises at the High School, where we took them mostly up. The womenkind were in a nervous twitter of talk and laughter, and the men tolerantly gay beyond their wont, "passing the time of day" with one another, and helping the more tumultuous sex to get settled in the overcrowded open car. They courteously made room for one another, and let the children stand between their knees, or took them in their laps, with that unfailing American kindness which I am prouder of than the American valor in battle, observing in all that American decorum which is no bad thing either. We had chanced upon the high and mighty occasion of the neighborhood year, when people might well have been a little off their balance, but there was not a boisterous note in the subdued affair. As we passed the school-house door, three dear, pretty maids in white gowns and white slippers stood on the steps and gently smiled upon our company. One could see that they were inwardly glowing and thrilling with the excitement of their graduation, but were controlling their emotions to a calm worthy of the august event, so that no one might ever have it to say that they had appeared silly.

The car swept on, and stopped to set down passengers at their doors or gates, where they severally left it, with an easy air as of private ownership, into some sense of which the trolley promptly flatters people along its obliging lines. One comfortable matron, in a cinnamon silk, was just such a figure as that in the Miss Wilkins's story where the bridegroom fails to come on the wedding-day; but, as I say, they made me think more of Miss Jewett's·people. The shore folk and the Down-Easters are specifically hers; and these were just such as might have belonged in *The Country of the Pointed Firs*, or *Sister Wisby's Courtship*, or *Dulham Ladies*, or *An Autumn Ramble*, or twenty other entrancing tales. Sometimes one of them would try her front door, and then, with a bridling toss of the head, express that she had forgotten locking it, and slip round to the kitchen; but most of the ladies made their way back at once between the roses and syringas of their grassy door-yards, which were as neat and prim as their own persons, or the best chamber in their white-walled, green-shuttered, story-and-a-half house, and as perfectly kept as the very kitchen itself.

## VI

The trolley-line had been opened only since the last September, but in an effect of familiar use it was as if it had always been there, and it climbed and crooked and clambered about with the easy freedom of the country road which it followed. It is a land of low hills, broken by frequent reaches of the sea, and it is most amusing, most amazing, to see how frankly the trolley-car takes and overcomes its difficulties. It scrambles up and down the little steeps like a cat, and whisks round a sharp and sudden curve with a feline screech, broadening into a loud caterwaul as it darts over the estuaries on its trestles. Its course does not lack excitement, and I suppose it does not lack danger;

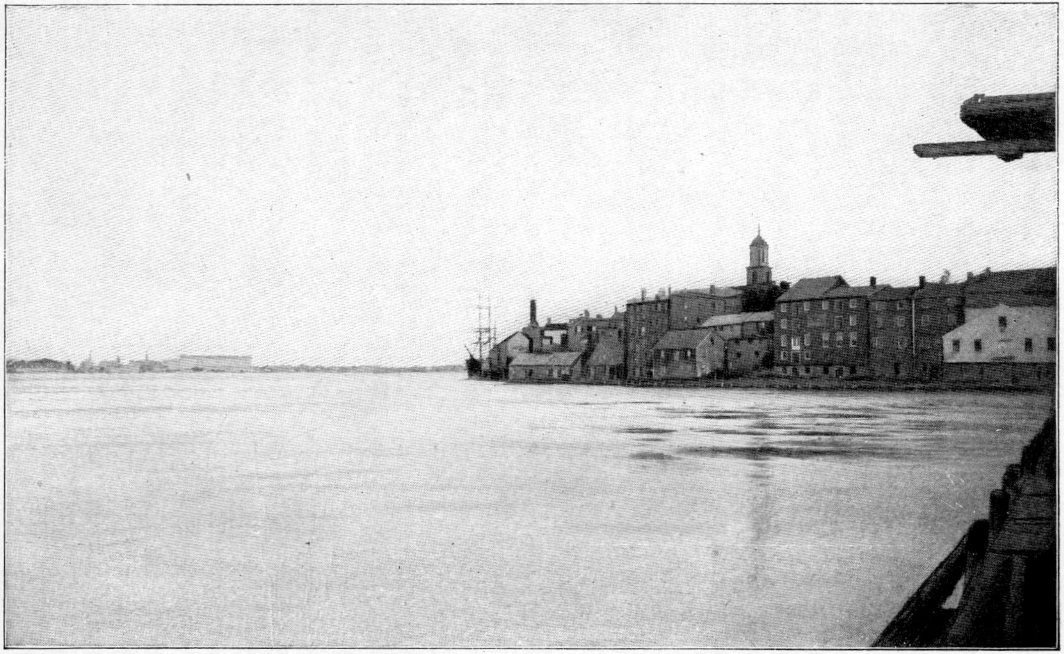

AN ASPECT OF PORTSMOUTH FROM THE PISCATAQUA

but as yet there have been no accidents, and it is not
so disfiguring as one would think. The landscape
has already accepted it, and is making the best of it;
and to the country people it is an inestimable convenience. It passes everybody's front door or back door,
and the farmers can get themselves or their produce
(for it runs an express car) into Portsmouth in an hour,
twice an hour, all day long. In summer the cars are
open, with transverse seats, and stout curtains that
quite shut out a squall of wind or rain. In winter the
cars are closed, and heated by electricity. The young
motorman whom I spoke with, while we waited on a
siding to let a car from the opposite direction get by,
told me that he was caught out in a blizzard last winter, and passed the night in a snow-drift. "But the
cah was so wa'm, I neva suff'ed a mite."

"Well," I summarized, "it must be a great advantage to all the people along the line."

"Well, you wouldn't 'a' thought so, from the kick
they made."

"I suppose the cottagers"— the summer colony—
"didn't like the noise."

"Oh yes; that's what I mean. The's whe' the kick
was. The natives like it. *I* guess the summa folks
'll like it, too."

He looked round at me with enjoyment of his joke
in his eye, for we both understood that the summer
folks could not help themselves, and must bow to the
will of the majority.

# THE STANDARD HOUSEHOLD-EFFECT
## COMPANY

MY friend came in the other day, before we had
left town, and looked round at the appointments
of the room in their summer shrouds, and said, with a
faint sigh, "I see you have had the eternal-womanly
with you, too."

## I

"Isn't the eternal-womanly everywhere? What has
happened to you?" I asked.

"I wish you would come to my house and see. Every
rug has been up for a month, and we have been living
on bare floors. Everything that could be tied up has
been tied up, everything that could be sewed up has
been sewed up. Everything that could be moth-balled
and put away in chests has been moth-balled and put
away. Everything that could be taken down has been
taken down. Bags with draw-strings at their necks
have been pulled over the chandeliers and tied. The
pictures have been hidden in cheese-cloth, and the mirrors veiled in gauze so that I cannot see my own miserable face anywhere."

"Come! That's something."

"Yes, it's something. But I have been thinking
this matter over very seriously, and I believe it is going from bad to worse. I have heard praises of the
thorough housekeeping of our grandmothers, but the

housekeeping of their granddaughters is a thousand times more intense."

"Do you really believe that?" I asked. "And if you do, what of it?"

"Simply this, that if we don't put a stop to it, at the gait it's going, it will put a stop to the eternal-womanly."

"I suppose we should hate that."

"Yes, it would be bad. It would be very bad; and I have been turning the matter over in my mind, and studying out a remedy."

"The highest type of philosopher turns a thing over in his mind and lets some one else study out a remedy."

"Yes, I know. I feel that I may be wrong in my processes, but I am sure that I am right in my results. The reason why our grandmothers could be such good housekeepers without danger of putting a stop to the eternal-womanly was that they had so few things to look after in their houses. Life was indefinitely simpler with them. But the modern improvements, as we call them, have multiplied the cares of housekeeping without subtracting its burdens, as they were expected to do. Every novel convenience and comfort, every article of beauty and luxury, every means of refinement and enjoyment in our houses, has been so much added to the burdens of housekeeping, and the granddaughters have inherited from the grandmothers an undiminished conscience against rust and the moth, which will not suffer them to forget the least duty they owe to the naughtiest of their superfluities."

"Yes, I see what you mean," I said. This is what one usually says when one does not quite know what another is driving at; but in this case I really did know, or thought I did. "That survival of the conscience is a very curious thing, especially in our eternal-womanly. I suppose that the North American conscience was evolved from the rudimental European conscience during the first centuries of struggle here, and was more or less religious and economical in its origin. But with the advance of wealth and the decay of faith among us, the conscience seems to be simply con- scientious, or, if it is otherwise, it is social. The eter- nal-womanly continues along the old lines of house- keeping from an atavistic impulse, and no one woman can stop because all the other women are going on. It is something in the air, or something in the blood. Perhaps it is something in both."

"Yes," said my friend, quite as I had said already, "I see what you mean. But I think it is in the air more than in the blood. I was in Paris, about this time last year, perhaps because I was the only thing in my house that had not been swathed in cheese-cloth, or tied up in a bag with draw-strings, or rolled up with moth-balls and put away in chests. At any rate, I was there. One day I left my wife in New York care- fully tagging three worn-out feather dusters, and put- ting them into a pillow-case, and tagging it, and put- ting the pillow-case into a camphorated self-sealing paper sack, and tagging it; and another day I was in Paris, dining at the house of a lady whom I asked how she managed with the things in her house when she went into the country for the summer. 'Leave them just as they are,' she said. 'But what about the dust and the moths, and the rust and the tarnish?' She said, 'Why, the things would have to be all gone over when I came back in the autumn, anyway, and why should I give myself double trouble?' I asked her if she didn't even roll anything up and put it away in closets, and she said: 'Oh, you mean that old Amer- ican horror of getting ready to go away. I used to go through all that at home, too, but I shouldn't dream of it here. In the first place, there are no closets in the house, and I couldn't put anything away if I wanted to. And really nothing happens. I scatter some Persian powder along the edges of things, and under the lower shelves, and in the dim corners, and I pull down the shades. When I come back in the fall I have the powder swept out, and the shades pulled up, and begin living again. Suppose a little dust *has* got in, and the moths *have* nibbled a little here and there? The whole damage would not amount to half the cost of putting everything away and taking everything out, not to speak of the weeks of discomfort, and the wear and tear of spirit. No, thank goodness! I left American housekeeping in America.' I asked her: 'But if you went back?' and she gave a sigh, and said: 'I suppose I should go back to that, along with all the rest. Everybody does it there.' So you see," my friend concluded, "it's in the air, rather than the blood."

"Then your famous specific is that our eternal-womanly should go and live in Paris?"

"Oh, dear, no!" said my friend. "Nothing so drastic as all that. Merely the extinction of household property."

"I see what you mean," I said. "But—what *do* you mean?"

"Simply that hired houses, such as most of us live in, shall all be furnished houses, and that the landlord shall own every stick in them, and every appliance down to the last spoon and ultimate towel. There must be no compromise, by which the tenant agrees to provide his own linen and silver; that would neutralize the effect I intend by the expropriation of the personal proprietor, if that says what I mean. It must be in the lease, with severe penalties against the tenant in case of violation, that the landlord is to furnish everything in perfect order when the tenant comes in, and is to put everything in perfect order when the tenant goes out, and the tenant is not to touch anything, to clean it, or dust it, or roll it up in moth-balls and put it away in chests. All is to be so sacredly and inalienably the property of the landlord that it shall constitute a kind of trespass if the tenant attempts to close the house for the summer or to open it for the winter in the usual way that houses are now closed and opened. Otherwise my scheme would be measurably vitiated."

"I see what you mean," I murmured. "Well?"

"Some years ago," my friend went on, "when we came home from Europe, we left our furniture in storage for a time, while we rather drifted about, and did not settle anywhere in particular. During that interval my wife opened and closed five furnished houses in two years."

"And she has lived to tell the tale?"

"She has lived to tell it a great many times. She can hardly be kept from telling it yet. But it is my belief that, although she brought to the work all the anguish of a quickened conscience, under the influence of the American conditions she had returned to, she suffered far less in her encounters with either of those furnished houses than she now does with our own furniture when she shuts up our house in the summer, and opens it for the winter. But if there had been a clause in the lease, as there should have been, forbidding her to put those houses in order when she left them, life would have been simply a rapture. Why, in Europe custom almost supplies the place of statute in such cases, and you come and go so lightly in and out of furnished houses that you do not mind taking them for a month, or a few weeks. We are very far behind in this matter, but I have no doubt that if we once came to do it on any extended scale we should do it, as we do everything else we attempt, more perfectly than any other people in the world. You see what I mean?"

"I am not sure that I do. But go on."

"I would invert the whole Henry George principle, and I would tax personal property of the household kind so heavily that it would necessarily pass out of private hands; I would make its tenure so costly that it would be impossible to any but the very rich, who are also the very wicked, and ought to suffer."

"Oh, come, now!"

"I refer you to your Testament. In the end, all household property would pass into the hands of the state."

"Aren't you getting worse and worse?"

"Oh, I'm not supposing there won't be a long interval when household property will be in the hands of powerful monopolies, and many millionaires will be made by letting it out to middle-class tenants like you and me, along with the houses we hire of them. I have no doubt that there will be a Standard Household-Effect Company, which will extend its relations to Europe, and get the household effects of the whole world into its grasp. It will be a fearful oppression, and we shall probably groan under it for generations, but it will liberate us from our personal ownership of them, and from the far more crushing weight of the moth-ball. We shall suffer, but—"

"I see what you mean," I hastened to interrupt at this point, "but these suggestive remarks of yours are getting beyond— Do you think you could defer the rest of your incompleted sentence for a week?"

"Well, for not more than a week," said my friend, with an air of discomfort in his arrest.

## II

—"We shall not suffer so much as we do under our present system," said my friend, completing his sentence after the interruption of a week. By this time we had both left town, and were taking up the talk again on the veranda of a sea-side hotel. "As for the eternal-womanly, it will be her salvation from herself. When once she is expropriated from her household effects, and forbidden under severe penalties from meddling with those of the Standard Household-Effect Company, she will begin to get back her peace of mind, and be the same blessing she was before she began housekeeping."

"That may all very well be," I assented, though I did not believe it, and I found something almost too fantastical in my friend's scheme. "But when we are expropriated from all our dearest belongings, what is to become of our tender and sacred associations with them?"

"What has become of devotion to the family gods, and the worship of ancestors? Once the graves of the dead were at the door of the living, so that libations might be conveniently poured out on them, and the ground where they lay was inalienable because it was supposed to be used by their spirits as well as their bodies. A man could not sell the bones, because he could not sell the ghosts, of his kindred. By-and-by, when religion ceased to be domestic and became social, and the service of the gods was carried on in temples common to all, it was found that the tombs of one's forefathers could be sold without violence to their spectres. I dare say it wouldn't be different in the case of our tender and sacred associations with tables and chairs, pots and pans, beds and bedding, pictures and bric-à-brac. We have only to evolve a little further. In fact we have already evolved far beyond the point that troubles you. Most people in modern towns and cities have changed their domiciles from ten to twenty times during their lives, and have not paid the slightest attention to the tender and sacred associations connected with them. I don't suppose you would say that a man has no such associations with the house that has sheltered him, while he has them with the stuff that has furnished it?"

"No, I shouldn't say that."

"If anything, the house should be dearer than the household gear. Yet at each remove we drag a lengthening chain of tables, chairs, side - boards, portraits, landscapes, bedsteads, washstands, stoves, kitchen utensils, and bric-à-brac after us, because, as my wife says, we cannot bear to part with them. At several times in our own lives we have accumulated stuff enough to furnish two or three houses and have paid a pretty stiff house - rent in the form of storage for the overflow. Why, I am doing that very thing now! Aren't you?"

"I am—in a certain degree," I assented.

"We all are, we well-to-do people, as we think ourselves. Once my wife and I revolted by a common impulse against the ridiculous waste and slavery of the thing. We went to the storage warehouse and sent three or four van-loads of the rubbish to the auctioneer. Some of the pieces we had not seen for years, and as each was hauled out for us to inspect and decide upon, we condemned it to the auction-block with shouts of rejoicing. Tender and sacred associations! We hadn't had such light hearts since we had put everything in storage and gone to Europe indefinitely as we had when we left those things to be carted out of our lives forever. Not one had been a pleasure to us ; the sight of every one had been a pang. All we wanted was never to set eyes on them again."

"I must say you have disposed of the tender and sacred associations pretty effectually, so far as they relate to things in storage. But the things that we have in daily use?"

"It is exactly the same with them. Why should they be more to us than the floors and walls of the houses we move in and move out of with no particular pathos? And I think we ought not to care for them, certainly not to the point of letting them destroy our eternal-womanly with the anxiety she feels for them. She is really much more precious, if she could but realize it, than anything she swathes in cheese-cloth or wraps up with moth-balls. The proof of the fact that the whole thing is a piece of mere sentimentality is that we may live in a furnished house for years, amid all the accidents of birth and death, joy and sorrow, and yet not form the slightest attachment to the furniture. Why should we have tender and sacred associations with a thing we have bought, and not with a thing we have hired?"

"I confess, I don't know. And do you really think we could liberate ourselves from our belongings if they didn't belong to us? Wouldn't the eternal - womanly still keep putting them away for summer and taking them out for winter?"

"At first, yes, there might be some such mechanical action in her; but it would be purely mechanical, and it would soon cease. When the Standard Household-Effect Company came down on the temporal-manly with a penalty for violation of the lease, the eternal-womanly would see the folly of her ways and stop; for the eternal - womanly is essentially economical, whatever we say about the dressmaker's bills; and the very futilities of putting away and taking out, that she now wears herself to a thread with, are founded in the instinct of saving."

"But," I asked, "wouldn't our household belongings lose a good deal of character if they didn't belong

248

to us? Wouldn't our domestic interiors become dreadfully impersonal?"

"How many houses now have character—personality? Most people let the different dealers choose for them, as it is. Why not let the Standard Household - Effect Company, and finally the state? I am sure that either would choose much more wisely than people choose for themselves, in the few cases where they even seem to choose for themselves. In most interiors the appointments are without fitness, taste, or sense; they are the mere accretions of accident in the greater number of cases; where they are the result of design, they are worse. I see what you mean by character and personality in them. You mean the sort of madness that let itself loose a few years ago in what was called household art, and has since gone to make the junk-shops hideous. Each of the eternal-womanly was supposed suddenly to have acquired a talent for decoration and a gift for the selection and arrangement of furniture, and each began to stamp herself upon our interiors. One painted a high - shouldered stone bottle with a stork and stood it at the right corner of the mantel on a scarf; another gilded the bottle and stood it at the left corner, and tied the scarf through its handle. One knotted a ribbon around the arm of a chair; another knotted it around the leg. In a day, an hour, a moment, the chairs suddenly became angular, cushionless, springless; and the sofas were stood across corners, or parallel with the fireplace, in slants expressive of the personality of the presiding genius. The walls became all frieze and dado; and instead of the simple and dignified ugliness of the impersonal period our interiors abandoned themselves to a hysterical chaos, full of character. Some people had their doors painted black, and the daughter or mother of the house then decorated them with morning-glories. I saw such a door in a house I looked at the other day, thinking I might hire it. The sight of that black door and its morning-glories made me wish to turn aside and live with the cattle, as Walt Whitman says. No, the less we try to get personality and character into our household effects the more beautiful and interesting they will be. As soon as we put the Standard Household-Effect Company in possession and render it a relentless monopoly, it will corrupt a competent architect and decorator in each of our large towns and cities, and when you hire a new house these will be sent to advise with the eternal - womanly concerning its appointments, and tell her what she wants, and what she will like; for at present the eternal womanly, as soon as she has got a thing she wants, begins to hate it. The company's agents will begin by convincing her that she does not need half the things she has lumbered up her house with, and that every useless thing is an ugly thing, even in the region of pure æsthetics. I once asked an Italian painter if he did not think a certain nobly imagined drawing-room was fine, and he said: ' Sì. Ma troppa roba.' There were too many rugs, tables, chairs, sofas, pictures, vases, statues, chandeliers. Troppa roba is the vice of all our household furnishing, and it will be the death of the eternal-womanly if it is not stopped. But the corrupt agents of a giant monopoly will teach the eternal-womanly something of the wise simplicity of the South, and she will end by returning to the ideal of housekeeping as it prevails among the Latin races, whom it began with, whom civilization began with. What of a harmless, necessary moth or two, or even a few fleas?"

"That might be all very well as far as furniture and carpets and curtains are concerned," I said, "but

surely you wouldn't apply it to pictures and objects of
art?"

"I would apply it to them first of all and above all,"
rejoined my friend, hardily. "Among all the people
who buy and own such things there is not one in a
thousand who has any real taste or feeling for them,
and the objects they choose are generally such as can
only deprave and degrade them further. The pictures, statues, and vases supplied by the Standard
Household-Effect Company would be selected by agents
with a real sense of art, and a knowledge of it. When
the house-letting and house-furnishing finally passed
into the hands of the state, these things would be lent
from the public galleries, or from immense municipal
stores for the purpose."

"And I suppose you would have ancestral portraits
supplied along with the other pictures?" I sneered.

"Ancestral portraits, of course," said my friend,
with unruffled temper. "So few people have ancestors of their own that they will be very glad to have
ancestral portraits chosen for them out of the collections of the company or the state. The agents of the
one, or the officers of the other, will study the existing
type of family face, and will select ancestors and an-
cestresses whose modelling, coloring, and expression
agree with it, and will keep in view the race and nationality of the family whose ancestral portraits are
to be supplied, so that there shall be no chance of the
grossly improbable effect which ancestral portraits
now have in many cases. Yes, I see no flaw in the
scheme," my friend concluded, "and no difficulty
that can't be easily overcome. We must alienate our
household furniture, and make it so sensitively and
exclusively the property of some impersonal agency
—company or community, I don't care which—that
any care of it shall be a sort of crime; any sense of

responsibility for its preservation a species of incivism punishable by fine or imprisonment. This, and nothing short of it, will be the salvation of the eternal-womanly."

"And the perdition of something even more precious than that!"

"What can be more precious?"

"Individuality."

"My dear friend," demanded my visitor, who had risen, and whom I was gradually edging to the door, "do you mean to say there is any individuality in such things now? What have we been saying about character?"

"Ah, I see what you mean," I said.

## STACCATO NOTES OF A VANISHED SUMMER

MONDAY afternoon the storm which had been beating up against the southeasterly wind nearly all day thickened, fold upon fold, in the northwest. The gale increased, and blackened the harbor and whitened the open sea beyond, where sail after sail appeared round the reef of Whaleback Light, and ran in a wild scamper for the safe anchorages within.

Since noon cautious coasters of all sorts had been dropping in with a casual air; the coal schooners and barges had rocked and nodded knowingly to one another, with their taper and truncated masts, on the breast of the invisible swell; and the flock of little yachts and pleasure-boats which always fleck the bay huddled together in the safe waters. The craft that came scurrying in just before nightfall were mackerel seiners from Gloucester. They were all of one graceful shape and one size; they came with all sail set, taking the waning light like sunshine on their flying-jibs, and trailing each two dories behind them, with their seines piled in black heaps between the thwarts. As soon as they came inside their jibs weakened and fell, and the anchor-chains rattled from their bows. Before the dark hid them we could have counted sixty or seventy ships in the harbor, and as the night fell they improvised a little Venice under the hill with their lights, which twinkled rhythmically, like the lamps in the basin of St. Mark, between the Maine and New Hampshire coasts.

There was a dash of rain, and we thought the storm had begun; but that ended it, as so many times this summer a dash of rain has ended a storm. The morning came veiled in a fog that kept the shipping at anchor through the day; but the next night the weather cleared. We woke to the clucking of tackle, and saw the whole fleet standing dreamily out to sea. When they were fairly gone, the summer, which had held aloof in dismay of the sudden cold, seemed to return and possess the land again; and the succession of silver days and crystal nights resumed the tranquil round which we thought had ceased.

### I

One says of every summer, when it is drawing near its end, "There never was such a summer"; but if the summer is one of those which slip from the feeble hold of elderly hands, when the days of the years may be reckoned with the scientific logic of the insurance tables and the sad conviction of the psalmist, one sees it go with a passionate prescience of never seeing its like again such as the younger witness cannot know. Each new summer of the few left must be shorter and swifter than the last: its Junes will be thirty days long, and its Julys and Augusts thirty-one, in compliance with the almanac; but the days will be of so small a compass that fourteen of them will rattle round in a week of the old size like shrivelled peas in a pod.

To be sure they swell somewhat in the retrospect, like the same peas put to soak; and I am aware now of some June days of those which we first spent at Kittery Point this year, which were nearly twenty-four hours long. Even the days of declining years linger a little here, where there is nothing to hurry

"THE WEATHER-BEATEN MANSION OF SIR WILLIAM PEPPERRELL."

them, and where it is pleasant to loiter, and muse beside the sea and shore, which are so netted together
at Kittery Point that they hardly know themselves
apart. The days, whatever their length, are divided,
not into hours, but into mails. They begin, without
regard to the sun, at eight o'clock, when the first mail
comes with a few letters and papers which had forgotten themselves the night before. At half-past eleven
the great mid-day mail arrives; at four o'clock there
is another indifferent and scattering post, much like
that at eight in the morning; and at seven the last
mail arrives with the Boston evening papers and the
New York morning papers, to make you forget any
letters you were looking for. The opening of the
mid-day mail is that which most throngs with summer folks the little post-office under the elms, opposite the weather-beaten mansion of Sir William Pepperrell; but the evening mail attracts a large and mainly disinterested circle of natives. The day's work on
land and sea is then over, and the village leisure,
perched upon fences and stayed against house walls,
is of a picturesqueness which we should prize if we saw
it abroad, and which I am not willing to slight on our
own ground.

II

The type is mostly of a seafaring brown, a complexion which seems to be inherited rather than personally acquired; for the commerce of Kittery Point
perished long ago, and the fishing fleets that used to
fit out from her wharves have almost as long ago passed
to Gloucester. All that is left of the fishing interest
is the weir outside which supplies, fitfully and uncer-
tainly, the fish shipped fresh to the nearest markets.
But in spite of this the tint taken from the suns and

255

winds of the sea lingers on the local complexion; and
the local manner is that freer and easier manner of
people who have known other coasts, and are in some
sort citizens of the world. It is very different from the
inland New England manner; as different as the gentle, slow speech of the shore from the clipped nasals
of the hill-country. The lounging native walk is not
the heavy plod taught by the furrow, but has the lurch
and the sway of the deck in it.

Nothing could be better suited to progress through
the long village, which rises and sinks beside the shore
like a landscape with its sea-legs on; and nothing could
be more charming and friendly than this village. It
is quite untainted as yet by the summer cottages which
have covered so much of the coast, and made it look as
if the æsthetic suburbs of New York and Boston had
gone ashore upon it. There are two or three old-fashioned summer hotels; but the summer life distinctly
fails to characterize the place. The people live where
their forefathers have lived for two hundred and fifty
years; and for the century since the baronial domain
of Sir William was broken up and his possessions con-
fiscated by the young Republic, they have dwelt in
small red or white houses on their small holdings along
the slopes and levels of the low hills beside the water,
where a man may pass with the least inconvenience
and delay from his threshold to his gunwale. Not all
the houses are small; some are spacious and ambi-
tious to be of ugly modern patterns; but most are
simple and homelike. Their gardens, following the
example of Sir William's vanished pleasaunce, drop
southward to the shore, where the lobster-traps and
the hen-coops meet in unembarrassed promiscuity.
But the fish-flakes which once gave these inclines the
effect of terraced vineyards have passed as utterly as
the proud parterres of the old baronet; and Kittery Point

no longer "makes" a cod or a haddock for the market.

Three groceries, a butcher shop, and a small variety store study the few native wants; and with a little money one may live in as great real comfort here as for much in a larger place. The street takes care of itself; the seafaring housekeeping of New England is not of the insatiable Dutch type which will not spare the stones of the highway; but within the houses are of almost terrifying cleanliness. The other day I found myself in a kitchen where the stove shone like oxidized silver; the pump and sink were clad in oil-cloth as with blue tiles; the walls were papered; the stainless floor was strewn with home-made hooked and braided rugs; and I felt the place so altogether too good for me that I pleaded to stay there for the transaction of my business, lest a sharper sense of my unfitness should await me in the parlor.

The village, with scarcely an interval of farm-lands, stretches four miles along the water-side to Portsmouth; but it seems to me that just at the point where our lines have fallen there is the greatest concentration of its character. This has apparently not been weakened, it has been accented, by the trolley-line which passes through its whole length, with gayly freighted cars coming and going every half-hour. I suppose they are not longer than other trolley-cars, but they each affect me like a procession. They are cheerful presences by day, and by night they light up the dim, winding street with the flare of their electric bulbs, and bring to the country a vision of city splendor upon terms that do not humiliate or disquiet. During July and August they are mostly filled with summer folks from a great summer resort beyond us, and their lights reveal the pretty fashions of hats and gowns in all the charm of the latest lines and tints. But there is an increasing

democracy in these splendors, and one might easily
mistake a passing excursionist from some neighboring inland town, or even a local native with the instinct
of clothes, for a social leader from York Harbor.

With the falling leaf, the bargelike open cars close
up into well-warmed saloons, and falter to hourly intervals in their course. But we are still far from the
falling leaf; we are hardly come to the blushing or
fading leaf. Here and there an impassioned maple
confesses the autumn; the ancient Pepperrell elms
fling down showers of the baronet's fairy gold in the
September gusts; the sumacs and the blackberry vines
are ablaze along the tumbling black stone walls; but
it is still summer, it is still summer: I cannot allow
otherwise!

### III

The other day I visited for the first time (in the opulent indifference of one who could see it any time) the
stately tomb of the first Pepperrell, who came from
Cornwall to these coasts, and settled finally at Kittery
Point. He laid there the foundations of the greatest
fortune in colonial New England, which revolutionary
New England seized and dispersed, as I cannot but
feel, a little ruthlessly. In my personal quality I am
of course averse to all great fortunes; and in my civic
capacity I am a patriot. But still I feel a sort of grace
in wealth a century old, and if I could now have my
way, I would not have had their possessions reft from
those kindly Pepperrells, who could hardly help being
loyal to the fountain of their baronial honors. Sir William, indeed, had helped, more than any other man, to
bring the people who despoiled him to a national consciousness. If he did not imagine, he mainly managed
the plucky New England expedition against Louis-

bourg at Cape Breton a half century before the War of Independence; and his splendid success in rending that stronghold from the French taught the colonists that they were Americans, and need be Englishmen no longer than they liked. His soldiers were of the stamp of all succeeding American armies, and his leadership was of the neighborly and fatherly sort natural to an amiable man who knew most of them personally. He was already the richest man in America, and his grateful king made him a baronet; but he came contentedly back to Kittery, and took up his old life in a region where he had the comfortable consideration of an unrivalled magnate. He built himself the dignified mansion which still stands across the way from the post-office on Kittery Point, within an easy stone's cast of the far older house, where his father wedded Margery Bray, when he came, a thrifty young Welsh fisherman, from the Isles of Shoals, and established his family on Kittery. The Bray house had been the finest in the region a hundred years before the Pepperrell mansion was built; it still remembers its consequence in the panelling and wainscoting of the large, square parlor where the young people were married and in the elaborate staircase cramped into the little, square hall; and the Bray fortune helped materially to swell the wealth of the Pepperrells.

I do not know that I should care now to have a man able to ride thirty miles on his own land; but I do not mind Sir William's having done it here a hundred and fifty years ago; and I wish the confiscations had left his family, say, about a mile of it. They could now, indeed, enjoy it only in the collateral branches, for all Sir William's line is extinct. The splendid mansion which he built his daughter is in alien hands, and the fine old house which Lady Pepperrell built herself after his death belongs to the remotest of kins-

men. A group of these, the descendants of a prolific
sister of the baronet, meets every year at Kittery Point
as the Pepperrell Association, and, in a tent hard
by the little grove of drooping spruces which shade
the admirable renaissance cenotaph of Sir William's
father, cherishes the family memories with due American "proceedings."

## IV

The meeting of the Pepperrell Association was by
no means the chief excitement of our summer. In
fact, I do not know that it was an excitement at all;
and I am sure it was not comparable to the presence
of our naval squadron, when for four days the mighty
dragon and kraken shapes of steel, which had crum-
bled the decrepit pride of Spain in the fight at Santiago, weltered in our peaceful waters, almost under my
window.

I try now to dignify them with handsome epithets;
but while they were here I had moments of thinking
they looked like a lot of whited locomotives, which had
broken through from some trestle, in a recent accident, and were waiting the offices of a wrecking-train.
The poetry of the man-of-war still clings to the "three-
decker out of the foam" of the past; it is too soon yet
for it to have cast a mischievous halo about the modern
battle-ship; and I looked at the *New York* and the
*Texas* and the *Brooklyn* and the rest, and thought,
"Ah, but for you, and our need of proving your dire
efficiency, perhaps we could have got on with the wickedness of Spanish rule in Cuba, and there had been
no war!" Under my reluctant eyes the great, dreadful
spectacle of the Santiago fight displayed itself in peaceful Kittery Harbor. I saw the Spanish ships drive
upon the reef where a man from Dover, New Hamp-

SIR WILLIAM PEPPERRELL

shire, was camping in a little wooden shanty unconscious; and I heard the dying screams of the Spanish
sailors, seethed and scalded within the steel walls of
their own wicked war-kettles.

As for the guns, battle or no battle, our ships, like
"kind Lieutenant Belay of the *Hot Cross-Bun*," seemed
to be "banging away the whole day long." They set
a bad example to the dreamy old fort on the Newcas-
tle shore, which, till they came, only recollected itself
to salute the sunrise and sunset with a single gun;
but which, under provocation of the squadron, formed
a habit of firing twenty or thirty times at noon.

Other martial shows and noises were not so bad. I
rather liked seeing the morning drill of the marines
and the blue-jackets on the iron decks, with the lively
music that went with it. The bugle calls and the bells
were charming; the week's wash hung out to dry had
its picturesqueness by day, and by night the spectral
play of the search-lights along the waves and shores,
and against the startled skies, was even more impressive. There was a band which gave us every evening
the airs of the latest coon-songs, and the national an-
thems which we have borrowed from various nations;
and yes, I remember the white squadron kindly, though
I was so glad to have it go, and let us lapse back into
our summer silence and calm. It was (I do not mind
saying now) a majestic sight to see those grotesque
monsters gather themselves together, and go wallowing, one after another, out of the harbor, and drop behind the ledge of Whaleback Light, as if they had sunk
into the sea.

## V

A deep peace fell upon us when they went, and it
must have been at this most receptive moment, when all

our sympathies were adjusted in a mood of hospitable expectation, that Jim appeared.

Jim was, and still is, and I hope will long be, a cat; but unless one has lived at Kittery Point, and realized, from observation and experience, what a leading part cats may play in society, one cannot feel the full import of this fact. Not only has every house in Kittery its cat, but every house seems to have its half-dozen cats, large, little, old, and young; of divers colors, tending mostly to a dark tortoise-shell. With a whole ocean inviting to the tragic rite, I do not believe there is ever a kitten drowned in Kittery; the illimitable sea rather employs itself in supplying the fish to which "no cat's averse," but which the cats of Kittery demand to have cooked. They do not like raw fish; they say it plainly, and they prefer to have the bones taken out for them, though they do not insist upon that point.

At least, Jim never did so from the time when he first scented the odor of delicate young mackerel in the evening air about our kitchen, and dropped in upon the maids there with a fine casual effect of being merely out for a walk, and feeling it a neighborly thing to call. He had on a silver collar, engraved with his name and surname, which offered itself for introduction like a visiting-card. He was too polite to ask himself to the table at once, but after he had been welcomed to the family circle, he formed the habit of finding himself with us at breakfast and supper, when he sauntered in like one who should say, "Did I smell *fish?*" but would not go further in the way of hinting.

He had no need to do so. He was made at home, and freely invited to our best not only in fish, but in chicken, for which he showed a nice taste, and in sweet-corn, for which he revealed a most surprising fondness when it was cut from the cob for him. After he had breakfasted or supped he gracefully suggested that he was thirsty by climbing to the table where the water-pitcher stood and stretching his fine feline head towards it. When he had lapped up his saucer of water, he marched into the parlor, and riveted the chains upon our fondness by taking the best chair and going to sleep in it in attitudes of Egyptian, of Assyrian majesty.

His arts were few or none; he rather disdained to practise any; he completed our conquest by maintaining himself simply a fascinating presence; and perhaps we spoiled Jim. It is certain that he came under my window at two o'clock one night, and tried the kitchen door. It resisted his efforts to get in, and then Jim began to use language which I had never heard from the lips of a cat before, and seldom from the lips of a man. I will not repeat it; enough that it carried to the listener the conviction that Jim was not sober. Where he could have got his liquor in the totally abstinent State of Maine I could not positively say, but probably of some sailor who had brought it from the neighboring New Hampshire coast. There could be no doubt, however, that Jim was drunk; and a dash from the water-pitcher seemed the only thing for him. The water did not touch him, but he started back in surprise and grief, and vanished into the night without a word.

His feelings must have been deeply wounded, for it was almost a week before he came near us again; and then I think that nothing but young lobster would have brought him. He forgave us finally, and made us of his party in the quarrel he began gradually to have with the large yellow cat of a next-door neighbor. This culminated one afternoon, after a long exchange of mediæval defiance and insult, in a battle upon a bed of rag-weed, with wild shrieks of rage, and prodigious feats of ground and lofty tumbling. It seemed to our anxious eyes that Jim was getting the worst of it; but when we afterwards visited the battle-field and picked up several tufts of blond fur, we were in a doubt which was afterwards heightened by Jim's invasion of the yellow cat's territory, where he stretched himself defiantly upon the grass and seemed to be challenging the yellow cat to come out and try to put him off the premises.

# THE ART OF THE ADSMITH

THE other day, a friend of mine, who professes all the intimacy of a bad conscience with many of my thoughts and convictions, came in with a bulky book under his arm, and said, "I see by a guilty look in your eye that you are meaning to write about spring."

"I am not," I retorted, "and if I were, it would be because none of the new things have been said yet about spring, and because spring is never an old story, any more than youth or love."

"I have heard something like *that* before," said my friend, "and I understand. The simple truth of the matter is that this is the fag-end of the season, and you have run low in your subjects. Now take my advice and don't write about spring; it will make everybody hate you, and will do no good. Write about advertising." He tapped the book under his arm significantly. "Here is a theme for you."

## I

He had no sooner pronounced these words than I began to feel a weird and potent fascination in his suggestion. I took the book from him and looked it eagerly through. It was called *Good Advertising*, and it was written by one of the experts in the business who have advanced it almost to the grade of an art, or a humanity.

"But I see nothing here," I said, musingly, "which would enable a self-respecting author to come to the help of his publisher in giving due hold upon the public interest those charming characteristics of his book which no one else can feel so penetratingly or celebrate so persuasively."

"I expected some such objection from you," said my friend. "You will admit that there is everything else here?"

"Everything but that most essential thing. You know how we all feel about it: the bitter disappointment, the heart-sickening sense of insufficiency that the advertised praises of our books give us poor authors. The effect is far worse than that of the reviews, for the reviewer is not your ally and copartner, while your publisher—"

"I see what you mean," said my friend. "But you must have patience. If the author of this book can write so luminously of advertising in other respects, I am sure he will yet be able to cast a satisfactory light upon your problem. The question is, I believe, how to translate into irresistible terms all that fond and exultant regard which a writer feels for his book, all his pervasive appreciation of its singular beauty, unique value, and utter charm, and transfer it to print, without infringing upon the delicate and shrinking modesty which is the distinguishing ornament of the literary spirit?"

"Something like that. But you understand."

"Perhaps a Röntgen ray might be got to do it," said my friend, thoughtfully, "or perhaps this author may bring his mind to bear upon it yet. He seems to have considered every kind of advertising except book-advertising."

"The most important of all!" I cried, impatiently.

"You think so because you are in that line. If

you were in the line of varnish, or bicycles, or soap, or typewriters, or extract of beef, or of malt—"

"Still I should be interested in book-advertising, because it is the most vital of human interests."

"Tell me," said my friend, "do you read the advertisements of the books of rival authors?"

"*Brother* authors," I corrected him.

"Well, brother authors."

I said, No, candidly, I did not; and I forbore to add that I thought them little better than a waste of the publishers' money.

## II

My friend did not pursue his inquiry to my personal disadvantage, but seemed to prefer a more general philosophy of the matter.

"I have often wondered," he said, "at the enormous expansion of advertising, and doubted whether it was not mostly wasted. But my author, here, has suggested a brilliant fact which I was unwittingly groping for. When you take up a Sunday paper" — I shuddered, and my friend smiled intelligence—"you are simply appalled at the miles of announcements of all sorts. Who can possibly read them? Who cares even to look at them? But if you want something in particular—to furnish a house, or buy a suburban place, or take a steamer for Europe, or go to the theatre—then you find out at once who reads the advertisements, and cares to look at them. They respond to the multifarious wants of the whole community. You have before you the living operation of that law of demand and supply which it has always been such a bore to hear about. As often happens, the supply seems to come before the demand; but that's only an appearance. You wanted something, and you found an offer to meet your want."

"Then you don't believe that the offer **to meet** your want suggested it?"

"I see that my author believes something of the kind. We *may* be full of all sorts of unconscious wants which merely need the vivifying influence of an advertisement to make them spring into active being; but I have a feeling that the money paid for advertising which appeals to potential wants is largely thrown away. You must want a thing, or think you want it; otherwise you resent the proffer of it as a kind of impertinence."

"There are some kinds of advertisements, all the same, that I read without the slightest interest in the subject matter. Simply the beauty of the style attracts me."

"I know. But does it ever move you to get what you don't want?"

"Never; and I should be glad to know what your author thinks of that sort of advertising: the literary, or dramatic, or humorous, or quaint."

"He doesn't contemn it, quite. But I think he feels that it may have had its day. Do you still read such advertisements with your early zest?"

"No; the zest for nearly everything goes. I don't care so much for Tourguénief as I used. Still, if I come upon the jaunty and laconic suggestions of a certain well-known clothing-house, concerning the season's wear, I read them with a measure of satisfaction. The advertising expert—"

"This author calls him the adsmith."

"Delightful! Ad is a loathly little word, but we must come to it. It's as legitimate as lunch. But as I was saying, the adsmith seems to have caught the American business tone, as perfectly as any of our novelists have caught the American social tone."

"Yes," said my friend, "and he seems to have prospered as richly by it. You know some of those chaps make fifteen or twenty thousand dollars by adsmithing. They have put their art quite on a level with fiction pecuniarily."

"Perhaps it *is* a branch of fiction."

"No; they claim that it is pure fact. My author discourages the slightest admixture of fable. The truth, clearly and simply expressed, is the best in an ad."

"It is best in a wof, too. I am always saying that."

"Wof?"

"Well, work of fiction. It's another new word, like lunch or ad."

"But in a wof," said my friend, instantly adopting it, "my author insinuates that the fashion of payment tempts you to verbosity, while in an ad the conditions oblige you to the greatest possible succinctness. In one case you are paid by the word; in the other you pay by the word. That is where the adsmith stands upon higher moral ground than the wofsmith."

"I should think your author might have written a recent article in *The* ——, reproaching fiction with its unhallowed gains."

"If you mean that for a sneer, it is misplaced. He would have been incapable of it. My author is no more the friend of honesty in adsmithing than he is of propriety. He deprecates jocosity in apothecaries and undertakers, not only as bad taste, but as bad business; and he is as severe as any one could be upon ads that seize the attention by disgusting or shocking the reader.

"He is to be praised for that, and for the other thing; and I shouldn't have minded his criticising the ready wofsmith. I hope he attacks the use of display type, which makes our newspapers look like the poster-plastered fences around vacant lots. In New York there is only one paper whose advertisements are not typographically a shock to the nerves."

"Well," said my friend, "he attacks foolish and ineffective display."

"It is all foolish and ineffective. It is like a crowd of people trying to make themselves heard by shouting each at the top of his voice. A paper full of display advertisements is an image of our whole congested and delirious state of competition; but even in competitive conditions it is unnecessary, and it is futile. Compare any New York paper but one with the London papers, and you will see what I mean. Of course I refer to the ad pages; the rest of our exception is as offensive with pictures and scare - heads as all the rest. I wish your author could revise his opinions and condemn all display in ads."

"I dare say he will when he knows what you think," said my friend, with imaginable sarcasm.

### III

"I wish," I went on, "that he would give us some philosophy of the prodigious increase of advertising within the last twenty-five years, and some conjecture as to the end of it all. Evidently, it can't keep on increasing at the present rate. If it does, there will presently be no room in the world for things; it will be filled up with the advertisements of things."

"Before that time, perhaps," my friend suggested, "adsmithing will have become so fine and potent an art that advertising will be reduced in bulk, while keeping all its energy and even increasing its effectiveness."

"Perhaps," I said, "some silent electrical process will be contrived, so that the attractions of a new line of dress-goods or the fascination of a spring or fall opening may be imparted to a lady's consciousness without even the agency of words. All other facts of commercial and industrial interest could be dealt with in the same way. A fine thrill could be made to go from the last new book through the whole community, so that people would not willingly rest till they had it. Yes, one can see an indefinite future for advertising in that way. The adsmith may be the supreme artist of the twentieth century. He may assemble in his grasp, and employ at will, all the arts and sciences."

"Yes," said my friend, with a sort of fall in his voice, "that is very well. But what is to become of the race when it is penetrated at every pore with a sense of the world's demand and supply?"

"Oh, that is another affair. I was merely imagining the possible resources of invention in providing for the increase of advertising while guarding the integrity of the planet. I think, very likely, if the thing keeps on, we shall all go mad; but then we shall none of us be able to criticise the others. Or possibly the thing may work its own cure. You know the ingenuity of the political economists in justifying the egotism to which conditions appeal. They do not deny that these foster greed and rapacity in merciless degree, but they contend that when the wealth-winner drops off gorged there is a kind of miracle wrought, and good comes of it all. I never could see how; but if it is true, why shouldn't a sort of ultimate immunity come back to us from the very excess and invasion of the appeals now made to us, and destined to be made to us still more by the adsmith? Come, isn't there hope in that?"

"I see a great opportunity for the wofsmith in some such dream," said my friend. "Why don't you turn it to account?"

"You know that isn't my line; I must leave that sort of wofsmithing to the romantic novelist. Besides, I have my well-known panacea for all the ills our state is heir to, in a civilization which shall legislate foolish and vicious and ugly and adulterate things out of the possibility of existence. Most of the adsmithing is now employed in persuading people that such things are useful, beautiful, and pure. But in *my* civilization they shall not even be suffered to be made, much less foisted upon the community by adsmiths."

"I see what you mean," said my friend; and he sighed gently. "I had much better let you write about spring."

# THE PSYCHOLOGY OF PLAGIARISM

A LATE incident in the history of a very wide-spread English novelist, triumphantly closed by the statement of his friend that the novelist had casually failed to accredit a given passage in his novel to the real author, has brought freshly to my mind a curious question in ethics. The friend who vindicated the novelist, or, rather, who contemptuously dismissed the matter, not only confessed the fact of adoption, but declared that it was one of many which could be found in the novelist's works. The novelist, he said, was quite in the habit of so using material in the rough, which he implied was like using any fact or idea from life, and he declared that the novelist could not bother to answer critics who regarded these exploitations as a sort of depredation. In a manner he brushed the impertinent accusers aside, assuring the general public that the novelist always meant, at his leisure, and in his own way, duly to ticket the flies preserved in his amber.

## I

When I read this haughty vindication, I thought at first that if the case were mine I would rather have several deadly enemies than such a friend as that; but since, I have not been so sure. I have asked myself upon a careful review of the matter whether plagiarism may not be frankly avowed, as in nowise dishonest, and I wish some abler casuist would take the affair into consideration and make it clear for me. If we are to suppose that offences against society disgrace the offender, and that public dishonor argues the fact of some such offence, then apparently plagiarism is not such an offence; for in even very flagrant cases it does not disgrace. The dictionary, indeed, defines it as "the crime of literary theft"; but as no penalty attaches to it, and no lasting shame, it is hard to believe it either a crime or a theft; and the offence, if it is an offence (one has to call it something, and I hope the word is not harsh), is some such harmless infraction of the moral law as white-lying.

The much-perverted saying of Molière, that he took his own where he found it, is perhaps in the consciousness of those who appropriate the things other people have rushed in with before them. But really they seem to need neither excuse nor defence with the impartial public if they are caught in the act of reclaiming their property or despoiling the rash intruder upon their premises. The novelist in question is by no means the only recent example, and is by no means a flagrant example. While the ratification of the treaty with Spain was pending before the Senate of the United States, a member of that body opposed it in a speech almost word for word the same as a sermon delivered in New York City only a few days earlier and published broadcast. He was promptly exposed by the parallel-column system; but I have never heard that his standing was affected or his usefulness impaired by the offence proven against him. A few years ago an eminent divine in one of our cities preached as his own the sermon of a brother divine, no longer living; he, too, was detected and promptly exposed by the parallel-column system, but nothing whatever happened from the exposure. Every one must recall like instances,

more or less remote. I remember one within my youth-
fuller knowledge of a journalist who used as his own
all the denunciatory passages of Macaulay's article
on Barrère, and applied them with changes of name
to the character and conduct of a local politician whom
he felt it his duty to devote to infamy. He was caught
in the fact, and by means of the parallel column pil-
loried before the community. But the community did
not mind it a bit, and the journalist did not either.
He prospered on amid those who all knew what he
had done, and when he removed to another city it
was to a larger one, and to a position of more com-
manding influence, from which he was long conspicuous in helping shape the destinies of the nation.

So far as any effect from these exposures was concerned, they were as harmless as those exposures of
fraudulent spiritistic mediums which from time to
time are supposed to shake the spiritistic superstition
to its foundations. They really do nothing of the
kind; the table-tippings, rappings, materializations,
and levitations keep on as before; and I do not believe
that the exposure of the novelist who has been the
latest victim of the parallel column will injure him a
jot in the hearts or heads of his readers.


II


I am very glad of it, being a disbeliever in punish-
ments of all sorts. I am always glad to have sinners
get off, for I like to get off from my own sins; and I have
a bad moment from my sense of them whenever another's have found him out. But as yet I have not
convinced myself that the sort of thing we have been
considering is a sin at all, for it seems to deprave no
more than it dishonors; or that it is what the dictionary

(with very unnecessary brutality) calls a "crime" and a "theft." If it is either, it is differently conditioned, if not differently natured, from all other crimes and thefts. These may be more or less artfully and hopefully concealed, but plagiarism carries inevitable detection with it. If you take a man's hat or coat out of his hall, you may pawn it before the police overtake you; if you take his horse out of his stable, you may ride it away beyond pursuit and sell it; if you take his purse out of his pocket, you may pass it to a pal in the crowd, and easily prove your innocence. But if you take his sermon, or his essay, or even his apposite reflection, you cannot escape discovery. The world is full of idle people reading books, and they are only too glad to act as detectives; they please their miserable vanity by showing their alertness, and are proud to bear witness against you in the court of parallel columns. You have no safety in the obscurity of the author from whom you take your own; there is always that most terrible reader, the reader of one book, who knows that very author, and will the more indecently hasten to bring you to the bar because he knows no other, and wishes to display his erudition. A man may escape for centuries and yet be found out. In the notorious case of William Shakespeare the offender seemed finally secure of his prey; and yet one poor lady, who ended in a lunatic asylum, was able to detect him at last, and to restore the goods to their rightful owner, Sir Francis Bacon.

In spite, however, of this almost absolute certainty of exposure, plagiarism goes on as it has always gone on; and there is no probability that it will cease as long as there are novelists, senators, divines, and journalists hard pressed for ideas which they happen not to have in mind at the time, and which they see going to waste elsewhere. Now and then it takes a more vio-

lent form and becomes a real mania, as when the plagi-
arist openly claims and urges his right to a well-known
piece of literary property. When Mr. William Allen
Butler's famous poem of "Nothing to Wear" achieved
its extraordinary popularity, a young girl declared and
apparently quite believed that she had written it and
lost the MS. in an omnibus. All her friends apparently believed so, too; and the friends of the different
gentlemen and ladies who claimed the authorship
of "Beautiful Snow" and "Rock Me to Sleep" were
ready to support them by affidavit against the real
authors of those pretty worthless pieces.

From all these facts it must appear to the philosophic
reader that plagiarism is not the simple "crime" or
"theft" that the lexicographers would have us believe.
It argues a strange and peculiar courage on the part
of those who commit it or indulge it, since they are sure
of having it brought home to them, for they seem to
dread the exposure, though it involves no punishment
outside of themselves. Why do they do it, or, having
done it, why do they mind it, since the public does not?
Their temerity and their timidity are things almost
irreconcilable, and the whole position leaves one quite
puzzled as to what one would do if one's own pla-
giarisms were found out. But this is a mere question
of conduct, and of infinitely less interest than that of
the nature or essence of the thing itself.

## PURITANISM IN AMERICAN FICTION

THE question whether the fiction which gives a vivid impression of reality does truly represent the conditions studied in it, is one of those inquiries to which there is no very final answer. The most baffling fact of such fiction is that its truths are self-evident; and if you go about to prove them you are in some danger of shaking the convictions of those whom they have persuaded. It will not do to affirm anything wholesale concerning them; a hundred examples to the contrary present themselves if you know the ground, and you are left in doubt of the verity which you cannot gainsay. The most that you can do is to appeal to your own consciousness, and that is not proof to anybody else. Perhaps the best test in this difficult matter is the quality of the art which created the picture. Is it clear, simple, unaffected? Is it true to human experience generally? If it is so, then it cannot well be false to the special human experience it deals with.

I

Not long ago I heard of something which amusingly, which pathetically, illustrated the sense of reality imparted by the work of one of our writers, whose art is of the kind I mean. A lady was driving with a young girl of the lighter-minded civilization of New York through one of those little towns of the North

Shore in Massachusetts, where the small, wooden houses cling to the edges of the shallow bay, and the schooners slip in and out on the hidden channels of the salt meadows as if they were blown about through the tall grass. She tried to make her feel the shy charm of the place, that almost subjective beauty, which those to the manner born are so keenly aware of in old-fashioned New England villages; but she found that the girl was not only not looking at the sad-colored cottages, with their weather - worn shingle walls, their grassy door-yards lit by patches of summer bloom, and their shutterless windows with their close-drawn shades, but she was resolutely averting her eyes from them, and staring straightforward until she should be out of sight of them altogether. She said that they were terrible, and she knew that in each of them was one of those dreary old women, or disappointed girls, or unhappy wives, or bereaved mothers, she had read of in Miss Wilkins's stories.

She had been too little sensible of the humor which forms the relief of these stories, as it forms the relief of the bare, duteous, conscientious, deeply individualized lives portrayed in them; and no doubt this cannot make its full appeal to the heart of youth aching for their stoical sorrows. Without being so very young, I, too, have found the humor hardly enough at times, and if one has not the habit of experiencing support in tragedy itself, one gets through a remote New England village, at nightfall, say, rather limp than otherwise, and in quite the mood that Miss Wilkins's bleaker studies leave one in. At mid-day, or in the bright sunshine of the morning, it is quite possible to fling off the melancholy which breathes the same note in the fact and the fiction; and I have even had some pleasure at such times in identifying this or that one-story cottage with its lean-to as a Mary

Wilkins house and in placing one of her muted dramas in it. One cannot know the people of such places without recognizing her types in them, and one cannot know New England without owning the fidelity of her stories to New England character, though, as I have already suggested, quite another sort of stories could be written which should as faithfully represent other phases of New England village life.

To the alien inquirer, however, I should be by no means confident that their truth would evince itself, for the reason that human nature is seldom on show anywhere. I am perfectly certain of the truth of Tolstoy and Tourguénief to Russian life, yet I should not be surprised if I went through Russia and met none of their people. I should be rather more surprised if I went through Italy and met none of Verga's or Fogazzaro's, but that would be because I already knew Italy a little. In fact, I suspect that the last delight of truth in any art comes only to the connoisseur who is as well acquainted with the subject as the artist himself. One must not be too severe in challenging the truth of an author to life; and one must bring a great deal of sympathy and a great deal of patience to the scrutiny. Types are very backward and shrinking things, after all; character is of such a mimosan sensibility that if you seize it too abruptly its leaves are apt to shut and hide all that is distinctive in it; so that it is not without some risk to an author's reputation for honesty that he gives his readers the impression of his truth.

II

The difficulty with characters in fiction is that the reader there finds them dramatized; not only their actions, but also their emotions are dramatized; and

the very same sort of persons when one meets them in
real life are recreantly undramatic. One might go
through a New England village and see Mary Wilkins
houses and Mary Wilkins people, and yet not witness
a scene nor hear a word such as one finds in her tales.
It is only too probable that the inhabitants one met
would say nothing quaint or humorous, or betray at
all the nature that she reveals in them; and yet I should
not question her revelation on that account. The life
of New England, such as Miss Wilkins deals with, and
Miss Sarah O. Jewett, and Miss Alice Brown, is not on
the surface, or not visibly so, except to the accustomed
eye. It is Puritanism scarcely animated at all by the
Puritanic theology. One must not be very positive
in such things, and I may be too bold in venturing to
say that while the belief of some New-Englanders approaches this theology the belief of most is now far
from it; and yet its penetrating individualism so deeply influenced the New England character that Puritanism survives in the moral and mental make of the
people almost in its early strength. Conduct and
manner conform to a dead religious ideal; the wish
to be sincere, the wish to be just, the wish to be right-
eous are before the wish to be kind, merciful, humble.
A people are not a chosen people for half a dozen generations without acquiring a spiritual pride that remains with them long after they cease to believe themselves chosen. They are often stiffened in the neck
and they are often hardened in the heart by it, to the
point of making them angular and cold; but they are
of an inveterate responsibility to a power higher than
themselves, and they are strengthened for any fate.
They are what we see in the stories which, perhaps,
hold the first place in American fiction.

As a matter of fact, the religion of New England is
not now so Puritanical as that of many parts of the

South and West, and yet the inherited Puritanism stamps the New England manner, and differences it from the manner of the straightest sects elsewhere. There was, however, always a revolt against Puritanism when Puritanism was severest and securest; this resulted in types of shiftlessness if not wickedness, which have not yet been duly studied, and which would make the fortune of some novelist who cared to do a fresh thing. There is also a sentimentality, or pseudo-emotionality (I have not the right phrase for it), which awaits full recognition in fiction. This efflorescence from the dust of systems and creeds, carried into natures left vacant by the ancestral doctrine, has scarcely been noticed by the painters of New England manners. It is often a last state of Unitarianism, which prevailed in the larger towns and cities when the Calvinistic theology ceased to be dominant, and it is often an effect of the spiritualism so common in New England, and, in fact, everywhere in America. Then, there is a wide-spread love of literature in the country towns and villages which has in great measure replaced the old interest in dogma, and which forms with us an author's closest appreciation, if not his best. But as yet little hint of all this has got into the short stories, and still less of that larger intellectual life of New England, or that exalted beauty of character which tempts one to say that Puritanism was a blessing if it made the New-Englanders what they are; though one can always be glad not to have lived among them in the disciplinary period. Boston, the capital of that New England nation which is fast losing itself in the American nation, is no longer of its old literary primacy, and yet most of our right thinking, our high thinking, still begins there, and qualifies the thinking of the country at large. The good causes, the generous causes, are first befriended there, and in a wholesome sort the New England culture, as well as the New England conscience, has imparted itself to the American people.

Even the power of writing short stories, which we suppose ourselves to have in such excellent degree, has spread from New England. That is, indeed, the home of the American short story, and it has there been brought to such perfection in the work of Miss Wilkins, of Miss Jewett, of Miss Brown, and of that most faithful, forgotten painter of manners, Mrs. Rose Terry Cook, that it presents upon the whole a truthful picture of New England village life in some of its more obvious phases. I say obvious because I must, but I have already said that this is a life which is very little obvious; and I should not blame any one who brought the portrait to the test of reality, and found it exaggerated, overdrawn, and unnatural, though I should be perfectly sure that such a critic was wrong.

# THE WHAT AND THE HOW IN ART

ONE of the things always enforcing itself upon
the consciousness of the artist in any sort is
the fact that those whom artists work for rarely care
for their work artistically. They care for it morally,
personally, partially. I suspect that criticism itself
has rather a muddled preference for the what over the
how, and that it is always haunted by a philistine
question of the material when it should, æsthetically
speaking, be concerned solely with the form.

## I

The other night at the theatre I was witness of a
curious and amusing illustration of my point. They
were playing a most soul-filling melodrama, of the
sort which gives you assurance from the very first
that there will be no trouble in the end, but everything
will come out just as it should, no matter what obstacles oppose themselves in the course of the action.
An over-ruling Providence, long accustomed to the
exigencies of the stage, could not fail to intervene at
the critical moment in behalf of innocence and virtue,
and the spectator never had the least occasion for
anxiety. Not unnaturally there was a black-hearted
villain in the piece; so very black-hearted that he
seemed not to have a single good impulse from first
to last. Yet he was, in the keeping of the stage Providence, as harmless as a blank cartridge, in spite

of his deadly aims. He accomplished no more mis-
chief, in fact, than if all his intents had been of the
best; except for the satisfaction afforded by the edi-
fying spectacle of his defeat and shame, he need not
have been in the play at all; and one might almost
have felt sorry for him, he was so continually baffled.
But this was not enough for the audience, or for that
part of it which filled the gallery to the roof. Perhaps
he was such an uncommonly black-hearted villain,
so very, very cold-blooded in his wickedness that the
justice unsparingly dealt out to him by the dramatist
could not suffice. At any rate, the gallery took such
a vivid interest in his punishment that it had out
the actor who impersonated the wretch between all
the acts, and hissed him throughout his deliberate
passage across the stage before the curtain. The
hisses were not at all for the actor, but altogether for
the character. The performance was fairly good,
quite as good as the performance of any virtuous part
in the piece, and easily up to the level of other villan-
ous performances (I never find much nature in them,
perhaps because there is not much nature in villany
itself; that is, villany pure and simple); but the mere
conception of the wickedness this bad man had attempted was too much for an audience of the average popular goodness. It was only after he had taken
poison, and fallen dead before their eyes, that the
spectators forbore to visit him with a lively proof of
their abhorrence; apparently they did not care to "give
him a realizing sense that there was a punishment
after death," as the man in Lincoln's story did with
the dead dog.

II

The whole affair was very amusing at first, but it
has since put me upon thinking (I like to be put upon

thinking; the eighteenth-century essayists were) that the attitude of the audience towards this deplorable reprobate is really the attitude of most readers of books, lookers at pictures and statues, listeners to music, and so on through the whole list of the arts. It is absolutely different from the artist's attitude, from the connoisseur's attitude; it is quite irreconcilable with their attitude, and yet I wonder if in the end it is not what the artist works for. Art is not produced for artists, or even for connoisseurs; it is produced for the general, who can never view it otherwise than morally, personally, partially, from their associations and preconceptions.

Whether the effect with the general is what the artist works for or not, he does not succeed without it. Their brute liking or misliking is the final test; it is universal suffrage that elects, after all. Only, in some cases of this sort the polls do not close at four o'clock on the first Tuesday after the first Monday of November, but remain open forever, and the voting goes on. Still, even the first day's canvass is important, or at least significant. It will not do for the artist to electioneer, but if he is beaten, he ought to ponder the causes of his defeat, and question how he has failed to touch the chord of universal interest. He is in the world to make beauty and truth evident to his fellow-men, who are as a rule incredibly stupid and ignorant of both, but whose judgment he must nevertheless not despise. If he can make something that they will cheer, or something that they will hiss, he may not have done any great thing, but if he has made something that they will neither cheer nor hiss, he may well have his misgivings, no matter how well, how finely, how truly he has done the thing.

This is very humiliating, but a tacit snub to one's artist-pride such as one gets from public silence is

not a bad thing for one. Not long ago I was talking
about pictures with a painter, a very great painter,
to my thinking; one whose pieces give me the same
feeling I have from reading poetry; and I was ex-
cusing myself to him with respect to art, and perhaps
putting on a little more modesty than I felt. I said
that I could enjoy pictures only on the literary side,
and could get no answer from my soul to those ex-
cellences of handling and execution which seemed
chiefly to interest painters. He replied that it was a
confession of weakness in a painter if he appealed
merely or mainly to technical knowledge in the spectator; that he narrowed his field and dwarfed his work
by it; and that if he painted for painters merely, or
for the connoisseurs of painting, he was denying his
office, which was to say something clear and appreciable to all sorts of men in the terms of art. He even
insisted that a picture ought to tell a story.

The difficulty in humbling one's self to this view of
art is in the ease with which one may please the general by art which is no art. Neither the play nor
the playing that I saw at the theatre when the actor
was hissed for the wickedness of the villain he was
personating, was at all fine; and yet I perceived, on
reflection, that they had achieved a supreme effect. If
I may be so confidential, I will say that I should be
very sorry to have written that piece; yet I should be
very proud if, on the level I chose and with the quality
I cared for, I could invent a villain that the populace
would have out and hiss for his surpassing wickedness. In other words, I think it a thousand pities
whenever an artist gets so far away from the general,
so far within himself or a little circle of amateurs, that
his highest and best work awakens no response in
the multitude. I am afraid this is rather the danger
of the arts among us, and how to escape it is not so

very plain. It makes one sick and sorry often to see how cheaply the applause of the common people is won. It is not an infallible test of merit, but if it is wanting to any performance, we may be pretty sure it is not the greatest performance.

### III

The paradox lies in wait here, as in most other human affairs, to confound us, and we try to baffle it, in this way and in that. We talk, for instance, of poetry for poets, and we fondly imagine that this is different from talking of cookery for cooks. Poetry is not made for poets; they have enough poetry of their own, but it is made for people who are not poets. If it does not please these, it may still be poetry, but it is poetry which has failed of its truest office. It is none the less its truest office because some very wretched verse seems often to do it.

The logic of such a fact is not that the poet should try to achieve this truest office of his art by means of doggerel, but that he should study how and where and why the beauty and the truth he has made manifest are wanting in universal interest, in human appeal. Leaving the drama out of the question, and the theatre which seems now to be seeking only the favor of the dull rich, I believe that there never was a time or a race more open to the impressions of beauty and of truth than ours. The artist who feels their divine charm, and longs to impart it, has now and here a chance to impart it more widely than ever artist had in the world before. Of course, the means of reaching the widest range of humanity are the simple and the elementary, but there is no telling when the complex and the recondite may not universally please.

The art is to make them plain to every one, for every one has them in him. Lowell used to say that Shakespeare was subtle, but in letters a foot high.

The painter, sculptor, or author who pleases the polite only has a success to be proud of as far as it goes, and to be ashamed of that it goes no further. He need not shrink from giving pleasure to the vulgar because bad art pleases them. It is part of his reason for being that he should please them, too; and if he does not it is a proof that he is wanting in force, however much he abounds in fineness. Who would not wish his picture to draw a crowd about it? Who would not wish his novel to sell five hundred thousand copies, for reasons besides the sordid love of gain which I am told governs novelists? One should not really wish it any the less because chromos and historical romances are popular.

Sometime, I believe, the artist and his public will draw nearer together in a mutual understanding, though perhaps not in our present conditions. I put that understanding off till the good time when life shall be more than living, more even than the question of getting a living; but in the mean time I think that the artist might very well study the springs of feeling in others; and if I were a dramatist I think I should quite humbly go to that play where they hiss the villain for his villany, and inquire how his wickedness had been made so appreciable, so vital, so personal. Not being a dramatist, I still cannot indulge the greatest contempt of that play and its public.

19

NO thornier theme could well be suggested than I was once invited to consider by an Englishman who wished to know how far American politicians were scholars, and how far American authors took part in politics. In my mind I first revolted from the inquiry, and then I cast about, in the fascination it began to have for me, to see how I might handle it and prick myself least. In a sort, which it would take too long to set forth, politics are very intimate matters with us, and if one were to deal quite frankly with the politics of a contemporary author, one might accuse one's self of an unwarrantable personality. So, in what I shall have to say in answer to the question asked me, I shall seek above all things not to be quite frank.

I

My uncandor need not be so jealously guarded in speaking of authors no longer living. Not to go too far back among these, it is perfectly safe to say that when the slavery question began to divide all kinds of men among us, Lowell, Longfellow, Whittier, Curtis, Emerson, and Bryant more or less promptly and openly took sides against slavery. Holmes was very much later in doing so, but he made up for his long delay by his final strenuousness; as for Hawthorne, he was, perhaps, too essentially a spectator of life to be

classed with either party, though his associations, if not
his sympathies, were with the Northern men who had
Southern principles until the civil war came.  After
the war, when our political questions ceased to be
moral and emotional and became economic and sociological, literary men found their standing with greater
difficulty.  They remained mostly Republicans, because the Republicans were the anti-slavery party,
and were still waging war against slavery in their
nerves.

I should say that they also continued very largely
the emotional tradition in politics, and it is doubtful
if in the nature of things the politics of literary men
can ever be otherwise than emotional.  In fact, though
the questions may no longer be so, the politics of vastly the greater number of Americans are so.  Nothing
else would account for the fact that during the last
ten or fifteen years men have remained Republicans
and remained Democrats upon no tangible issues except of office, which could practically concern only a
few hundreds or thousands out of every million voters.
Party fealty is praised as a virtue, and disloyalty to
party is treated as a species of incivism next in wickedness to treason.  If any one were to ask me why then
American authors were not active in American politics,
as they once were, I should feel a certain diffidence in
replying that the question of other people's accession
to office was, however emotional, unimportant to them
as compared with literary questions.  I should have
the more diffidence because it might be retorted that
literary men were too unpractical for politics when
they did not deal with moral issues.

Such a retort would be rather mild and civil, as
things go, and might even be regarded as compliment-
ary.  It is not our custom to be tender with any one
who doubts if any actuality is right, or might not be

bettered, especially in public affairs. We are apt to call such a one out of his name and to punish him for opinions he has never held. This may be a better reason than either given why authors do not take part in politics with us. They are a thin-skinned race, fastidious often, and always averse to hard knocks; they are rather modest, too, and distrust their fitness to lead, when they have quite a firm faith in their convictions. They hesitate to urge these in the face of practical politicians, who have a confidence in their ability to settle all affairs of State not surpassed even by that of business men in dealing with economic questions.

I think it is a pity that our authors do not go into politics at least for the sake of the material it would yield them; but really they do not. Our politics are often vulgar, but they are very picturesque; yet, so far, our fiction has shunned them even more decidedly than it has shunned our good society—which is not picturesque or apparently anything but a tiresome adaptation of the sort of drama that goes on abroad under the same name. In nearly the degree that our authors have dealt with our politics as material, they have given the practical politicians only too much reason to doubt their insight and their capacity to understand the mere machinery, the simplest motives, of political life.

II

There are exceptions, of course, and if my promise of reticence did not withhold me I might name some striking ones. Privately and unprofessionally, I think our authors take as vivid an interest in public affairs as any other class of our citizens, and I should be sorry to think that they took a less intelligent interest. Now and then, but only very rarely, one of them speaks out, and usually on the unpopular side. In this event he is spared none of the penalties with which we like to visit difference of opinion; rather they are accumulated on him.

Such things are not serious, and they are such as no serious man need shrink from, but they have a bearing upon what I am trying to explain, and in a certain measure they account for a certain attitude in our literary men. No one likes to have stones, not to say mud, thrown at him, though they are not meant to hurt him badly and may be partly thrown in joke. But it is pretty certain that if a man not in politics takes them seriously, he will have more or less mud, not to say stones, thrown at him. He might burlesque or caricature them, or misrepresent them, with safety; but if he spoke of public questions with heart and conscience, he could not do it with impunity, unless he were authorized to do so by some practical relation to them. I do not mean that then he would escape; but in this country, where there were once supposed to be no classes, people are more strictly classified than in any other. Business to the business man, law to the lawyer, medicine to the physician, politics to the politician, and letters to the literary man; that is the rule. One is not expected to transcend his function, and commonly one does not. We keep each to his last, as if there were not human interests, civic interests, which had a higher claim than the last upon our thinking and feeling. The tendency has grown upon us severally and collectively through the long persistence of our prosperity; if public affairs were going ill, private affairs were going so well that we did not mind the others; and we Americans are, I think, meridional in our improvidence. We are so essentially of to-day that we behave as if to-morrow no more concerned us than yesterday. We have taught ourselves to believe that it will all come out right in the end so long that we have come to act upon our belief; we are optimistic fatalists.

### III

The turn which our politics have taken towards economics, if I may so phrase the rise of the questions of labor and capital, has not largely attracted literary men. It is doubtful whether Edward Bellamy himself, whose fancy of better conditions has become the abiding faith of vast numbers of Americans, supposed that he was entering the field of practical politics, or dreamed of influencing elections by his hopes of economic equality. But he virtually founded the Populist party, which, as the vital principle of the Democratic party, came so near electing its candidate for the Presidency some years ago; and he is to be named first among our authors who have dealt with politics on their more human side since the days of the old anti-slavery agitation. Without too great disregard of the reticence concerning the living which I promised myself, I may mention Dr. Edward Everett Hale and Colonel Thomas Wentworth Higginson as prominent authors who encouraged the Nationalist movement eventuating in Populism, though they were never Populists. It may be interesting to note that Dr. Hale and Colonel Higginson, who later came together in their sociological sympathies, were divided by the schism of 1884, when the first remained with the Republicans and the last went off to the Democrats. More remotely, Colonel Higginson was anti-slavery almost to the point of Abolitionism, and he led a negro regiment in the war. Dr. Hale was of those who were less radically opposed to slavery before the war, but hardly so after it came. Since the war a sort of refluence of the old anti-slavery politics carried from his moorings in Southern tradition Mr. George W. Cable, who, against the white sentiment of his section, sided with the former slaves, and would, if the indignant renunciation of his fellow-Southerners could avail, have consequently ceased to be the first of Southern authors, though he would still have continued the author of at least one of the greatest American novels.

If I must burn my ships behind me in alleging these modern instances, as I seem really to be doing, I may mention Mr. R. W. Gilder, the poet, as an author who has taken part in the politics of municipal reform. Mr. Hamlin Garland has been known from the first as a zealous George man, or single-taxer. Mr. John Hay, Mr. Theodore Roosevelt, and Mr. Henry Cabot Lodge are Republican politicians, as well as recognized literary men. Mr. Joel Chandler Harris, when not writing *Uncle Remus*, writes political articles in a leading Southern journal. Mark Twain is a leading anti-imperialist.

## IV

I am not sure whether I have made out a case for our authors or against them; perhaps I have not done so badly; but I have certainly not tried to be exhaustive; the exhaustion is so apt to extend from the subject to the reader, and I wish to leave him in a condition to judge for himself whether American literary men take part in American politics or not. I think they bear their share, in the quieter sort of way which we hope (it may be too fondly) is the American way. They are none of them politicians in the Latin sort. Few, if any, of our statesmen have come forward with small volumes of verse in their hands as they used to do in Spain; none of our poets or historians have been chosen

Presidents of the republic as has happened to their French *confrères;* no great novelist of ours has been exiled as Victor Hugo was, or atrociously mishandled as Zola has been, though I have no doubt that if, for instance, one had once said the Spanish war wrong he would be pretty generally *conspué.* They have none of them reached the heights of political power, as several English authors have done; but they have often been ambassadors, ministers, and consuls, though they may not often have been appointed for political reasons. I fancy they discharge their duties in voting rather faithfully, though they do not often take part in caucuses or conventions.

As for the other half of the question—how far American politicians are scholars—one's first impulse would be to say that they never were so. But I have always had an heretical belief that there *were* snakes in Ireland; and it may be some such disposition to question authority that keeps me from yielding to this impulse. The law of demand and supply alone ought to have settled the question in favor of the presence of the scholar in our politics, there has been such a cry for him among us for almost a generation past. Perhaps the response has not been very direct, but I imagine that our politicians have never been quite so destitute of scholarship as they would sometimes make appear. I do not think so many of them now write a good style, or speak a good style, as the politicians of forty, or fifty, or sixty years ago; but this may be merely part of the impression of the general worsening of things, familiar after middle life to every one's experience, from the beginning of recorded time. If something not so literary is meant by scholarship, if a study of finance, of economics, of international affairs is in question, it seems to go on rather more to their own satisfaction than that of their critics. But without

being always very proud of the result, and without
professing to know the facts very profoundly, one
may still suspect that under an outside by no means
academic there is a process of thinking in our statesmen which is not so loose, not so unscientific, and not
even so unscholarly as it might be supposed. It is
not the effect of specific training, and yet it is the effect
of training. I do not find that the matters dealt with
are anywhere in the world intrusted to experts; and
in this sense scholarship has not been called to the aid
of our legislation or administration; but still I should
not like to say that none of our politicians were scholars.
That would be offensive, and it might not be true. In
fact, I can think of several whom I should be tempted
to call scholars if I were not just here recalled to a sense
of my purpose not to deal quite frankly with this inquiry.

## STORAGE

IT has been the belief of certain kindly philosophers that if the one half of mankind knew how the other half lived, the two halves might be brought together in a family affection not now so observable in human relations. Probably if this knowledge were perfect, there would still be things to bar the perfect brotherhood; and yet the knowledge itself is so interesting, if not so salutary as it has been imagined, that one can hardly refuse to impart it if one has it, and can reasonably hope, in the advantage of the ignorant, to find one's excuse with the better informed.

I

City and country are still so widely apart in every civilization that one can safely count upon a reciprocal strangeness in many every-day things. For instance, in the country, when people break up house-keeping, they sell their household goods and gods, as they did in cities fifty or a hundred years ago; but now in cities they simply store them; and vast warehouses in all the principal towns have been devoted to their storage. The warehouses are of all types, from dusty lofts over stores, and ammoniacal lofts over stables, to buildings offering acres of space, and carefully planned for the purpose. They are more or less fire-proof, slow-burning, or briskly combustible, like the dwellings they have devastated. But the modern tendency is to a type where flames do not destroy, nor moth corrupt,

nor thieves break through and steal. Such a warehouse is a city in itself, laid out in streets and avenues,
with the private tenements on either hand duly num-
bered, and accessible only to the tenants or their order.
The aisles are concreted, the doors are iron, and the
roofs are ceiled with iron; the whole place is heated by
steam and lighted by electricity. Behind the iron
doors, which in the New York warehouses must number hundreds of thousands, and throughout all our
other cities, millions, the furniture of a myriad house-
holds is stored—the effects of people who have gone
to Europe, or broken up house-keeping provisionally
or definitively, or have died, or been divorced. They
are the dead bones of homes, or their ghosts, or their
yet living bodies held in hypnotic trances, destined
again in some future time to animate some house or
flat anew. In certain cases the spell lasts for many
years, in others for a few, and in others yet it prolongs
itself indefinitely.

I may mention the case of one owner whom I saw
visiting the warehouse to take out the household stuff
that had lain there a long fifteen years. He had been
all that while in Europe, expecting any day to come
home and begin life again in his own land. That
dream had passed, and now he was taking his stuff
out of storage and shipping it to Italy. I did not envy
him his feelings as the parts of his long-dead past rose
round him in formless resurrection. It was not that
they were all broken or defaced. On the contrary,
they were in a state of preservation far more heart-
breaking than any decay. In well-managed storage
warehouses the things are handled with scrupulous
care, and they are so packed into the appointed rooms
that if not disturbed they could suffer little harm in
fifteen or fifty years. The places are wonderfully
well kept, and if you will visit them, say in midwinter,

after the fall influx of furniture has all been hidden away behind the iron doors of the several cells, you shall find their far-branching corridors scrupulously swept and dusted, and shall walk up and down their concrete length with some such sense of secure finality as you would experience in pacing the aisle of your family vault.

That is what it comes to. One may feign that these storage warehouses are cities, but they are really cemeteries: sad columbaria on whose shelves are stowed exanimate things once so intimately of their owners' lives that it is with the sense of looking at pieces and bits of one's dead self that one revisits them. If one takes the fragments out to fit them to new circumstance, one finds them not only uncomfortable and incapable, but so volubly confidential of the associations in which they are steeped, that one wishes to hurry them back to their cell and lock it upon them forever. One feels then that the old way was far better, and that if the things had been auctioned off, and scattered up and down, as chance willed, to serve new uses with people who wanted them enough to pay for them even a tithe of their cost, it would have been wiser. Failing this, a fire seems the only thing for them, and their removal to the cheaper custody of a combustible or slow-burning warehouse the best recourse. Desperate people, aging husbands and wives, who have attempted the reconstruction of their homes with these

"Portions and parcels of the dreadful past"

have been known to wish for an earthquake, even, that would involve their belongings in an indiscriminate ruin.

## II

In fact, each new start in life should be made with material new to you, if comfort is to attend the enterprise. It is not only sorrowful but it is futile to store your possessions, if you hope to find the old happiness in taking them out and using them again. It is not that they will not go into place, after a fashion, and perform their old office, but that the pang they will inflict through the suggestion of the other places where they served their purpose in other years will be only the keener for the perfection with which they do it now. If they cannot be sold, and if no fire comes down from heaven to consume them, then they had better be stored with no thought of ever taking them out again.

That will be expensive, or it will be inexpensive, according to the sort of storage they are put into. The inexperienced in such matters may be surprised, and if they have hearts they may be grieved, to learn that the fire-proof storage of the furniture of the average house would equal the rent of a very comfortable domicile in a small town, or a farm by which a family's living can be earned, with a decent dwelling in which it can be sheltered. Yet the space required is not very great; three fair-sized rooms will hold everything; and there is sometimes a fierce satisfaction in seeing how closely the things that once stood largely about, and seemed to fill ample parlors and chambers, can be packed away. To be sure they are not in their familiar attitudes; they lie on their sides or backs, or stand upon their heads; between the legs of library or dining tables are stuffed all kinds of minor movables, with cushions, pillows, pictures, cunningly adjusted to the environment; and mattresses pad the walls, or interpose their soft bulk between pieces of furniture that would otherwise rend each other. Carpets sewn in cotton against moths, and rugs in long rolls; the piano hovering under its ample frame a whole brood of helpless little guitars, mandolins, and banjos, and supporting on its broad back a bulk of lighter cases to the fire-proof ceiling of the cell; paintings in boxes indistinguishable outwardly from their companioning mirrors; barrels of china and kitchen utensils, and all the what-not of householding and house-keeping contribute to the repletion.

There is a science observed in the arrangement of the various effects; against the rear wall and packed along the floor, and then in front of and on top of these, is built a superstructure of the things that may be first wanted, in case of removal, or oftenest wanted in some exigency of the homeless life of the owners, pending removal. The lightest and slightest articles float loosely about the door, or are interwoven in a kind of fabric just within, and curtaining the ponderous mass behind. The effect is not so artistic as the mortuary mosaics which the Roman Capuchins design with the bones of their dead brethren in the crypt of their church, but the warehousemen no doubt have their just pride in it, and feel an artistic pang in its provisional or final disturbance.

It had better never be disturbed, for it is disturbed only in some futile dream of returning to the past; and we never can return to the past on the old terms. It is well in all things to accept life implicitly, and when an end has come to treat it as the end, and not vainly mock it as a suspense of function. When the poor break up their homes, with no immediate hope of founding others, they must sell their belongings because they cannot afford to pay storage on them. The rich or richer store their household effects, and cheat themselves with the illusion that they are going some time to rehabilitate with them just such a home as they have dismantled. But the illusion probably deceives nobody so little as those who cherish the vain hope. As long as they cherish it, however

—and they must cherish it till their furniture or themselves fall to dust—they cannot begin life anew, as the poor do who have kept nothing of the sort to link them to the past. This is one of the disabilities of the prosperous, who will probably not be relieved of it till some means of storing the owner as well as the furniture is invented. In the immense range of modern ingenuity, this is perhaps not impossible. Why not, while we are still in life, some sweet oblivious antidote which shall drug us against memory, and after time shall elapse for the reconstruction of a new home in place of the old, shall repossess us of ourselves as unchanged as the things with which we shall again array it? Here is a pretty idea for some dreamer to spin into the filmy fabric of a romance, and I handsomely make a present of it to the first comer. If the dreamer is of the right quality he will know how to make the reader feel that with the universal longing to return to former conditions or circumstances it must always be a mistake to do so, and he will subtly insinuate the disappointment and discomfort of the stored personality in resuming its old relations. With that just mixture of the comic and pathetic which we desire in romance, he will teach convincingly that a stored personality is to be desired only if it is permanently stored, with the implication of a like finality in the storage of its belongings.

Save in some signal exception, a thing taken out of storage cannot be established in its former function without a sense of its comparative inadequacy. It stands in the old place, it serves the old use, and yet a new thing would be better; it would even in some subtle wise be more appropriate, if I may indulge so audacious a paradox; for the time is new, and so will be all the subconscious keeping in which our lives are mainly passed. We are supposed to have associa-

tions with the old things which render them precious,
but do not the associations rather render them painful?
If that is true of the inanimate things, how much truer
it is of those personalities which once environed and
furnished our lives! Take the article of old friends,
for instance: has it ever happened to the reader to
witness the encounter of old friends after the lapse of
years? Such a meeting is conventionally imagined
to be full of tender joy, a rapture that vents itself in
manly tears, perhaps, and certainly in womanly tears.
But really is it any such emotion? Honestly is not
it a cruel embarrassment, which all the hypocritical
pretences cannot hide? The old friends smile and
laugh, and babble incoherently at one another, but
are they genuinely glad? Is not each wishing the
other at that end of the earth from which he came?
Have they any use for each other such as people of
unbroken associations have?

I have lately been privy to the reunion of two old
comrades who are bound together more closely than
most men in a community of interests, occupations,
and ideals. During a long separation they had kept
account of each other's opinions as well as experiences;
they had exchanged letters, from time to time, in which
they opened their minds fully to each other, and found
themselves constantly in accord. When they met
they made a great shouting, and each pretended that
he found the other just what he used to be. They
talked a long, long time, fighting the invisible enemy
which they felt between them. The enemy was habit,
the habit of other minds and hearts, the daily use of
persons and things which in their separation they had
not had in common. When the old friends parted
they promised to meet every day, and now, since their
lines had been cast in the same places again, to repair
the ravage of the envious years, and become again

to each other all that they had ever been. But though they live in the same town, and often dine at the same table, and belong to the same club, yet they have not grown together again. They have grown more and more apart, and are uneasy in each other's presence, tacitly self-reproachful for the same effect which neither of them could avert or repair. They had been respectively in storage, and each, in taking the other out, has experienced in him the unfitness which grows upon the things put away for a time and reinstated in a former function.

### III

I have not touched upon these facts of life, without the purpose of finding some way out of the coil. There seems none better than the counsel of keeping one's face set well forward, and one's eyes fixed steadfastly upon the future. This is the hint we will get from nature if we will heed her, and note how she never recurs, never stores or takes out of storage. Fancy rehabilitating one's first love: how nature would mock at that! We cannot go back and be the men and women we were, any more than we can go back and be children. As we grow older, each year's change in us is more chasmal and complete. There is no elixir whose magic will recover us to ourselves as we were last year; but perhaps we shall return to ourselves more and more in the times, or the eternity, to come. Some instinct or inspiration implies the promise of this, but only on condition that we shall not cling to the life that has been ours, and hoard its mummified image in our hearts. We must not seek to store ourselves, but must part with what we were for the use and behoof of others, as the poor part with their worldly gear when they move from one place to another. It is a curious and significant property of our outworn characteristics that, like our old furniture, they will serve admirably in the life of some other, and that this other can profitably make them his when we can no longer keep them ours, or ever hope to resume them. They not only go down to successive generations, but they spread beyond our lineages, and serve the turn of those whom we never knew to be within the circle of our influence.

Civilization imparts itself by some such means, and the lower classes are clothed in the cast conduct of the upper, which if it had been stored would have left the inferiors rude and barbarous. We have only to think how socially naked most of us would be if we had not had the beautiful manners of our exclusive society to put on at each change of fashion when it dropped them.

All earthly and material things should be worn out with use, and not preserved against decay by any unnatural artifice. Even when broken and disabled from overuse they have a kind of respectability which must commend itself to the observer, and which partakes of the pensive grace of ruin. An old table with one leg gone, and slowly lapsing to decay in the woodshed, is the emblem of a fitter order than the same table, with all its legs intact, stored with the rest of the furniture from a broken home. Spinning-wheels gathering dust in the garret of a house that is itself falling to pieces have a dignity that deserts them when they are dragged from their refuge, and furbished up with ribbons and a tuft of fresh tow, and made to serve the hollow occasions of bric-à-brac, as they were a few years ago. A pitcher broken at the fountain, or a battered kettle on a rubbish heap, is a venerable object, but not crockery and copper-ware stored in the possibility of future need. However carefully handed down from one generation to another, the old objects have a forlorn incongruity in their successive surroundings which appeals to the compassion rather than the veneration of the witness.

It was from a truth deeply mystical that Hawthorne declared against any sort of permanence in the dwellings of men, and held that each generation should newly house itself. He preferred the perishability of the wooden American house to the durability of the piles of brick or stone which in Europe affected him as with some moral miasm from the succession of sires and sons and grandsons that had died out of them. But even of such structures as these it is impressive how little the earth makes with the passage of time. Where once a great city of them stood, you shall find a few tottering walls, scarcely more mindful of the past than "the cellar and the well" which Holmes marked as the ultimate monuments, the last witnesses, to the existence of our more transitory habitations. It is the law of the patient sun that everything under it shall decay, and if by reason of some swift calamity, some fiery cataclysm, the perishable shall be overtaken by a fate that fixes it in unwasting arrest, it cannot be felt that the law has been set aside in the interest of men's happiness or cheerfulness. Neither Pompeii nor Herculaneum invites the gayety of the spectator, who as he walks their disinterred thoroughfares has the weird sense of taking a former civilization out of storage, and the ache of finding it wholly unadapted to the actual world. As far as his comfort is concerned, it had been far better that those cities had not been stored, but had fallen to the ruin that has overtaken all their contemporaries.

## IV

No, good friend, sir or madam, as the case may be, but most likely madam: if you are about to break

up your household for any indefinite period, and are not so poor that you need sell your things, be warned against putting them in storage, unless of the most briskly combustible type. Better, far better, give them away, and disperse them by that means to a continuous use that shall end in using them up; or if no one will take them, then hire a vacant lot, somewhere, and devote them to the flames. By that means you shall bear witness against a custom that insults the order of nature, and crowds the cities with the cemeteries of dead homes, where there is scarcely space for the living homes. Do not vainly fancy that you shall take your stuff out of storage and find it adapted to the ends that it served before it was put in. You will not be the same, or have the same needs or desires, when you take it out, and the new place which you shall hope to equip with it will receive it with cold reluctance, or openly refuse it, insisting upon forms and dimensions that render it ridiculous or impossible. The law is that nothing taken out of storage is the same as it was when put in, and this law, hieroglyphed in those rude *graffiti* apparently inscribed by accident in the process of removal, has only such exceptions as prove the rule.

The world to which it has returned is not the same, and that makes all the difference. Yet, truth and beauty do not change, however the moods and fashions change. The ideals remain, and these alone you can go back to, secure of finding them the same, to-day and to-morrow, that they were yesterday. This perhaps is because they have never been in storage, but in constant use, while the moods and fashions have been put away and taken out a thousand times. Most people have never had ideals, but only moods and fashions, but such people, least of all, are fitted to find in them that pleasure of the rococo which consoles the idealist when the old moods and fashions reappear.

# "FLOATING DOWN THE RIVER ON THE O-HI-O"

THERE was not much promise of pleasure in the sodden afternoon of a mid-March day at Pittsburg, where the smoke of a thousand foundry chimneys gave up trying to rise through the thick, soft air, and fell with the constant rain which it dyed its own black. But early memories stirred joyfully in the two travellers in whose consciousness I was making my tour, at sight of the familiar stern-wheel steamboat lying beside the wharf-boat at the foot of the dilapidated levee, and doing its best to represent the hundreds of steamboats that used to lie there in the old days. It had the help of three others in its generous effort, and the levee itself made a gallant pretence of being crowded with freight, and succeeded in displaying several saturated piles of barrels and agricultural implements on the irregular pavement whose wheel-worn stones, in long stretches, were sunken out of sight in their parent mud. The boats and the levee were jointly quite equal to the demand made upon them by the light-hearted youngsters of sixty-five and seventy, who were setting out on their journey in fulfilment of a long-cherished dream, and for whom much less freight and much fewer boats would have rehabilitated the past.

I

When they mounted the broad stairway, tidily strewn with straw to save it from the mud of careless boots, and entered the long saloon of the steamboat, the promise of their fancy was more than made good for them. From the clerk's office, where they eagerly paid their fare, the saloon stretched two hundred feet by thirty away to the stern, a cavernous splendor of white paint and gilding, starred with electric bulbs, and fenced at the stern with wide windows of painted glass. Midway between the great stove in the bow where the men were herded, and the great stove at the stern where the women kept themselves in the seclusion which the tradition of Western river travel still guards, after wellnigh a hundred years, they were given ample state-rooms, whose appointments so exactly duplicated those they remembered from far-off days that they could have believed themselves awakened from a dream of insubstantial time, with the events in which it had seemed to lapse, mere feints of experience. When they sat down at the supper-table and were served with the sort of belated steamboat dinner which it recalled as vividly, the kind, sooty faces and snowy aprons of those who served them were so quite those of other days that they decided all repasts since were mere Barmecide feasts, and made up for the long fraud practised upon them with the appetites of the year 1850.

## II

A rigider sincerity than shall be practised here might own that the table of the good steamboat *Avonek* left something to be desired, if tested by more sophisticated cuisines, but in the article of corn-bread it was of an inapproachable pre-eminence. This bread was made of the white corn which North knows not, nor the hapless East; and the buckwheat cakes at break-

"THE HILLS . . . THAT CHANGE WITH THE STEAMER'S COURSE"

fast were without blame, and there was a simple variety in the abundance which ought to have satisfied if it did not flatter the choice. The only thing that seemed strangely, that seemed sadly, anomalous in a land flowing with ham and bacon was that the *Avonek* had not imagined providing either for the guests, no one of whom could have had a religious scruple against them.

The thing, indeed, which was first and last conspicuous in the passengers, was their perfectly American race and character. At the start, when with an acceptable observance of Western steamboat tradition the *Avonek* left her wharf eight hours behind her appointed time, there were very few passengers; but they began to come aboard at the little towns of both shores as she swam southward and westward, till all the tables were so full that, in observance of another Western steamboat tradition, one did well to stand guard over his chair lest some other who liked it should seize it earlier. The passengers were of every age and condition, except perhaps the highest condition, and they seemed none the worse for being more like Americans of the middle of the last century than of the beginning of this. Their fashions were of an approximation to those of the present, but did not scrupulously study detail; their manners were those of simpler if not sincerer days.

The women kept to themselves at their end of the saloon, aloof from the study of any but their husbands or kindred, but the men were everywhere else about, and open to observation. They were not so open to conversation, for your mid-Westerner is not a facile, though not an unwilling, talker. They sat by their tall, cast-iron stove (of the oval pattern unvaried since the earliest stove of the region), and silently ruminated their tobacco and spat into the clustering cuspidors at their feet. They would always answer civilly if questioned, and oftenest intelligently, but they asked nothing in return, and they seemed to have none of that curiosity once known or imagined in them by Dickens and other averse aliens. They had mostly faces of resolute power, and such a looking of knowing exactly what they wanted as would not have promised well for any collectively or individually opposing them. If ever the sense of human equality has expressed itself in the human countenance it speaks unmistakably from American faces like theirs.

They were neither handsome nor unhandsome; but for a few striking exceptions, they had been impartially treated by nature; and where they were notably plain their look of force made up for their lack of beauty. They were notably handsomest in a tall young fellow of a lean face, absolute Greek in profile, amply thwarted with a branching mustache, and slender of figure, on whom his clothes, lustrous from much sitting down and leaning up, grew like the bark on a tree, and who moved slowly and gently about, and spoke with a low, kind voice. In his young comeliness he was like a god, as the gods were fancied in the elder world: a chewing and a spitting god, indeed, but divine in his passionless calm.

He was a serious divinity, and so were all the mid-Western human-beings about him. One heard no joking either of the dapper or cockney sort of cities, or the quaint graphic phrasing of Eastern country folk; and it may have been not far enough West for the true Western humor. At any rate, when they were not silent these men still were serious.

The women were apparently serious, too, and where they were associated with the men were, if they were not really subject, strictly abeyant, in the spectator's eye. The average of them was certainly not above the American woman's average in good looks, though one young mother of six children, well grown save for the baby in her arms, was of the type some masters loved to paint, with eyes set wide under low-arched brows. She had the placid dignity and the air of motherly goodness which goes fitly with such beauty, and the sight of her was such as to disperse many of the misgivings that beset the beholder who looketh upon the woman when she is New. As she seemed, so any man might wish to remember his mother seeming.

All these river folk, who came from the farms and villages along the stream, and never from the great towns or cities, were well mannered, if quiet manners are good; and though the men nearly all chewed tobacco and spat between meals, at the table they were of an exemplary behavior. The use of the fork appeared strange to them, and they handled it strenuously rather than agilely, yet they never used their knives .shovelwise, however they planted their forks like daggers in the steak: the steak deserved no gentler usage, indeed. They were usually young, and they were constantly changing, bent upon short journeys between the shore villages; they were mostly farm youth, apparently, though some were said to be going to find work at the great potteries up the river for wages fabulous to home-keeping experience.

One personality which greatly took the liking of one of our tourists was a Kentucky mountaineer who, after three years' exile in a West Virginia oil town, was gladly returning to the home for which he and all his brood—of large and little comely, red-haired boys and girls—had never ceased to pine. His eagerness to get back was more than touching; it was awing; for it was founded on a sort of mediæval patriotism that could own no excellence beyond the borders of

313

the natal region. He had prospered at high wages in his trade at that oil town, and his wife and children had managed a hired farm so well as to pay all the family expenses from it, but he was gladly leaving opportunity behind, that he might return to a land where, if you were passing a house at meal-time, they came out and made you come in and eat. "When you eat where I've been living you pay fifty cents," he explained. "And are you taking all your household stuff with you?" "Only the cook-stove. Well, I'll tell you: we made the other things ourselves; made them out of plank, and they were not worth moving." Here was the backwoods surviving into the day of Trusts; and yet we talk of a world drifted hopelessly far from the old ideals!

### III

The new ideals, the ideals of a pitiless industrialism, were sufficiently expressed along the busy shores, where the innumerable derricks of oil-wells silhouetted their gibbet shapes against the horizon, and the myriad chimneys of the foundries sent up the smoke of their torment into the quiet skies and flamed upon the forehead of the evening like baleful suns. But why should I be so violent of phrase against these guiltless means of millionairing? There must be iron and coal as well as wheat and corn in the world, and without their combination we cannot have bread. If the combination is in the form of a trust, such as has laid its giant clutch upon all those warring industries beside the Ohio and swept them into one great monopoly, why, it has still to show that it is worse than competition; that it is not, indeed, merely the first blind stirrings of the universal co-operation of which the

"IN THE SPRING . . . THE RIVER SCALES ITS BANKS"

dreamers of ideal commonwealths have always had the vision.

The derricks and the chimneys, when one saw them, seemed to have all the land to themselves; but this was an appearance only, terrifying in its strenuousness, but not, after all, the prevalent aspect. That was rather of farms, farms, and evermore farms, lying along the rich levels of the stream, and climbing as far up its beautiful hills as the plough could drive. In the spring and in the fall, when it is suddenly swollen by the earlier and the later rains, the river scales its banks and swims over those levels to the feet of those hills, and when it recedes it leaves the cornfields enriched for the crop that has never failed since the forests were first cut from the land. Other fertilizing the fields have never had any, but they teem as if the guano islands had been emptied into their laps. They feel themselves so rich that they part with great lengths and breadths of their soil to the river, which is not good for the river, and is not well for the fields; so that the farmers, whose ease learns slowly, are beginning more and more to fence their borders with the young willows which form a hedge in the shallow wash such a great part of the way up and down the Ohio. Elms and maples wade in among the willows, and in time the river will be denied the indigestion which it confesses in shoals and bars at low water, and in a difficulty of channel at all stages.

Meanwhile the fields flourish in spite of their unwise largesse to the stream, whose shores the comfortable farmsteads keep so constantly that they are never out of sight. Most commonly they are of brick, but sometimes of painted wood, and they are set on little eminences high enough to save them from the freshets, but always so near the river that they cannot fail of its passing life. Usually a group of planted evergreens half hides the house from the boat, but its inmates will not lose any detail of the show, and come down to the gate of the paling fence to watch the *Avonek* float by: motionless men and women, who lean upon the supporting barrier, and rapt children who hold by their skirts and hands. There is not the eager New England neatness about these homes; now and then they have rather a sloven air, which does not discord with their air of comfort; and very, very rarely they stagger drunkenly in a ruinous neglect. Except where a log cabin has hardily survived the pioneer period, the houses are nearly all of one pattern; their façades front the river, and low chimneys point either gable, where a half-story forms the attic of the two stories below. Gardens of pot-herbs flank them, and behind cluster the corn-cribs, and the barns and stables stretch into the fields that stretch out to the hills, now scantily wooded, but ever lovely in the lines that change with the steamer's course.

Except in the immediate suburbs of the large towns, there is no ambition beyond that of rustic comfort in the buildings on the shore. There is no such thing, apparently, as a summer cottage, with its mock humility of name, up or down the whole tortuous length of the Ohio. As yet the land is not openly depraved by shows of wealth; those who amass it either keep it to themselves or come away to spend it in European travel, or pause to waste it unrecognized on the ungrateful Atlantic seaboard. The only distinctions that are marked are between the homes of honest industry above the banks and the homes below them of the leisure, which it is hoped is not dishonest. But, honest or dishonest, it is there apparently to stay in the house-boats which line the shores by thousands, and repeat on Occidental terms in our new land the river-life of old and far Cathay.

They formed the only feature of their travel which our tourists found absolutely novel; they could clearly or dimly recall from the past every other feature but the house-boats, which they instantly and gladly naturalized to their memories of it. The houses had in common the form of a freight-car set in a flat-bottomed boat; the car would be shorter or longer, with one, or two, or three windows in its sides, and a section of stovepipe softly smoking from its roof. The windows might be curtained or they might be bare, but apparently there was no other distinction among the house-boat dwellers, whose sluggish craft lay moored among the willows, or tied to an elm or a maple, or even made fast to a stake on shore. There were cases in which they had not followed the fall of the river promptly enough, and lay slanted on the beach, or propped up to a more habitable level on its slope; in a sole, sad instance, the house had gone down with the boat and lay wallowing in the wash of the flood. But they all gave evidence of a tranquil and unhurried life which the soul of the beholder envied within him, whether it manifested itself in the lord of the house-boat fishing from its bow, or the lady coming to cleanse some household utensil at its stern. Infrequently a group of the house-boat dwellers seemed to be drawing a net, and in one high event they exhibited a good-sized fish of their capture, but nothing so strenuous characterized their attitude on any other occasion. The accepted theory of them was that they did by day as nearly nothing as men could do and live, and that by night their forays on the bordering farms supplied the simple needs of people who desired neither to toil nor to spin, but only to emulate Solomon in his glory with the least possible exertion. The joyful witness of their ease would willingly have sacrificed to them any amount of the facile industrial or agricultural pros-

317

perity about them and left them slumberously afloat, unmolested by dreams of landlord or tax-gatherer. Their existence for the fleeting time seemed the true interpretation of the sage's philosophy, the fulfilment of the poet's aspiration.

" Why should we only toil, that are the roof and crown of
    things?"

How did they pass their illimitable leisure, when they rested from the fishing-net by day and the chicken-coop by night? Did they read the new historical fictions aloud to one another? Did some of them even meditate the thankless muse and not mind her ingratitude? Perhaps the ladies of the house-boats, when they found themselves—as they often did—in companies of four or five, had each other in to " evenings," at which one of them read a paper on some artistic or literary topic.

## IV

The trader's boat, of an elder and more authentic tradition, sometimes shouldered the house-boats away from a village landing, but it, too, was a peaceful home, where the family life visibly went hand-in-hand with commerce. When the trader has supplied all the wants and wishes of a neighborhood, he unmoors his craft and drops down the river's tide to where it meets the ocean's tide in the farthermost Mississippi, and there either sells out both his boat and his stock, or hitches his home to some returning steamboat, and climbs slowly, with many pauses, back to the upper Ohio. But his home is not so interesting as that of the house-boatman, nor so picturesque as that of the raftsman, whose floor of logs rocks flexibly under his shanty, but securely rides the current. As the pilots said, a

"THE HOUSE-BOAT DWELLERS, WHOSE SLUGGISH CRAFT LAY MOORED AMONG THE WILLOWS"

steamboat never tries to hurt a raft of logs, which is
adapted to dangerous retaliation; and by night it always gives a wide berth to the lantern tilting above
the raft from a swaying pole. By day the raft forms
one of the pleasantest aspects of the river-life, with its
convoy of skiffs always searching the stream or shore
for logs which have broken from it, and which the
skiffmen recognize by distinctive brands or stamps.
Here and there the logs lie in long ranks upon the
shelving beaches, mixed with the drift of trees and
fence-rails, and frames of corn-cribs and hen-coops,
and even house walls, which the freshets have brought
down and left stranded. The tops of the little willows
are tufted gayly with hay and rags, and other spoil of
the flood; and in one place a disordered mattress was
lodged high among the boughs of a water-maple, where
it would form building material for countless generations of birds. The fat cornfields were often littered
with a varied wreckage which the farmers must soon
heap together and burn, to be rid of it, and everywhere
were proofs of the river's power to devastate as well as
enrich its shores. The dwellers there had no power
against it, in its moments of insensate rage, and the
land no protection from its encroachments except in
the simple device of the willow hedges, which, if planted, sometimes refused to grow, but often came of themselves and kept the torrent from the loose, unfathom-
able soil of the banks, otherwise crumbling helplessly
into it.

The rafts were very well, and the house-boats and
the traders' boats, but the most majestic feature of the
river-life was the tow of coal-barges which, going or
coming, the *Avonek* met every few miles. Whether
going or coming they were pushed, not pulled, by the
powerful steamer which gathered them in tens and
twenties before her, and rode the mid-current with

them, when they were full, or kept the slower water near shore when they were empty. They claimed the river where they passed, and the *Avonek* bowed to an unwritten law in giving them the full right of way, from the time when their low bulk first rose in sight, with the chimneys of their steamer towering above them and her gay contours gradually making themselves seen, till she receded from the encounter, with the wheel at her stern pouring a cataract of yellow water from its blades. It was insurpassably picturesque always, and not the tapering masts or the swelling sails of any sea-going craft could match it.

## V

So at least the travellers thought who were here revisiting the earliest scenes of childhood, and who perhaps found them unduly endeared. They perused them mostly from an easy seat at the bow of the hurricane-deck, and, whenever the weather favored them, spent the idle time in selecting shelters for their declining years among the farmsteads that offered themselves to their choice up and down the shores. The weather commonly favored them, and there was at least one whole day on the lower river when the weather was divinely flattering. The soft, dull air lulled their nerves while it buffeted their faces, and the sun, that looked through veils of mist and smoke, gently warmed their aging frames and found itself again in their hearts. Perhaps it was there that the water-elms and water-maples chiefly budded, and the red-birds sang, and the drifting flocks of blackbirds called and clattered; but surely these also spread their gray and pink against the sky and filled it with their voices. There were meadow-larks and robins without as well

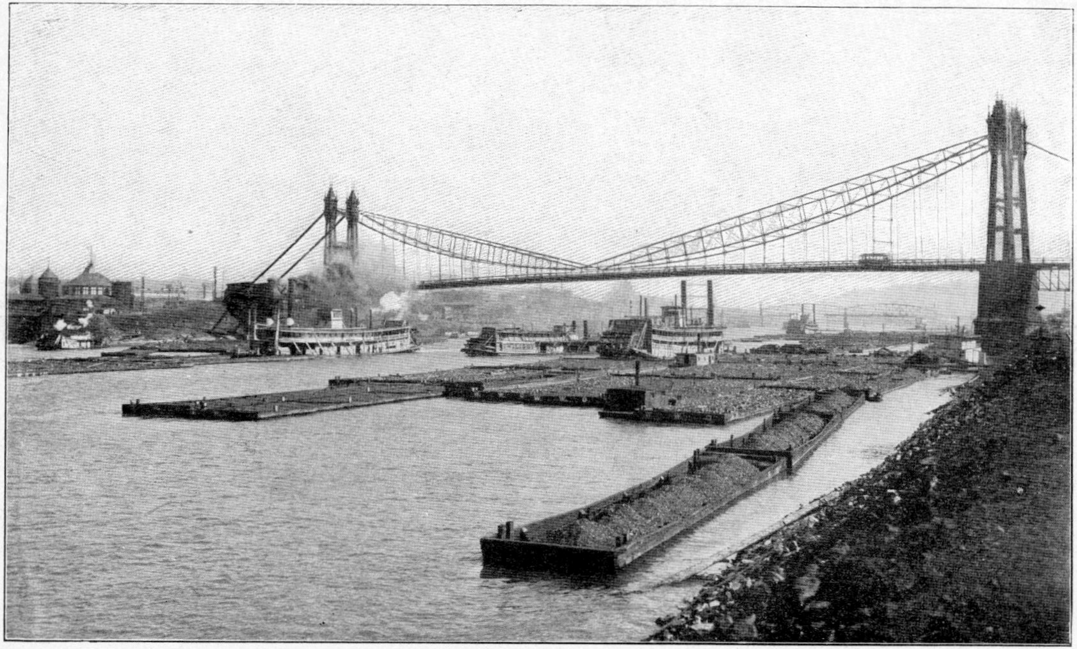

TOWS OF COAL BARGES

as within, and it was no subjective plough that turned the earliest furrows in those opulent fields.

When they were tired of sitting there, they climbed, invited or uninvited, but always welcomed, to the pilot-house, where either pilot of the two who were always on watch poured out in an unstinted stream the lore of the river on which all their days had been passed. They knew from indelible association every ever-changing line of the constant hills; every dwelling by the low banks; every aspect of the smoky towns; every caprice of the river; every tree, every stump; probably every bud and bird in the sky. They talked only of the river; they cared for nothing else. The Cuban cumber and the Philippine folly were equally far from them; the German prince was not only as if he had never been here, but as if he never had been; no public question concerned them but that of abandoning the canals which the Ohio legislature was then foolishly debating. Were not the canals water-ways, too, like the river, and if the State unnaturally abandoned them would not it be for the behoof of those railroads which the rivermen had always fought, and which would have made a solitude of the river if they could?

But they could not, and there was nothing more surprising and delightful in this blissful voyage than the evident fact that the old river traffic had strongly survived, and seemed to be more strongly reviving. Perhaps it was not; perhaps the fondness of those Ohio-river-born passengers was abused by an illusion (as subjective as that of the buds and birds) of a vivid variety of business and pleasure on the beloved stream. But again, perhaps not. They were seldom out of sight of the substantial proofs of both in the through or way packets they encountered, or the nondescript steam craft that swarmed about the mouths of the contributory rivers, and climbed their shallowing courses into the recesses of their remotest hills, to the last lurking-places of their oil and coal.

## VI

The *Avonek* was always stopping to put off or take on merchandise or men. She would stop for a single passenger, planted in the mud with his telescope valise or gripsack under the edge of a lonely cornfield, or to gather upon her decks the few or many casks or bales that a farmer wished to ship. She lay long hours by the wharf-boats of busy towns, exchanging one cargo for another, in that anarchic fetching and carrying which we call commerce, and which we drolly suppose to be governed by laws. But wherever she paused or parted, she tested the pilot's marvellous skill, for no landing, no matter how often she landed in the same place, could be twice the same. At each return the varying stream and shore must be studied, and every caprice of either divined. It was always a triumph, a miracle, whether by day or by night, a constant wonder how under the pilot's inspired touch she glided softly to her moorings, and without a jar slipped from them again and went on her course.

But the landings by night were of course the finest. Then the wide fan of the search-light was unfurled upon the point to be attained and the heavy staging lowered from the bow to the brink, perhaps crushing the willow hedges in its fall, and scarcely touching the land before a black, ragged deck-hand had run out through the splendor and made a line fast to the trunk of the nearest tree. Then the work of lading or unlading rapidly began in the witching play of the light, that set into radiant relief the black, eager faces and

322

"STOPPING TO PUT OFF OR TAKE ON MERCHANDISE OR MEN"

the black, eager figures of the deck-hands struggling up or down the staging under boxes of heavy wares, or kegs of nails, or bales of straw, or blocks of stone, steadily mocked or cursed at in their shapeless effort, till the last of them reeled back to the deck down the steep of the lifting stage, and dropped to his broken sleep wherever he could coil himself, doglike, down among the heaps of freight.

No dog, indeed, leads such a hapless life as theirs; and ah! and ah! why should their sable shadows intrude in a picture that was meant to be all so gay and glad? But ah! and ah! where, in what business of this hard world, is not prosperity built upon the struggle of toiling men, who still endeavor their poor best, and writhe and writhe under the burden of their brothers above, till they lie still under the lighter load of their mother earth?

THE END